Vauxhall Magnum Owners Workshop Manual

by J H Haynes
Member of the Guild of Motoring Writers

and Peter Ward

Models covered:

Magnum 1800 and 2300 Saloon
Magnum 1800 and 2300 Coupe } 1759 and 2279cc
Magnum 1800 and 2300 Estate

ISBN 0 85696 294 5

ABCDE FGHIJ KLMNO

Printed in England

HAYNES PUBLISHING GROUP
SPARKFORD YEOVIL SOMERSET ENGLAND
distributed in the USA by
HAYNES PUBLICATIONS INC
861 LAWRENCE DRIVE
NEWBURY PARK
CALIFORNIA 91320
USA

Acknowledgements

Thanks are due to Vauxhall Motors Limited for the provision of technical information and certain illustrations. Castrol Limited supplied lubrication data.

Car Mechanics magazine kindly provided many of the photographs used in the bodywork repair section of Chapter 12.

Lastly thanks are due to all of those people at Sparkford who helped in the production of this manual. Particularly Brian Horsfall and Les Brazier, who carried out the mechanical work and took the photographs respectively; and Rod Grainger the editor.

About this manual

Its aims

This is a manual by a practical owner for other practical owners. The author, and those assisting him, learned about this range of models the only thorough way, by studying all available information and then going ahead and doing the work, under typical domestic conditions and with a typical range of tools, (metric sized spanners are needed on these cars) backed only by their experience as keen car men over a number of years.

Unlike other books of this nature, therefore, the hands in most of the photographs are those of the author, and the instructions cover every step in full detail, assuming no special knowledge on the part of the reader except how to use tools and equipment in a proper manner, firmly and positively but with due respect for precise control.

Using the manual

The manual is divided into twelve Chapters, each covering a logical sub-division of the car. The Chapters are each divided into numbered Sections, and the Sections into numbered paragraphs.

It is freely illustrated especially in those parts where there is a detailed sequence of operations to be carried out. There are two forms of illustration: figures and photographs. The figures are numbered in sequence with decimal numbers, according to their position in the Chapter, (eg: Fig. 6.4 is the 4th drawing/illustration in Chapter 6). Photographs are numbered in their captions. These numbers pinpoint the relevant Section and photograph number within the Chapter in which the photographs appear.

There is an alphabetical index at the back of the manual as well as a contents list at the front.

References to the 'left' or 'right' of the vehicle are in the sense of a person in a seat facing forwards towards the engine.

Where appropriate, fault diagnosis instructions are given at the end of Chapters. Accurate diagnosis of troubles depends on a careful, and above all, systematic approach, so avoid the attitude "If all else fails, read the manual." It is better, and almost always quicker, to say: "This could be one of several things, so let's have a look at the *Haynes* manual before trying anything."

Certain jobs require special tools and where these are essential the manual points this out. Otherwise, alternative methods are given.

Please note that whilst every care is taken to ensure that the information in this manual is correct bearing in mind the changes in design and specification which are a continuous process, even within a model range, no liability can be accepted by the authors and publishers for any loss, damage or injury caused by any errors in or omissions from the information given.

Contents

Chapter	Page
Acknowledgements	2
About this manual	2
Introduction to the Vauxhall Magnum	4
Buying spare parts and vehicle identification numbers	4
Lubrication chart	6
Routine maintenance	7
1 Engine	11-39
2 Cooling system	40-46
3 Carburation; fuel and exhaust systems	47-64
4 Ignition system	65-73
5 Clutch	74-78
6 Manual gearbox and automatic transmission	79-96
7 Propeller shaft	97-99
8 Rear axle	100-102
9 Braking system	103-114
10 Electrical system	115-143
11 Suspension and steering	144-161
12 Bodywork and fittings	162-181
Metric conversion table	182
Index	184

Introduction to the Vauxhall Magnum

At first glance the Magnum models may be mistaken for Vivas or Firenza Coupés, since their body styling has been around for several years. However, although twin-headlamps were previously featured on Firenza models, these are used throughout the Magnum range and, together with the styled wheels, provide a touch of elegance and style to these high performance small cars.

Introduced in September 1973, the models were powered by the well-proven overhead-camshaft engine originally introduced for the Victor models. These are of 1759 and 2279cc and are used in the 1800 and 2300 models respectively. An improvement in running efficiency has been gained by the use of a thermostatically controlled air cleaner and a viscous coupled cooling fan, but in other respects the power unit is conventional. A 4-speed, all synchromesh gearbox drives a hypoid rear axle via a two-piece propeller shaft; GM 3-speed automatic transmission is available as an option.

A high standard of interior trim and instrumentation is used and is in keeping with the general standard of luxury and sporty styling.

Buying spare parts

Buying spare parts

Spare parts are available from many sources, for example Vauxhall garages, other garages and accessory stores, and motor factors. Our advice regarding spare parts is as follows:

Officially appointed Vauxhall garages — This is the best source of parts which are peculiar to your car and otherwise not generally available (eg: complete cylinder heads, internal gearbox components, badges, interior trim etc.). It is also the only place at which you should buy parts if your car is still under warranty; non-Vauxuall components may invalidate the warranty. To be sure of obtaining the correct parts it will always be necessary to give the storeman your car's engine and chassis number, and if possible, to take the old part along for positive identification. Remember that many parts are available on a factory exchange scheme — any parts returned should always be clean! It obviously makes good sense to go straight to the specialists on your car for this type of part for they are best equipped to supply you.

Other garages and accessory stores — These are often very good places to buy material and components needed for the maintenance of your car (eg: oil filters, spark plugs, bulbs, fan belts, oils and grease, touch-up paint, filler paste etc.). They also sell general accessories, usually have convenient opening hours, often charge lower prices and can usually be found not far from home.

Motor factors — Good factors will stock all of the more important components which wear out relatively quickly (eg: clutch components, pistons, valves, exhaust systems, brake cylinders/pipes/hoses/seals/shoes and pads etc.). Motor factors will often provide new or reconditioned components on a part exchange basis — this can save a considerable amount of money.

Vehicle identification numbers

The *car identification number* is attached to the top of the instrument panel on the left-hand side and can be read through the windscreen.

A further *identification plate,* giving the *model designation* and service numbers with other code numbers, is fitted to the right-hand wheel arch panel on front of the battery.

The *engine number* is stamped on a pad at the right-hand rear of the engine block together with the capacity and compression code references. '23' denotes 2300cc, '18' denotes 1800cc, 'H' denotes high compression and 'L' denotes low compression.

Engine Number, Capacity Code and Compression Code References

Car identification number

Model Designation, Serial and Code Numbers

Vauxhall Magnum 1800 Saloon

Vauxhall Magnum 1800 Estate (Inset: Vauxhall Magnum 2300 Coupe)

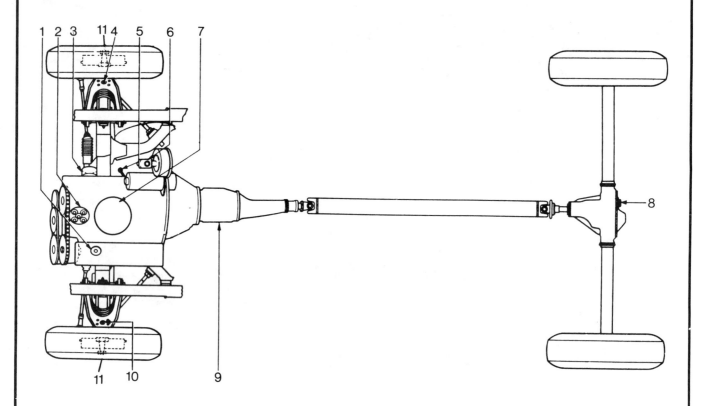

Maintenance and lubrication points

Maintenance points

1 Oil filler cap, engine
2 Distributor
3 Oil filter, engine
4 Suspension ball joint
5 Engine dipstick
6 Brake master cylinder

7 Air cleaner
8 Rear axle
9 Gearbox
10 Suspension ball joint
11 Front wheel bearings

Recommended lubricants and fluids

Engine (1)	Castrol GTX
Gearbox (9):	
Manual	Castrol Hypoy (90 EP)
Automatic	Castrol TQ Dexron ®
Rear axle (8)	Castrol Hypoy (90 EP) *
Front wheel bearings (11)	Castrol LM Grease
Chassis, general	Castrol MS.3 Grease
Distributor cam	Castrol LM Grease
Carburettor dashpot (Stromberg) & general body lubrication	Castrol GTX or Everyman
Brake Master cylinder	Castrol Girling Universal Brake and Clutch Fluid

Note: The above are general recommendations. Lubrication requirements vary from territory-to-territory and also depend on vehicle usage — consult the operators handbook supplied with your vehicle.

* If the car has covered less than 10,000 miles or new differential gears are fitted, a special lubricant is required. Consult your Vauxhall dealer.

Routine maintenance

The manufacturers base their own servicing operation on a time rather than mileage factor (see diagram). They take 1200 miles per annum as an average to base this service plan. This system is very satisfactory as it enables both owner and service station to plan servicing in advance on a regular basis and confirm that deterioration of a vehicle's performance and safety is not necessarily connected with the number of miles covered. Where mileage is consistently and significantly in excess of the average the time intervals between services may be reduced in proportion.

By implication the servicing cycle recommended by the manufacturers gives a 6000 mile interval between engine oil changes. Many owners prefer to change the oil more frequently particularly where much of the driving is in short runs, or stop/start situations, where the engine either does not get many opportunities to warm up completely or operates constantly in heavy traffic. These conditions take far more out of an engine than steady runs along motorways in top gear.

The maintenance information given is not detailed (apart from lubrication guidelines) in this Section as the full information is given in the appropriate Chapters of the book.

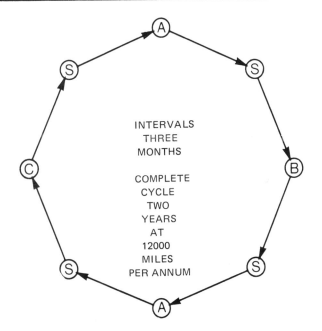

INTERVALS THREE MONTHS

COMPLETE CYCLE TWO YEARS AT 12000 MILES PER ANNUM

Maintenance cycle

Weekly

Check coolant level in radiator
  1 inch (25mm) below bottom edge of filler neck.

Check engine oil level with dipstick
  Level must be above 'Add oil' mark. Quantity required from 'Add oil' to 'Full' is 2 Imp. pints (1.13 litres).

Check battery electrolyte level
  Electrolyte should just cover the plate separators. Wipe away any moisture or dirt.

Check tyre pressures
  Also examine tread depth and for signs of damage.

Safety check service 'S'

Brakes
  Master cylinder fluid level
  Hydraulic pipes and hose — inspection
  Wheel cylinder — inspection
  Linings and pads — inspection
  Handbrake lever setting.

Steering
  Tyre condition
  Front wheel hub bearings — adjustment
  Trackrods and ball joints damage and/or wear.

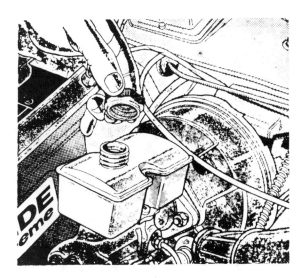

Brake master cylinder fluid level check

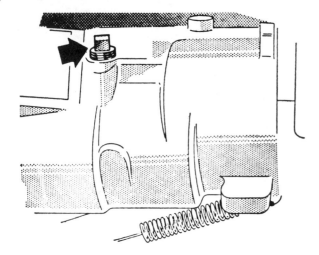

Gearbox filler/level plug

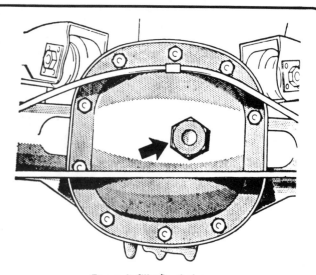

Rear axle filler/level plug

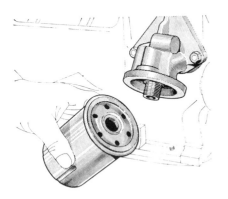

Engine oil filter renewal

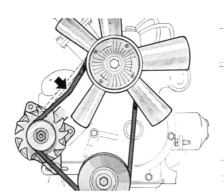

Fan belt check and adjustment

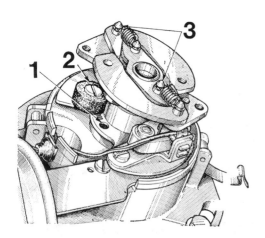

Distributor lubrication

1 Lubrication hole   3 Balance weight pivots
2 Lubricator pad

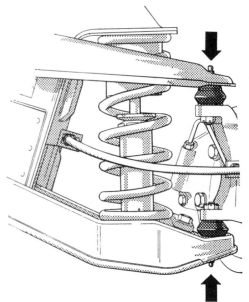

Suspension arm lubrication points

Suspension
Suspension arm upper and lower ball joints — wear
Springs — level and unbroken.

Automatic transmission
Fluid level correct.

General
Lights in order
Exhaust system intact
Windscreen wipers — blades serviceable
Seat belts and anchorage points in order
Check for oil and water leaks
Check operation of all gauges, instruments and warning lights.

Service 'A'

Brakes
Master cylinder fluid level
Front brake pads — inspection.

Clutch and transmission
Check and adjust clutch pedal free-play
Gearbox oil level — check and top-up
Automatic transmission fluid level — check and top-up
Rear axle oil level — check and top-up.

Engine
Renew oil and oil filter
Carburettor damper dashpots (Stromberg carburettors) — check oil level
Fuel pump — clean filter
Spark plugs — remove, clean and reset
Distributor contact breaker points — adjust gap. Clean or renew if necessary
Valve clearances — check and adjust
Fan belt — adjust tension if required
Engine idling speed — adjust carburettor if required.

Steering
Front wheel hub bearings — adjustment
Front wheel alignment.

General
Check wheel nuts for tightness
Lubricate all linkages and pivots of the throttle controls, gearshift mechanism, clutch and parking brake
Lights in order
Exhaust system intact
Windscreen wipers — blades serviceable
Seat belts and anchorage points in order
Check for oil and water leaks.

Service 'B'

Service 'A' to be carried out with the following additions:

Brakes
Brake servo filter — renew.

Suspension
Grease upper and lower arm ball joints.

Automatic transmission
Clean all ventilation holes and slots around the torque converter cover. Scrape all accumulations of dirt from surrounding areas also.

Engine
Renew spark plugs
Renew paper element in air cleaner
Clean crankcase ventilation hose and filter
Lubricate distributor.

General
Lubricate all hinges, strikers and door locks
Check link pins.

Service 'C'

Service 'B' to be carried out with the following additions:

Steering
Remove front wheel bearings — clean and repack with grease.

Brakes
Renew hydraulic fluid.

Automatic transmission
Renew fluid
Renew oil pump suction screen
Adjust low band servo.

Engine
Renew antifreeze.

Lubrication procedures

Engine oil
Weekly
Check the oil level using the dipstick (5) and if necessary add sufficient engine oil through the filler orifice (1) to bring the level up to the 'FULL' mark. 2.85 Imp. pints (1.62 litres) will raise the level from the 'ADD oil' to 'FULL' marks.
Service 'A'
When warm, undo the sump drain plug and drain the old oil. Renew the oil filter (3). Replace the drain plug and refill with fresh engine oil. Under abnormal conditions (city traffic, excess mileage, dusty or extreme temperature conditions) change the oil more frequently.
Capacity (dry) — 8.5 Imp. pints/4.83 litres.
Capacity (refill incl. filter) — 8 Imp. pints/4.55 litres.

Gearbox oil
Service 'A'
Remove the filler plug (9) and top-up if necessary to the level of the plug orifice with correct grade of oil. Examine for any signs of leaks.
Capacity (3 speed) — 2.1 Imp. pints/1.9 litres.
Capacity (4 speed) — 2.4 Imp. pints/1.36 litres.
with overdrive — 3.0 Imp. pints/1.17 litres.

Automatic transmission fluid
Service 'A'
Check the fluid level on the dipstick whilst the engine is running at normal working temperature. Top-up as necessary with correct ATF.
Service 'C'
Drain and refill.
Capacity refill: — 4.5 Imp. pints/2.56 litres.

Rear axle oil
Service 'A'
Remove filler plug (8) and top-up if necessary to the level of the plug orifice with correct grade of oil. Examine the casing for any signs of leakage.

Air filter
Service 'B'
   Renew paper element (7).

Front suspension arm ball joints
Service 'B'
   Grease two nipples each side, top and bottom (4 and 10) with correct grade of grease.

Hydraulic brake master cylinder reservoir
Service 'S'
   Clean cap and surrounding area (6) and after removing cap top-up if necessary to ¼ inch (6mm) below the lower edge of the filler neck. Use correct grade of brake fluid.

Distributor
Service 'B'
   Remove the distributor cap and rotor, and apply a few drops of engine oil to the lubrication hole, lubrication pad and balance weight pivots.

Chapter 1 Engine

Contents

Auxiliary shaft - removal, inspection and renovation ...	17
Auxiliary shaft - replacement	34
Bellhousing and cover plate - removal and replacement ...	9
Camshaft, camshaft housing and tappets - reassembly ...	32
Camshaft housing assembly - replacement	33
Camshaft housing, camshaft and tappets - removal and inspection	13
Connecting rods (big-ends) - refitting to crankshaft ...	27
Crankshaft pulley, auxiliary shaft pulley and camshaft pulley - removal and replacement	12
Crankshaft - removal and inspection	22
Crankshaft and seals - replacement	86
Cylinder head - replacement	31
Cylinder head, valves and springs - removal, inspection and renovation	15
Drive belt for camshaft and auxiliary shaft - removal ...	11
Drive belt replacement and valve timing	36
Engine ancillaries - removal	6
Engine dismantling - general	5
Engine final reassembly after major overhaul	38
Engine mountings - removal and replacement	7
Engine reassembly - general	24
Engine removal	4
Engine replacement in car	39
Fault diagnosis - engine	40
Flywheel - removal, inspection and renovation	10
Flywheel - replacement	89
General description	1
Inlet and exhaust manifolds - removal and replacement ...	14
Main and big-end bearing shells - inspection and renewal ...	23
Major operations possible with the engine installed ...	2
Major operations requiring engine removal	3
Oil filter and adaptor - removal and replacement ...	8
Oil pump - removal and inspection	16
Oil pump - replacement	35
Oil suction pipe and strainer - removal and replacement ...	19
Pistons and connecting rods - replacement in cylinders ...	25
Pistons, connecting rods and bearings - removal	20
Pistons, piston rings and cylinder bores - inspection and renovation	21
Sump - removal	18
Sump - replacement	28
Valves and springs - reassembly to cylinder head ...	30
Valve tappet clearances - adjustment	37

Specifications

Engine — general

	1800	2300
Type	4 cylinder, in-line, inclined OHC	
Cubic capacity	1759 cc	2279 cc
Bore	87.5mm (3.375 cu in)	97.54mm (3.84 cu in)
Stroke	76.2mm (300 cu in)	76.20mm (300 cu in)
Compression ratio:		
hc (Standard)	8.5 : 1	8.5 : 1
lc	7.3 : 1	
Compression pressure: (minimum)		
hc	125 lb/in^2 (8.76 kg/cm^2)	125 lb/in^2 (8.76 kg/cm^2)
lc	110 lb/in^2 (7.7 kg/cm^2)	
Torque (gross) — hc	104 lb ft at 3000 rpm	150 lb ft at 3200 rpm
bhp (gross):		
hc	90 bhp at 5500 rpm	128 bhp at 5000 rpm
lc	86 bhp at 5500 rpm	
Firing order	1-3-4-2	1-3-4-2
Oil pressure - hot	45-55 lbs in^2 at 3000 rpm	45-55 lbs in^2 at 3000 rpm

Camshaft

Journal diameter:	
No 1 (front)	2.3735 - 2.3740 in (60.28 - 60.30 mm)
No 2	2.3575 - 2.3580 in (59.88 - 58.90 mm)
No 3	2.3425 - 2.3430 in (59.50 - 59.52 mm)
No 4	2.3265 - 2.3270 in (59.09 - 59.11 mm)
No 5	2.0605 - 2.0610 in (52.33 - 52.35 mm)
Clearance in housing	0.0010 - 0.0025 in (0.03 - 0.06 mm)

Endfloat ... ...   0.001 - 0.007 in (0.02 - 0.18 mm)
Thrust washer thickness ... ...   0.157 - 0.160 in (3.99 - 4.06 mm)
Permissible dimension - cam peak to base:
1800:
    Inlet ... ...   1.877 in (47.93 mm) minimum
    Exhaust ... ...   1.868 in (47.45 mm) minimum
2300:
    Inlet ... ...   1.902 in (48.31 mm) minimum
    Exhaust ... ...   1.893 in (48.08 mm) minimum

Auxiliary shaft

Front journal diameter ... ...   1.749 - 1.750 in (44.42 - 44.44 mm)
Rear journal diameter ... ...   1.686 - 1.687 in (42.82 - 42.84 mm)
Bearing clearance ... ...   0.001 - 0.003 in (0.02 - 0.08 mm)
Thrust washer thickness ... ...   0.116 - 0.118 in (2.95 - 3.00 mm)
Endfloat ... ...   0.002 - 0.008 in (0.05 - 0.20 mm)

Cylinder block

Cylinder bore diameter - nominal standard:
    1800 ... ...   3.375 in (85.73 mm)
    2300 ... ...   3.84 in (97.54 mm)
Top face distortion - max permissible:
    Longitudinally ... ...   0.005 in (0.13 mm)
    Transversely ... ...   0.003 in (0.08 mm)
Permissible depth of block after refacing (Top face to
centre of main bearing housing) ... ...   8.567 in (217.6 mm)

Cylinder liners (1800)

Cylinder bore diameter for liner fitment ... ...   3.553 - 3.554 in (90.26 - 90.27 mm)

Piston rings

Number per piston   3
Ring gap in cylinder bore:
1800:
    Top ring ... ...   0.014 - 0.025 in (0.36 - 0.63 mm)
    Centre ring ... ...   0.007 - 0.024 in (0.19 - 0.60 mm)
2300:
    Top ring ... ...   0.015 - 0.026 in (0.37 - 0.65 mm)
    Centre ring ... ...   0.009 - 0.026 in (0.24 - 0.65 mm)
Thickness (top to bottom face) Top and centre rings ... ... 0.077 - 0.078 in (1.95 - 1.98 mm)
Clearance in piston groove:
    Top ring ... ...   0.0015 - 0.0035 in (0.04 - 0.09 mm)
    Centre ring ... ...   0.001 - 0.003 in (0.03 - 0.08 mm)

Pistons

Type ... ...   Aluminium alloy solid skirt
Clearance in cylinder bore ... ...   0.0015 - 0.0020 in (0.04 - 0.05 mm)

Piston pins

Clearance in piston bosses at 20° C (68° F) ... ...   0.0003 - 0.0005 in (0.008 - 0.013 mm)

Connecting rods

Bearing housing bore ... ...   2.1460 - 2.1465 in (54.51 - 54.52 mm)
Endfloat on crankpin ... ...   0.008 - 0.014 in (0.20 - 0.36 mm)

Crankshaft and bearings

Type ... ...   5 bearing, cast iron - copper/lead shells
Crankpin diameter — standard ... ...   1.9975 - 1.9985 in (50.75 - 50.76 mm)
Crankpin clearance in bearing ... ...   0.0010 - 0.0032 in (0.03 - 0.08 mm)
Crankpin fillet radius ... ...   0.125 in (3.18 mm)
Crank throw ... ...   1.497 - 1.502 in (38.02 - 38.15 mm)
Main journal diameter - standard:
    No 1,2,3,4 journals ... ...   2.4995 - 2.5005 in (63.49 - 63.51 mm)
    No 5 (rear) journal ... ...   2.5000 - 2.5005 in (63.50 - 63.51 mm)
Main journal clearance in bearing:
    No 1,2,3,4 journals ... ...   0.0008 - 0.0028 in (0.02 - 0.07 mm)
    No 5 (rear) journal ... ...   0.0008 - 0.0025 in (0.02 - 0.06 mm)
Main journal fillet radius ... ...   0.125 in (3.18 mm)
Crankshaft endfloat ... ...   0.002 - 0.010 in (0.05 - 0.25 mm)

Permissible crankshaft run-out ... ...   0.0015 in (0.04 mm) max.
Main bearing housing bores ... ...   2.6655 - 2.6660 in (67.70 - 67.72 mm)
Rear main journal - required length:
    0.010 in undersize ... ...   1.346 - 1.350 in (34.19 - 34.29 mm)
    0.020 in undersize ... ...   1.351 - 1.355 in (34.32 - 34.42 mm)
    0.040 in undersize ... ...   1.356 - 1.360 in (34.44 - 34.54 mm)
Rear main bearing width:
    Standard ... ...   1.337 - 1.339 in (33.96 - 34.01 mm)
    0.010 in undersize ... ...   1.342 - 1.344 in (34.09 - 34.14 mm)
    0.020 in undersize ... ...   1.347 - 1.349 in (34.21 - 34.26 mm)
    0.040 in undersize ... ...   1.352 - 1.354 in (34.34 - 34.39 mm)

Cylinder head
    Minimum depth after lapping ... ...   3.624 in (92.05 mm)

Valves and valve seats
    Valve seat angle ... ...   45°
    Valve seat width:
        Inlet ... ...   0.03 - 0.060 in (0.89 - 1.52 mm)
        Exhaust ... ...   0.055 - 0.85 in (1.40 - 2.16 mm)
    Stem diameter — standard:
        Inlet ... ...   0.3410 - 0.3417 in (8.66 - 8.68 mm)
        Exhaust ... ...   0.3403 - 0.3410 in (8.64 - 8.66 mm)
    Stem clearance in guide:
        Inlet ... ...   0.0010 - 0.0027 in (0.03 - 0.07 mm)
        Exhaust ... ...   0.0017 - 0.0034 in (0.04 - 0.09 mm)
    Seat angle ... ...   44°
    Valve head thickness:
        Inlet ... ...   0.025 in (0.6 mm) minimum
        Exhaust ... ...   0.035 in (0.9 mm) minimum
    Assembled length of valve in head ... ...   1.13 in (28.5 mm) maximum

Valve springs
    Free length - nominal:
        Inner ... ...   1.40 in (35.5 mm)
        Outer ... ...   1.64 in (41.5 mm)
    Spring force:
        Inner at 0.83 in (21 mm) ... ...   72 lb (32.4 kg)
        Outer at 1.00 in (25.5 mm) ... ...   139 lb (62.55 kg)

Valve tappets
    Diameter ... ...   1.4365 - 1.437 in (36.49 - 36.57 mm)
    Clearance in guide ... ...   0.0010 - 0.0015 in (0.03 - 0.04 mm)

Valve clearance (hot)
    Inlet ... ...   0.007 - 0.010 in (0.18 - 0.25 mm)
    Exhaust ... ...   0.015 - 0.018 in (0.38 - 0.46 mm)

Valve timing
    Inlet valve maximum opening point ... ...   106° after TDC

Capacities
    Dry engine ... ...   8.5 pints (Imperial)/4.8 litres
    Refill with new oil filter ... ...   8.0 pints (Imperial)/4.6 litres
    Refill ... ...   7.5 pints (Imperial)/4.3 litres

Torque wrench settings

	lb ft	kg fm
Connecting rod cap bolts*	47	6.47
Main bearing cap bolts*	83	11.45
Flywheel and flex plate bolts	48	6.6
Cylinder head bolts	83	11.45
Camshaft housing bolts	15	2.07
Clutch to flywheel bolts	14	1.94
Torque converter to flex plate bolts	42	5.81

*Oiled threads

1 General description

The engine fitted to models covered by this manual is available in two capacities, 1759cc (1800) and 2279cc (2300). They are basically identical with the exception of the cylinder bore which has been increased on the larger capacity version.

It is of the four cylinder, water cooled, overhead camshaft design and is mounted with the clutch and gearbox within the engine compartment on flexible mountings.

The cylinder block and crankcase are cast together and have integral cylinder liners each one being surrounded by the water jacket. One unusual feature is that when fitted the cylinder axis is inclined to the left at an angle of 45°. The solid skirt pistons are made from aluminium alloy and have two compression rings and one steel rail type compression/oil control ring fitted, all above the gudgeon pin. The connecting rod is attached by this piston pin which is a running fit with piston bosses and shrunk into the little end.

The crankshaft is of cast iron and runs in five renewable copper/lead steel backed shells. Endfloat control is at the rear main bearing (no. 5).

The 'I' section steel forged connecting rods are fitted to the crankshaft by means of renewable copper lead steel backed shells at the big-end. No bush is used in the connecting rod small end as the gudgeon pin is a shrink fit to the connecting rod.

The cast iron camshaft is positioned on the top of the cylinder head and is driven from the crankshaft by a special internally toothed reinforced rubber belt. The camshaft rotates in five bearings which are machined in the aluminium camshaft housing. Endfloat is controlled by a thrust washer located between the rear face of the rear bearing and the retaining washer which is bolted to the end of the camshaft.

Also driven by the rubber toothed drivebelt is the auxiliary shaft and this runs in two steel backed white metal bearings positioned in a housing within the cylinder block. The fuel pump operates from this shaft as does the distributor and oil pump. Endfloat of the auxiliary shaft is taken by a thrust washer which is located in a groove at the front of its main journal.

The drive belt is tensioned by a smooth surface jockey pulley which runs on double row type ball bearings.

The crossflow type cast iron cylinder head is mounted on the cylinder block and carries the aluminium camshaft housing and valve assemblies. The overhead valves are retained in position with split type cotters which are located in the tapered bore of the valve spring retaining cap and double coil type valve springs. The valve guides are integral with the cylinder head. Because of the overhead mounted camshaft the valves are actuated directly by means of 'bucket-type' tappets which move in bores in the camshaft housing. Each tappet incorporates an angled wedge type adjusting screw.

The oil pump is driven via the distributor from the auxiliary shaft and may be of either the rotor or vane type. It has a special built in pressure relief valve which opens when the oil pressure exceeds normal operating pressure. The oil filter is of the disposable cartridge type and is mounted on the outside, right hand side of the cylinder block. The majority of nuts, bolts and screws used on the engine are to Unified standard specifications so before any work is started make sure that a selection of suitable spanners and sockets is available.

2 Major operations possible with the engine installed

The following work may be carried out with the engine in the car (in addition to ancillaries):
1 *Removal and replacement of camshaft and housing*
2 *Removal and replacement of the cylinder head*
3 *Removal and replacement of the front mountings*
4 *Removal of sump (after removing front suspension cross-member assembly).*
5 *Removal of flywheel not recommended without availability of raised ramps or a pit.*

6 *Removal of crankshaft front oil seal.*

3 Major operations requiring engine removal

The following work can only be carried out with the engine removed from the car:
1 *Crankshaft and bearings removal.*
2 *Pistons and connecting rods removal.*

4 Engine removal

1 The engine should only be lifted out after the gearbox has been taken of the bellhousing, as described in Chapter 6.
2 With few exceptions it is simplest to lift out the engine with all the ancillaries — alternator, distributor, carburettor still attached.
3 The average do-it-yourself owner should be able to remove the engine fairly easily in about 3½ hours. It is essential to have a good hoist, and two strong axle stands if an inspection pit is not available. Engine removal will be much easier if there is someone to help. Before beginning work it is worthwhile to get all the accumulated dirt cleaned off the engine unit at a service station equipped with steam or high pressure air and water cleaning equipment. It helps to make the job quicker, easier and, of course, much cleaner.
4 Remove the windscreen washer pipe from the bonnet jet connection and then mark the position of the upper hinge brackets, undo the bolts and lift the bonnet off. Help will be needed.
5 Disconnect and remove the battery.
6 Disconnect the exhaust pipe at the manifold.
7 Remove the gearbox as described in Chapter 6, and then disconnect the clutch cable (Chapter 5).
8 Undo the radiator drain tap and drain the cooling system. A drain plug is fitted in later models. Drain into containers to prevent mess and keep the coolant for re-use if it contains anti-freeze. Then remove radiator cap.
9 Drain off the engine oil.
10 Disconnect the two heater hoses, one from the engine and the other from the junction with the lower radiator hose.
11 Disconnect the top and bottom radiator hoses from the engine, undo the two screws at each side of the radiator holding it to the body panel and lift it out complete with hoses. (Detail Chapter 2).
12 Disconnect the choke and throttle cables from the carburettor assembly. (Details in Chapter 3).
13 Disconnect the leads from the end of the starter motor.
14 Pull off the connections for the wires to the coil, oil pressure sender unit, and water temperature sender unit. These four leads are grouped together on the right hand side of the engine.
15 Pull off the connections to the alternator at the front left of the engine.
16 Disconnect the earth strap which runs from the front right of the body frame. (Photo)
17 Pull off the four spark plug leads and the HT lead from the centre of the coil. Unclip the leads from the cam box cover, undo the distributor cap clips and remove the cap and leads together.
18 Undo the fuel pipe union at the carburettor and remove the engine mounting bracket bolt securing the clip holding the pipe to the side of the engine.
19 Remove the air cleaner (Chapter 3) and the viscous coupling fan and pulley (Chapter 2).
20 Above the starter motor mounting will be seen a blanked off hole in the casting. Use one of the bolts holding the blanking plate to fix a suitable lifting bracket.
21 Certain other makes of car have suitable brackets installed and it should be possible to get hold of one. This lifting bracket is important as there is nowhere else suitable to fix a sling if the engine is to be lifted easily at a reasonable angle. It is worthwhile making a bracket if necessary or fixing a suitable eye bolt in the hole. (Photo)
22 Sling the engine from this bracket to the front end of the exhaust

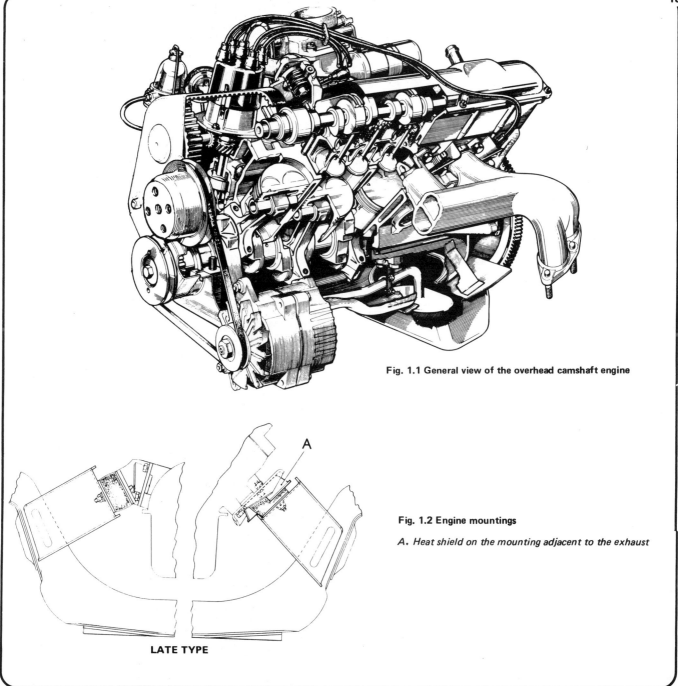

Fig. 1.1 General view of the overhead camshaft engine

Fig. 1.2 Engine mountings

A. Heat shield on the mounting adjacent to the exhaust

LATE TYPE

4.16 Disconnecting the earth cable from the engine block

4.20 Fitting a lifting bracket to the right rear of the block

4.21 Engine slung round exhaust manifold at front

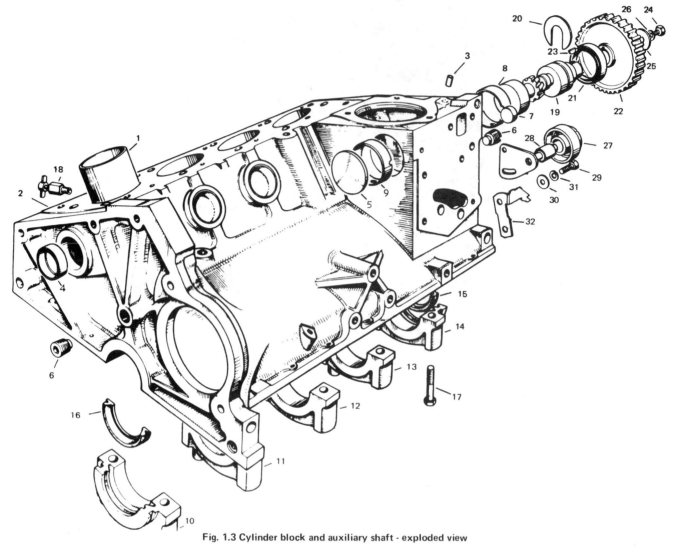

Fig. 1.3 Cylinder block and auxiliary shaft - exploded view

1 Cylinder liner	9 Rear bearing - auxiliary shaft	17 Main bearing cap bolt
2 Cylinder block	10 Main bearing cap No 5	18 Drain cock
3 Plug - cylinder block	11 Main bearing cap No 4	19 Auxiliary shaft
4 Plug - cylinder block	12 Main bearing cap No 3	20 Thrust washer
5 Plug - auxiliary shaft	13 Main bearing cap No 2	21 Oil seal
6 Plug - screwed	14 Main bearing cap No 1	22 Pulley
7 Plug - oil galley	15 Crankshaft oil seal - front	23 Woodruff key
8 Front bearing - auxiliary shaft	16 Crankshaft oil seal - rear	24 Pulley bolt
		25 Washer

26 Lockwasher
27 Drive belt jockey pulley
28 Bearing
29 Bolt
30 Washer
31 Lockwasher
32 Timing pointer

manifold diagonally opposite. Do not worry about the heater ducting that overhangs the rear of the engine. This does not have to be moved.

23 Undo the nut securing the shear type mountings to the front suspension crossmember. (Details in Section 7).

24 After the mountings have been released, take the weight of the engine on the hoist and bring it forward and upwards a little to get the mounting brackets clear, then remove the right-hand bracket from the engine. It will be necessary to swing the rear round in order to get the head clear of the heater duct. The engine can then be lifted up and brought out. Watch out that the heater valve control cable does not get caught up.

25 Place the engine as soon as possible where you are going to work on it. Plenty of space is a great advantage. A free standing bench (rather than one against a wall) that you can work round is ideal.

5 Engine dismantling - general

1 Keen owners who dismantle a lot of engines will probably have a

stand on which to put them but most will make do with a work bench which should be large enough to spread the inevitable bits and pieces and tools around on, and strong enough to support the engine weight. If the floor is the only possible place try and ensure that the engine rests on a hardwood platform or similar rather than concrete (or beaten earth!!).

2 Spend some time on cleaning the unit. If you have been wise this will have been done before the engine was removed, at a service bay. Good solvents such as 'Gunk' will help to 'float' off caked dirt/grease under a water jet. Once the exterior is clean, dismantling may begin. As parts are removed clean them in petrol or paraffin (do not immerse parts with oilways in paraffin — clean them with a petrol soaked cloth and clear oilways with pipe cleaners. If an air line is available so much the better for final cleaning off. Paraffin, which could possibly remain in oilways would dilute the oil for initial lubrication after reassembly).

3 Where components are fitted with seals and gaskets it is always best to fit new ones — but **do not** throw the old ones away until you have the new ones to hand. A pattern is then available if they have to be

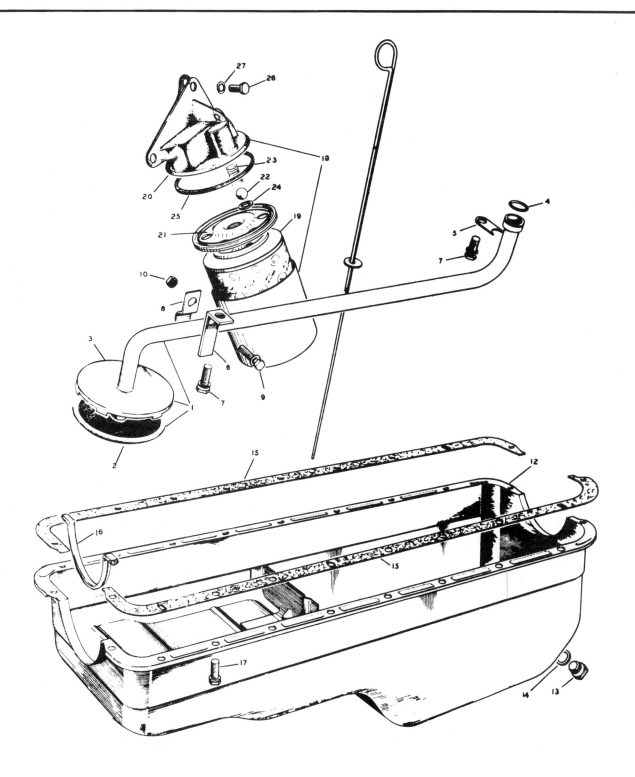

Fig. 1.4 Sump, oil suction pipe and filter assemblies

1 Screw and suction pipe assembly	7 Bolt	14 Washer	21 Valve seat
2 Screw	8 Clamp plate	15 Gasket	22 Steel ball
3 Cover	9 Clamp bolt	16 Seal	23 Spring
4 'O' ring	10 Nut	17 Screw and lockwasher	24 Sealing ring
5 Clamp plate	11 Gasket	18 Oil filter assembly	25 Gasket
6 Support bracket	12 Sump	19 Filter element	26 Bolt
	13 Drain plug	20 Adaptor lead	27 Lockwasher

made specially. Hang them on a convenient hook.

4   In general it is best to work from the top of the engine downwards. In any case support the engine firmly so that it does not topple over when you are undoing stubborn nuts and bolts.

5   Always place nuts and bolts back with their components or place of attachment if possible — it saves so much confusion later. Otherwise put them in small, separate pots or jars so that their groups are easily identified.

6   If you are lucky enough to have an area where parts can be laid out on sheets of paper do so — putting the nuts and bolts with them. If you are able to look at all the components in this way it helps to avoid missing something on reassembly because it is tucked away on a shelf or whatever.

7   Even though you may be dismantling the engine only partly — possibly with it still in the car — the principles still apply. It is appreciated that most people prefer to do engine repairs if possible with the engine in position. Consequently an indication will be given as to what is necessary to lead up to carrying out repairs on a particular component. Generally speaking the engine is easy enough to get at as far as repairs and renewals of the ancillaries are concerned. When it comes to repair of the major engine components, however, it is only fair to say that repairs with the engine in position are more difficult than with it out.

6   Engine ancillaries - removal

1   If you are stripping the engine completely or preparing to install a reconditioned unit, all the ancillaries must be removed first. If you are going to obtain a reconditioned 'short' motor (block, crankshaft, pistons and connecting rods) then obviously the cambox, cylinder head and associated parts will need retention for fitting to the new engine. It is advisable to check just what you will get with a reconditioned unit as changes are made from time to time.

2   The removal of all those items connected with fuel, ignition and charging systems are detailed in the respective Chapters so for brevity they are merely listed here.

Distributor
Carburettor (can be removed together with inlet manifold)
Alternator
Fuel pump
Water pump
Starter motor
Thermostat

7   Engine mountings - removal and replacement

1   Mountings may be renewed with the engine in the car.

2   Place a wooden load spreader under the engine sump and jack up the engine just enough to take the weight of the brackets off the mounting. The bracket bolts and lower mounting nut are then removed and the bracket and mounting removed together. Fit a new mounting to the bracket and replace the bracket and mounting together. It must be ensured that the cut-away portion of heat shield (A) engages the locating dowel on the top face of the left-hand mounting (Fig. 1.2).

8   Oil filter and adaptor - removal and replacement

1   The oil filter is a throwaway cartridge which is changed regularly under service procedures. The adaptor into which it screws is held to the block by three bolts. A gasket is used.

2   The adaptor may be removed for cleaning and checking of the spring loaded bypass valve. The bypass valve opens to permit oil to flow in the event that the filter should get blocked.

3   Always fit a new gasket when refitting the adaptor (photo).

4   Smear the filter element sealing ring with lubricant before fitting to prevent binding and removal difficulty later (photos).

9   Bellhousing and cover plate - removal and replacement

1   The bellhousing can be removed with the engine in the car but first the gearbox has to be removed and the engine disengaged from its left mounting in order to get at the top two securing bolts on the left side. Unless a hoist or pit is available this operation is very difficult and it is recommended the engine be taken from the car first.

2   Remove all the bolts holding the bellhousing to the block and the lower cover plate to the bellhousing including those of the starter motor if not removed already. The housing will have the clutch actuating arm attached to it. Pull the housing off the dowel pegs. The clutch actuating arm can be pulled off the pivot pin — it is held by a spring clip.

3   Replacement is a reversal of this procedure.

4   Note that the bellhousing is never removed or replaced together with the gearbox.

10   Flywheel - removal, inspection and renovation

1   The flywheel is held to the rear of the crankshaft by five bolts and located by two dowel pegs. It can be removed with the engine in the car but the bellhousing has to come off first and this is not recommended for the reasons given in last Section 9.

2   If the engine is removed from the car take the bellhousing off first followed by the flywheel. Undo the bolts with a socket spanner and, taking great care to avoid damaging the mating surfaces, dowel pegs and holes, remove the flywheel.

3   The flywheel clutch friction surface should be shiny and unscored. Minor blemishes and scratches can be overlooked but deep grooves will probably cause clutch problems in time. Renewal may be advisable.

If the starter gear teeth are badly worn the ring can be removed by first splitting it between two teeth with a chisel. Do not try and drive it off because it rests in a shallow groove. If you have never fitted a new ring gear yourself it is best to have it done for you. It needs heating to a temperature of 200°C (392°F) evenly in order to shrink fit it in the flywheel. The chamfers on the ring gear must face the direction the flywheel normally rotates. On later models the chamfer is on one side of the teeth only and this must be towards the clutch side of the flywheel.

11   Drivebelt for camshaft and auxiliary shaft - removal

1   The drivebelt may be removed with the engine installed. On later models it will be necessary to remove the cover first and this, in turn, will involve removal of the fan and crankshaft V belt pulleys.

The crankshaft pulley is held by a central bolt which can be undone with a socket. The V-section is separate from the toothed section but located on the common crankshaft Woodruff key. It should pull off easily. The fan pulley is held to the water pump shaft by the four bolts which also carry the fan blades.

2   Before removing the belt certain precautions should be taken, depending on the reasons for removing it, so as to minimise the risk of making mistakes on replacement, and, of course, to save time. For all conditions mark the belt with a piece of chalk to indicate the direction of travel. This ensures that the wear pattern of the teeth stays the same and wear does not become excessive. (Photo)

3   In all situations other than complete engine dismantling, refer to the Section on 'Valve timing and drivebelt replacement' and set the pulleys in position before taking the belt off. In such situations do not move any pulleys (other than the one you may have to) until the belt is replaced.

If any of the pulleys are to be removed from their shafts later, first slacken the centre retaining bolt before removing the belt. Note that independent movement of the camshaft and crankshaft will do no harm since the valves cannot contact the pistons under any circumstances.

4   Slacken the bolts securing the belt jockey pulley mounting bracket.

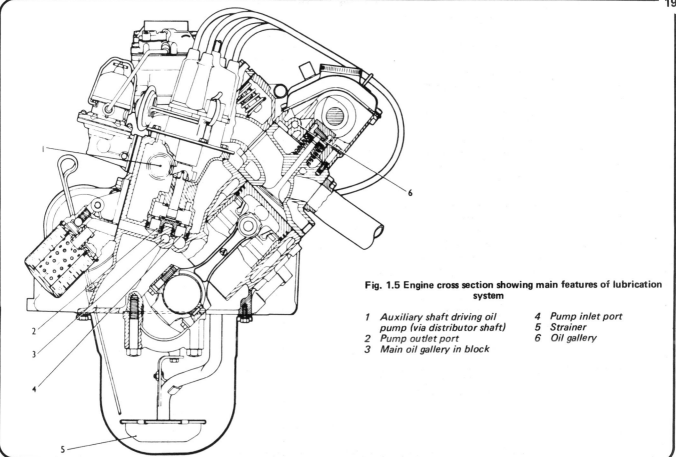

Fig. 1.5 Engine cross section showing main features of lubrication system

1 *Auxiliary shaft driving oil pump (via distributor shaft)*
2 *Pump outlet port*
3 *Main oil gallery in block*
4 *Pump inlet port*
5 *Strainer*
6 *Oil gallery*

8.3 Replace oil filter adaptor bracket to block

8.4a Lubricating the oil filter cartridge sealing ring before replacement

8.4b Replacing the oil filter cartridge

11.2 Mark on timing belt to show direction of travel before removal

12.1 Levering off the crankshaft pulley

13.12 Camshaft housing - the punch is indicating the fine oil spray orifice

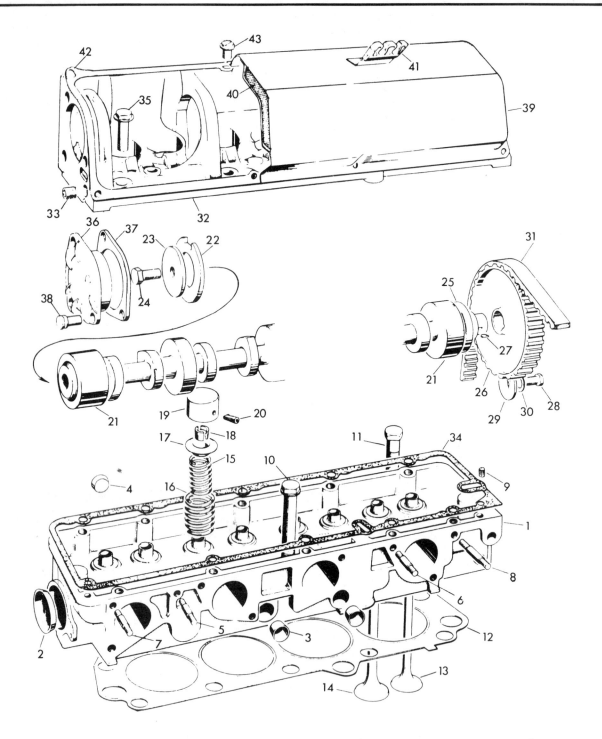

Fig. 1.6 Cylinder head, camshaft and housing

1 Cylinder head
2 Cup plug 1½ in.
3 Cup plug ¾ in.
4 Cup plug 5/8 in.
5 Stud - inlet manifold 1.5/16 in.
6 Stud - inlet manifold 1.7/16 in.
7 Stud-inlet manifold 1.5/8 in.
8 Stud - inlet manifold 2.1/8 in.
9 Knurled dowel peg

10 Cylinder head bolt - long
11 Cylinder head bolt - short
12 Head gasket
13 Exhaust valve
14 Inlet valve
15 Inner valve spring
16 Outer valve spring
17 Valve spring cap
18 Valve collets
19 Tappet
20 Adjuster screw

21 Camshaft
22 Camshaft thrust washer
23 Retaining washer
24 Self locking bolt
25 Oil seal
26 Camshaft pulley
27 Woodruff key
28 Pulley bolt
29 Washer
30 Lockwasher
31 Drive belt
32 Camshaft housing
33 Oil gallery plug

34 Gasket
35 Housing bolts
36 Rear cover
37 Gasket
38 Cover bolt
39 Housing cover
40 Breather element
41 Spark plug lead bracket
42 Cover gasket
43 Cover screw and washer

The belt may then be slid off the pulleys. Do not let it get kinked, damaged or contaminated. It is expensive. Normally it should last indefinitely and require no adjustment.

12 Crankshaft pulley, auxiliary shaft pulley and camshaft pulley - removal and replacement

1 All three pulleys are held onto their respective shafts in the same way — namely by a Woodruff key in a parallel shaft. They should all pull or lever off easily once the centre bolt is removed. (Photo)

2 The centre bolt should be slackened before the drivebelt is removed — and then the drive belt should be taken off, as described in Section 11.

3 The crankshaft pulley is pressed steel with a timing mark on its rear face. It is fitted with a dished flange washer which is assembled with its convex side towards the camshaft pulley. With this type of assembly, the securing bolt has a nylon-insert type of thread and is used without a lockwasher (Fig. 1.6).

4 It should be remembered that if any one of the three shafts is moved when the belt is off, the timing must be reset before replacing the belt.

13 Camshaft housing, camshaft and tappets - removal and inspection

1 The operation described can be carried out with the engine installed.

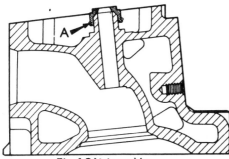

Fig. 1.7 The crankshaft pulley wheel assembly

The arrow shows the dished flange washer

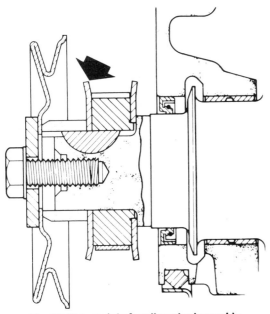

Fig. 1.8 Valve guides

A valve stem seal is fitted round the guide boss of the head and secured by a circlip 'A'

2 The camshaft is removed together with the housing from the top of the cylinder head (ie you cannot move the camshaft with the housing fitted to the head).

3 Disconnect the leads from the spark plugs and then unclip them from the cambox cover.

4 Slacken the camshaft pulley bolt and remove the timing belt as described in Section 12.

5 The camshaft housing is held to the head by ten bolts inside the housing. After removing the cover each bolt should be slackened a little at a time, evenly over the whole area until the valve springs held under tension are completely relaxed. Due to the narrow access to the bolt heads it will be found that a ½ in. drive socket set will be too big so unless you have a 3/8 in. or ¼ in. drive set buy a tubular spanner to fit. The bolts are not very tight.

6 Having loosened all bolts lift them out. Before lifting the cam housing you should be aware that the tappets can all fall out and this must be prevented. As soon as the tappets are clear of the valves, therefore, tip the housing so that they will stay in their locations. When they are removed from the housing place them in a suitable container which marks clearly which position they are from.

7 To remove the camshaft first take off the pulley which is keyed to the shaft. Under no circumstances grip the pulley in a vice. If you forget to slacken the bolt use the timing belt to grip the pulley when removing it. Alternatively, grip the camshaft on an unmachined portion with a pair of self grips to hold it.

8 Remove the housing end cover from the rear. The thrust washer retaining bolt underneath is then undone and for this it is all right to clamp the nose of the camshaft in a vice with the jaws suitably covered with soft material.

9 The oil seal at the front end should now be prised out of the housing. Make sure you have a new one available as the old one will no longer be of any use.

10 The camshaft can be drawn out of the front of the housing. Take care not to catch the bearings with the cam lobes.

11 The bearing surfaces of the cam lobes and tappets should be flat and unpitted. If otherwise you may expect rapid wear to occur in the future. Badly worn cam lobes affect the opening of the valves and consequently engine performance. If lack of lubrication has occurred the

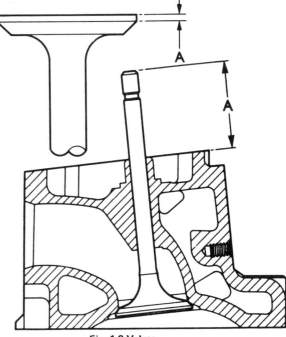

Fig. 1.9 Valves

Left — Head thickness 'A' should not be less than .025 for inlet and .035 for exhaust.
Right — Valve stem protrusion through head not to be more than 1.13 inches.

tappets may have become badly worn in the housing bores. In any of these circumstances it will be necessary to renew the affected parts.

12 The camshaft housing has an oil gallery running its full length with fine jet holes opposite each tappet bore. It is essential that this is perfectly clean. To clean the gallery properly unscrew the blanking plugs at each end and blow out the five jets and gallery with an air line. Do not try to enlarge the jet holes — they are of a particular size in order to maintain oil pressure and an adequate spray to the tappets and cams. (Photo)

13 Each tappet contains a screw with a wedge shaped flat on it for the purposes of adjusting the valve tappet clearances. Should these be damaged or need renewal for other reasons (see 'Valve clearance adjustment') they may be screwed out of the tappets using an Allen key.

14 Inlet and exhaust manifolds - removal and replacement

Details of how to remove the exhaust and inlet manifold are given in Chapter 3.

15 Cylinder head, valves and springs - removal, inspection and renovation

1 The cylinder head can be removed with the engine in the car. Remove the camshaft housing as described in Section 15, and drain the cooling system of about four pints.

2 Undo the exhaust pipe from the manifold by removing the two nuts with a socket and extension from underneath (where applicable)

3 Remove the exhaust manifold. Refer to Chapter 3 for details.

4 Remove the inlet manifold. Refer to Chapter 3 for details.

5 The cylinder head bolts are tight and if the engine is out of the car it must be securely supported whilst they are slackened. Use only a good quality socket spanner for this job. Bolts should be slackened from the ends towards the centre — preferably in the reverse sequence of tightening as shown in Fig. 1.18.

6 Undo the bolt holding the inlet elbow for the water pump to the front of the head.

7 The head is located on two small dowels to the block and should lift straight off. Tapping the sides will not do much good if it sticks and no form of lever should be forced between the head and block. A lever can be arranged across the lower front cover however, where it projects over the block.

8 Even if the valves are not being removed it is best to remove all carbon deposits from the combustion chamber with a wire brush in a power drill. If no power drill is available scrape the carbon off with an old screwdriver.

9 To remove the valves from the cylinder head requires a special 'G' clamp spring compressor. This is positioned with the screw head on the head of the valve and the claw end over the valve spring collar. The screw is turned until the two split collars round the valve stem are freed and can be removed. If the spring collar tends to stick so that the compressor cannot be tightened, tap the top of the spring (while the clamp is on) to free it.

Slacken off the compressor and the valve springs and collar will be released and can be lifted off. (An oil seal cup is fitted round each valve guide shoulder and retained by a circlip. These should be renewed.) Valves should be drawn out from the guides with care. Any tightness is probably caused by burring at the end of the stem so clean this up before drawing the valves through. The guides will not then be scored.

10 Valves, seats and guides should be examined simultaneously. Any valve which is cracked or burnt away at the edges must be discarded. Valves which are a slack fit in the guides should be discarded also if further rapid deterioration and poor seating are to be avoided. To decide whether a valve is a slack fit replace it in its bore and feel how much it rocks at the end. Then judge if this represents a gap of more than 0.003 in. (0.076 mm) between stem and bore.

11 If valves are obviously a very slack fit the remedy is to ream the guides out to an oversize to accept oversize valves. Valves are available

in oversizes of 0.003, 0.006, 0.012 and 0.024 in. Reaming should be done from the top of the head. Unless you have the proper reamers and experience of their use you are strongly advised to have this work done by a specialist. It will not be possible to decide what oversize valves will be required until the guide bore oversize is established by reaming out.

12 Where a valve has deteriorated badly at the seat the corresponding seat in the cylinder head must be examined. Light pitting or scoring may be removed by grinding the valve into the seat with carborundum paste. If worse then the seat may need recutting with a special tool. Check again, if you do not have the correct tool it is best to have the work done by a specialist.

13 When grinding in valves to their seats all carbon must first of all be removed from the head end of the stem. This is effectively done by fitting the valve in a power drill chuck, clamping the drill in a vice and then scraping the carbon off the rotating valve with an old screwdriver. It is essential to protect the eyes with suitable goggles when doing this. (Photo)

New valves may also be ground into their seats but check first whether the ones you get have any special coating on them. The procedure for grinding in valves is as follows: Obtain a tin of carborundum paste which contains coarse and fine varieties and a grinding tool consisting of a rubber suction cup on the end of a wooden handle. Smear a trace of coarse carborundum paste on the seat face and apply a suction grinder tool to the valve head. With a semi-rotary motion, grind the valve head to its seat, lifting the valve occasionally to redistribute the grinding paste. When a dull matt even surface finish is produced on both the valve seat and the valve, then wipe off the paste and repeat the process with fine carborundum paste, lifting and turning the valve to redistribute the paste as before. A light spring placed under the valve head will greatly ease this operation. When a smooth unbroken ring of light grey matt finish is produced, on both valve seat faces, the grinding operation is complete.

14 After grinding, the thickness of the valve head (as indicated in Fig. 1.9) should be not less than specified. Also the width of the seating should be not more than specified. If it is it means that the seating in the head may need recutting.

15 After the valve seats have been recut in the head the valve will naturally protrude further above the head. This protrusion should not exceed specification either (Fig. 1.9) if you think of remedying this by grinding something off the end of the valve stem you could get into difficulties with valve clearances. It may be possible to fit valve seat inserts but the manufacturers do not recommend it.

16 When the grinding in process has finished all traces of carborundum paste must be removed. This is best done by flushing the head with paraffin and hosing out with water.

17 If the reason for removal of the head has been a blown gasket make sure that the surface is perfectly flat before a new gasket is refitted. This requires an accurate steel straight edge and a feeler gauge for checking. If there is any sign of warp over 0.003in. (0.076 mm) it is worthwhile getting it machined flat.

18 Each valve has an inner and outer spring and these should, of course, not have any broken coils. The overall length of each spring must be no less than that specified and if it is it must be discarded. The normal practice is to renew all springs when some are defective.

16 Oil pump - removal and inspection

1 The oil pump may be removed after the distributor has been taken off as described in Chapter 4, and the fuel pump removed as described in Chapter 3.

2 To lift the pump out insert a suitable lever into the fuel pump lever hole and prise the pump upwards so as to draw the bottom of the pump out of the two ports in the block. Do not try and prise it by the upper flange which may bend or break.

3 Once the pump is clear it should be turned 90° clockwise so that it can be lifted out.

4 Two types of pump are used — bi-rotor or vane. To check the pump it is necessary to remove the bottom cover. Mark it first in relation to

15.13 Cleaning carbon from a valve. Power drill held in vice

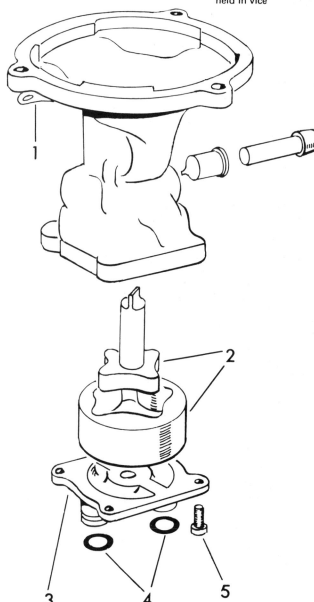

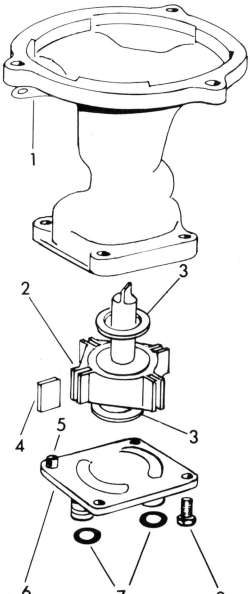

Fig. 1.10 Rotor type oil pump

Fig. 1.11 Vane type oil pump

1 Gasket	4 'O' rings	1 Gasket	5 Locating sleeve
2 Shaft and rotors assembly	5 Cover screw (four off)	2 Rotor and shaft	6 Cover
3 Cover plate		3 Vane locating washer	7 'O' rings
		4 Rotor vane (four off)	8 Cover screw (four off)

the main body and remove the four screws. Using a feeler gauge and straight edge the clearances between rotors and vanes, and the body housing them should be checked. On bi-rotor types the clearance between the tip of inner rotor and convex radius of outer rotor should not exceed 0.005 in. (0.127 mm). The clearance between the outer rotor and the housing should not exceed 0.010 in. (0.254 mm). End-float of rotors is 0.005 in. (0.127 mm) maximum — measured with feeler blade and straight edge across the housing.

5   On vane type pumps the clearances between vanes and rotor, rotor body (on the high point of the eccentric) and rotor end float should not exceed 0.005 in. (0.127 mm). Tip clearance of the vanes opposite the high point of the rotor eccentric should not exceed 0.010 in. (0.254 mm).

6   If any or all of the clearances are excessive and the shaft is a slack fit in the body then it is best to obtain a new pump.

7   After checking the pump make sure that both the upper and lower rotor centre rings are properly located in relation to the vanes in the vane type pump and that the radiused edges of the vanes face outwards. On rotor type pumps the outer rotor is assembled with the chamfered edge inwards. In the side of the pump body below the gear opening there is a small hole which delivers oil to lubricate the auxiliary gears. Make sure it is quite clear.

8   Ensure that the O-rings are assembled on the pump bottom cover before installing the pump. Oil should be smeared in the cylinder block ports to assist entry of the pump O-rings.

17 Auxiliary shaft - removal, inspection and renovation

1   The auxiliary shaft may be removed after removing the drivebelt, the shaft pulley, distributor and fuel pump. Refer to the appropriate Chapter and Sections for details on their removal.

2   The shaft is held in position by the oil seal. The oil seal cannot be removed without damage to it so make sure a new one is available beforehand.

3   Prise it out with a suitable tool and avoid scratching the shaft or the bore in the housing.

4   The shaft complete with thrust washer will then come out.

5   If the shaft gear is damaged or badly worn calling for renewal of the shaft then the distributor drive gear should also be renewed.

6   Wear on the thrust washer will be indicated by grooves and this also calls for renewal.

7   Endfloat should be as specified and if there is any noticeable play between the shaft and bearings new bearing shells should be fitted.

8   The front and rear bearing shells can be driven out although the rear one will come out with the block sealing plug.

9   When fitting new bearings see that the rear one has the offset hole and that the hole lines up with the passageway in the block.

10 The cut-out on the edge of the rear bearing may face either to the front or rear. Line up the hole for the front bearing with the cut-out facing the front.

11 Fit a new sealing plug at the rear using jointing compound to make it oil tight.

18 Sump - removal

1   To remove the sump means either lifting the engine out of the car or removing the front crossmember assembly.

2   If the engine is undergoing overhaul then, of course, it will be removed anyway.

3   If the problem is only leaking sump gaskets it is probably easiest to lower the front suspension. It is essential, however, to have proper stands to support the front of the car. Remove all the screws, marking the position of the one which holds the clutch cable clip. The sump can then be taken off.

19 Oil suction pipe and strainer - removal and replacement

1   The suction pipe and strainer can be removed when the sump is off.

2   It is held by a bolted clip to No 4 main bearing cap and a retaining plate held by a bolt at the elbow where the pipe goes into the block. (Photos)

3   With these removed the pipe can be pulled out.

4   Note the sealing ring round the pipe which is very important and should be renewed on removal. (Photo)

5   Refitting is a straightforward reversal of these procedures.

20 Pistons, connecting rods and bearings - removal

1   To remove the pistons and connecting rods the engine should be removed from the car and the sump and cylinder head removed first as already described.

2   It is possible to make a preliminary examination of the state of the pistons relative to the bores with the engine in the car after removal of the cylinder head, so bear this in mind where the inspection details are given in the next Section.

3   Each connecting rod, bearing cap and piston is matched to each other and the cylinder, and must be replaced in the same position. Before removing anything mark each connecting rod near the cap with a light punch mark to indicate which cylinder it comes from. There is usually a makers number on the rod and cap so there should be no need to worry about mixing them up. If no numbers are apparent then mark the cap as well.

4   It is also important to ensure that the connecting rods and pistons go on the crankshaft the proper way round (the pistons are offset to the thrust side on the gudgeon pins). The best way to record this is by noting which side of the engine block the marks you have made, or the existing number, face. Provided the pistons are not being renewed then they can be arrowed with chalk on the crown pointing to the front but if they are separated from the connecting rods you still want to know which way the rods go.

5   Having made quite sure that positions are clear undo the connecting rod cap bolts with a socket spanner. A normal 7/16 in. AF socket does not fit properly — a flank drive is needed — but an 11 mm metric socket is quite satisfactory.

6   Having removed the bearing caps, the connecting rods and pistons may be pushed out through the top of the block.

7   The shell bearings may be slid round to remove them from the connecting rods and caps.

8   To separate the pistons from the connecting rods a great deal of pressure is needed to free the pins from the small ends. This is not possible with anything other than a proper press and tools. Attempts with other methods will probably result in bent connecting rods or broken pistons. If new pistons are needed anyway it will need an experienced man to heat the connecting rods to fit the new gudgeon pins so the same man may as well take the old ones off.

21 Pistons, piston rings and cylinder bores - inspection and renovation

1   Examine the piston for signs of damage on the crown and around the top edge. If any of the piston rings have broken there could be quite noticeable damage to the grooves, in which case the piston must be renewed. Deep scores in the piston walls also call for renewal. If the cylinders are being rebored new oversize pistons and rings will be needed anyway. If the cylinders do not need reboring and the pistons are in good condition only the rings need to be checked.

2   Unless new rings are to be fitted for certain, care has to be taken that rings are not broken on removal. Starting with the top ring first (all rings are to be removed from the top of the piston) ease one end out of its groove and place a thin piece of metal behind it. A feeler gauge will often suffice.

Then move the metal strip carefully round behind the ring, at the

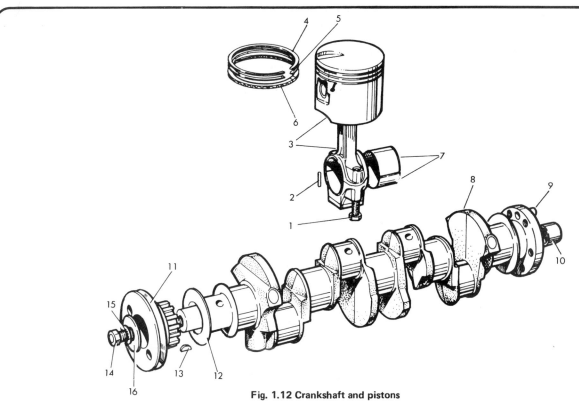

Fig. 1.12 Crankshaft and pistons

1 Big-end bearing cap bolt	5 Lower compression ring	9 Dowel peg	13 Woodruff key
2 Dowel pin	6 Oil control ring	10 Input shaft pilot bush	14 Crankshaft pulley bolt
3 Piston and connecting rod	7 Big end shell bearings	11 Crankshaft pulley	15 Lockwasher
4 Top compression ring	8 Crankshaft	12 Pulley flange	16 Large plain washer

19.2a Oil pump suction pipe securing bracket

19.2b Oil pump suction pipe securing plate

19.4 Oil pump suction pipe 'O' ring seal

21.6 Checking a new ring gap above the ridge in an un rebored cylinder

21.8 Cleaning out the ring groove in a piston with a piece of broken ring

21.9 Fitting a 3 part oil control ring in the bottom groove

same time nudging the ring upwards so that it rests on the surface of the piston above until the whole ring is clear and can be slid off. With the second and third rings which must also come off the top, arrange the strip of metal to carry them over the other grooves.

Note where each ring has come from (pierce a piece of paper with each ring showing 'top 1', 'middle 1' etc).

3   To check the existing rings, place them in the cylinder bore and press each one down in turn to the bottom of the stroke. In this case a distance of 2½ in. (6.35 mm) from the top of the cylinder will be satisfactory. Use an inverted piston to press them down square. With a feeler gauge measure the gap for each ring which should be as given in the specifications at the beginning of this Chapter. If the gap is too large, the rings will need renewal.

4   Check that each ring gives a clearance in the piston groove according to specifications. If the gap is too great, new pistons and rings will be required if Vauxhall spares are used. However, independent specialist producers of pistons and rings can normally provide the rings required separately. If new Vauxhall pistons and rings are being obtained it will be necessary to have the ridge ground away from the top of each cylinder bore. If specialist oil control rings are being obtained from an independent supplier the ridge removal will not be necessary as the top rings will be stepped to provide the necessary clearance. If the top ring of a new set is not stepped it will hit the ridge made by the former ring and break.

5   If new pistons are obtained the rings will be included, so it must be emphasised that the top ring be stepped if fitted to an un-reground bore (or un-deridged bore).

6   The new rings should be placed in the bores and the gap checked. If an un-reground bore check the gap above the line of the ridge. (Photo) Any gaps which are too small should be increased by filing one end of the ring with a fine file. Be careful not to break the ring as they are brittle (and expensive). On no account make the gap less than specification. If the gap should close when under normal operating temperatures the ring will break.

7   The groove clearance of new rings in old pistons should be within the specified tolerances. If it is not enough, the rings could stick in the piston grooves causing loss of compression. The piston grooves in this case will need machining out to accept the new rings.

8   Before putting new rings onto an old piston clean out the grooves with a piece of old broken ring. (Photo)

9   Refit the new rings with care, in the same order as the old ones were removed. The top compression ring has a chrome-plated outer face and may be installed in the piston groove either way up. The centre ring is externally stepped on its lower face. The steel rail scraper ring is unchanged. Note that some special oil control rings are supplied in three separate pieces. (Photo) The cylinder bores must be checked for ovality, scoring, scratching and pitting. Starting from the top, look for a ridge where the top piston ring reaches the limit of its upward travel. The depth of this ridge will give a good indication of the degree of wear and can be checked with the engine in the car and the cylinder head removed.

10 Measure the bore diameter across the block and just below any ridge. This can be done with an internal micrometer or a Mercer gauge. Compare this with the diameter of the bottom of the bore, which is not subject to wear. If no micrometer measuring instruments are available, use a piston from which the rings have been removed and measure the gap between it and the cylinder wall with a feeler gauge.

11 If the difference in bore diameters at top and bottom is 0.010 in. (0.254 mm) or more, then the cylinders need reboring. If less than 0.010 in. (0.254 mm) then the fitting of new and special rings to the pistons can cure the trouble.

12 If the cylinders have already been bored out to their maximum it may be possible to have liners fitted. This situation will not often be encountered.

13 As mentioned in the previous section, new pistons should be fitted to the connecting rods by the firm which rebores the block.

22 Crankshaft - removal and inspection

1   With the engine removed from the car, remove the sump and oil suction pipe as described in Section 18. If the cylinder head is also removed so much the better as the engine can be stood firmly in an inverted position.

2   Remove the connecting rod bearing caps. This will already have been done if the pistons are removed.

3   Using a good quality socket wrench remove the two cap bolts from each of the five main bearing caps.

4   Lift off each cap carefully. Each one is marked with the bearing number.

5   The bearing cap shells will probably come off with the caps, in which case they can be removed by pushing them round from the end opposite the notch and lifting them out.

6   Grip the crankshaft firmly at each end and lift it out. Put it somewhere safe where it cannot fall. Remove the shell bearings from the inner housings noting that No 5 has a flange on each side. There is a two piece oil seal embedded in grooves of the crankcase and bearing cap of No 5 (rear) bearing. These should be levered out and the grooves properly cleaned. The circular oil seal on the front of the shaft should be pulled off.

7   Examine all the crankpins and main bearing journals for signs of scoring or scratches. If all surfaces are undamaged check next that all the bearing journals are round. This can be done with a micrometer or caliper gauge, taking readings across the diameter at 6 or 7 points for each journal. If you do not own or know how to use a micrometer, take the crankshaft to your local engineering works and ask them to 'mike it up' for you.

8   If the crankshaft is ridged or scored it must be reground. If the ovality exceeds 0.002 in. (0.051 mm) on measurement, but there are no signs of scoring or scratching on the surfaces, regrinding may still be necessary. It would be advisable to ask the advice of the engineering works to whom you entrust the work of regrinding in such instances.

23 Main and big-end bearing shells - inspection and renewal

1   Big end bearing failure is normally indicated by a pronounced knocking from the crankcase and a slight drop in oil pressure. Main bearing failure is normally accompanied by vibration, which can be quite severe at high engine speeds, and a more significant drop in oil pressure.

2   The shell bearing surfaces should be matt grey in colour with no sign of pitting or scoring. If they are obviously in bad condition it is essential to examine the crankshaft before fitting new ones.

3   Replacement shell bearings are supplied in a series of thicknesses dependent on the degree of regrinding that the crankshaft requires, which is done in multiples of 0.010 in. (0.254 mm). Thus depending on how much it is necessary to grind off, so bearing shells are supplied as 0.010 in. (0.254 mm) undersize, and so on. The engineering works regrinding the crankshaft will normally supply the correct shells with the reground crank.

4   If an engine is removed for overhaul regularly it is worthwhile renewing big end bearings every 30,000 miles as a matter of course and main bearings every 50,000 miles. This will add many thousands of miles to the life of the engine before any regrinding of the crankshaft is necessary. Make sure that bearing shells renewed are standard dimensions if the crankshaft has not been reground.

5   It is very important, if in doubt, to take the old bearing shells along if you want replacements of the same size. Some original crankshafts are 0.010 in. (0.254 mm) undersize on journals or crankpin and the appropriate bearings must be used.

24 Engine reassembly - general

1   To ensure maximum life with minimum trouble from a rebuilt

engine, not only must everything be correctly assembled, but everything must be spotlessly clean, all the oilways must be clear, locking washers and spring washers must always be fitted where indicated and all bearing and other working surfaces must be thoroughly lubricated during assembly.

2   Before assembly begins renew any bolts or studs, the threads of which are in any way damaged, and whenever possible use new spring washers.

3   Apart from your normal tools, a supply of clean rag, an oil can filled with engine oil (an empty plastic detergent bottle thoroughly cleaned and washed out, will invariably do just as well), a new supply of assorted spring washers, a set of new gaskets, and a torque spanner should be collected together.

4   It is well worthwhile sitting down with a pencil and paper and listing all those items which you intend to renew and acquire all of them before beginning reassembly. If you have little experience of shopping around for parts you will appreciate that they cannot all be obtained quickly. Do not underestimate the cost either. Spare parts are relatively much more expensive now than they were a few years ago.

25 Pistons and connecting rods - replacement in cylinders

1   If the crankshaft has been removed, fit the pistons in the bores before replacing it. The pistons, complete with connecting rods and new shell bearings can be fitted to the cylinder bores in the following sequence:

2   With a wad of clean rag wipe the cylinder bores clean. If new rings are being fitted any surface oil 'glaze' on the walls should be removed by rubbing with a very fine abrasive. This can be a very fine (400 grade) 'wet and dry' paper as used for rubbing down paintwork. This enables new rings to bed into the cylinders properly which would otherwise be prevented or at least delayed for a long time. Make sure that all traces

of abrasive are confined to the cylinder bores and are completely cleaned off before assembling the pistons into the cylinders. Then oil the pistons, rings, and cylinder bores generously with engine oil. Space the piston ring gaps equally around the piston. (Photo)

3   The pistons, complete with connecting rods, are fitted to their bores from above.

4   Before each piston is inserted into its bore ensure that it is the correct piston/connecting rod assembly for that particular bore and that the connecting rod is the right way round. Ensure that the front of the piston which is marked with an 'L' or an arrowhead is towards the front of the engine.

5   The piston will only slide into the bore as far as the oil control ring. It is necessary to compress the piston rings into a clamp and to gently tap the piston into the cylinder bore with a wooden or plastic hammer. If a proper piston ring clamp is not available then a hose clip may be used. (Photo)

6   If new pistons and rings are being fitted to a rebored block the clearances are very small and care has to be taken to make sure that no part of a piston ring catches the edge of the bore before being pressed down. They are very brittle and easily broken. For this reason it is acceptable practice to chamfer the lip of the cylinder very slightly to provide a lead for the rings into the cylinder. The chamfer should be at an angle of 45° and should not be cut back more than 0.010 in. (0.254 mm). If some form of hose clip is being used to compress the piston rings it may be found that the screw housing prevents the clip from lying exactly flush with the cylinder head. Here again watch carefully to ensure that no part of the ring slips from under the control of the clamp. Make sure also that the clamp is not gripping the piston tightly otherwise you will not be able to move it into the bore. (Photo).

7   When all four assemblies have been inserted position the connecting rods so that they will not interfere with the crankshaft when it is replaced. Check that the connecting rod bearing shells are properly positioned with the notches engaging in their respective positions.

25.2 Ring gaps spaced equally round the piston

Fig. 1.13 Pistons

A — Low compression piston (1759 cc engine)
B — High compression piston (1759 cc engine)
The lower, plain crown, piston is used in the 2279 cc engine.
These type of pistons are all high compression

25.5 Clamping piston rings and putting the pistons and connecting rods into the cylinders

25.6 Tapping the piston into the bore

26.5a Main bearing showing plain centre shell No. 3

26.5b Main bearing showing flanged rear shell No. 5

26.10 Fit half the seal into the crankcase seal groove with the ends protruding above the face of the crankcase

26.11a Lubricate the bearing shells

26.11b Crankshaft ready to go into the bearings

26.11c Crankshaft in position

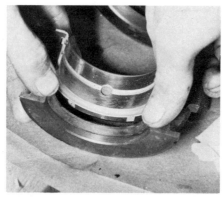

26.12 Fitting the other half of the rear bearing oil seal

26.14 Smearing jointing compound on the bearing caps

26.15 Lubricating the crankshaft journals

26.16a Replacing bearing caps

26.16b Note number on bearing cap

26 Crankshaft and seals - replacement

1 It is simpler to replace the pistons and connecting rods before the crankshaft. Ensure that the crankcase is thoroughly clean and that all oilways are clear. If possible blow the drillings out with compressed air.

2 It is best to take out the plug at each end of the main oil gallery in the cylinder block and so clean out the oilways to the crankshaft bearing housings. Replace the plugs using jointing compound to make an oil tight seal.

3 Treat the crankshaft in the same fashion and then inject engine oil into the crankshaft oilways.

4 Thoroughly clean the main bearing shell locations in the crankcase and carefully fit each half shell into the five locations.

5 The centre bearing shell has no oil groove and No 5 is a two-piece flanged bearing to control the crankshaft endfloat. (Photos)

6 New bearings may have over-thick flanges which will need reducing in order to permit the crankshaft to be fitted with the correct amount of endfloat, which is from 0.002 in. to 0.010 in. (0.051 to 0.254 mm). Endfloat, which is the amount a crankshaft can move endways, is measured between the centre bearing upper shell flange and the bearing surface on the web of the crankshaft, with the crankshaft moved to one extreme of its endfloat travel.

7 It will be necessary to reduce the shell bearing flange thickness by rubbing it down evenly on an engineer's flat bed covered with fine emery cloth. This is done progressively until a feeler blade of 0.002 in. (0.051 mm) thickness can be placed between the flange and the crankshaft web.

8 **Note** that at the back of each bearing is a tab which engages in locating grooves in either the crankcase or the main bearing cap housings.

9 If new bearings are being fitted, carefully clean away all traces of any protective grease or coating with which they may have been treated.

10 With the upper bearing shells securely in place, wipe the lower bearing cap housing and fit the five lower shell bearings to their caps ensuring that the right shell goes into the right cap. Check that the rear oil seal groove in the crankcase is completely free of old jointing compound and that the bearing cap faces throughout are similarly clean. Remove all traces of oil. When quite clean and dry, apply Silastic 732 RTV jointing compound sparingly into the crankcase seal groove. Then fit the half of the seal into the groove firmly and with the ends protruding above the face of the crankcase. (Photo). Make sure it is pressed fully into place — use a wooden hammer handle. The ends must be carefully trimmed to protrude no more than 0.020 in. (0.51 mm) and no frayed threads must be left to get trapped between the bearing cap and crankcase. Coat the seal with molybdenum paste or grease (Castrol MS3).

11 Thoroughly lubricate the main bearing shells with engine oil and lower the crankshaft carefully into position. Check the endfloat with a feeler gauge as described in paragraph 7.

12 Next fit the other half of the rear bearing oil seal into the groove in the cap, having first lightly smeared the groove with Silastic 732 RTV

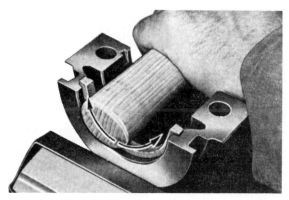

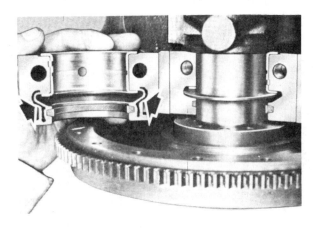

Fig. 1.14 Crankshaft rear bearing fabric seal. Using a hammer handle to press seal into groove

Fig. 1.15 Crankshaft front and rear main bearing caps. Application of 'Silastic' jointing compound (arrowed)

26.17 Tightening main bearing cap bolts with a torque wrench

26.22 Preparing the crankshaft front oil seal

26.33a Refitting the crankshaft front oil seal

26.23b Drifting the oil seal home

27.3a Fitting big end cap

27.3b Check the numbers match

27.5 Tightening big end bearing bolts with a torque spanner

28.3 Fitting the sump end seals into the bearing cap grooves

28.4 Putting 'Bostik' 771 sealing compound onto the sump seal ends

28.5 Positioning the sump gasket

28.6a Fitting sump gasket and sump

28.6b Tightening down sump

29.1 Flywheel replacement

29.3a Tightening flywheel bolts

29.3b Holding the flywheel tightening the bolts

jointing compound. Take the same precautions as for the other half. (Photo).

13 Clean the bearing surface of the caps and position all the five shell bearings to them in the same way as was done for the others.

14 The front and rear main bearing caps need a trace of Silastic 732 RTV jointing compound across them to prevent oil leaks. It should be sparingly applied in the position indicated in Fig. 1.15.

15 Next lubricate all the journals with the engine oil and fit the front and rear caps in position with the flat end faces flush with the ends of the crankcase. (Photo).

16 Place the other three caps in position the correct way round — as a guide the members should all be the same way. (Photos).

17 Replace the cap bolts in all bearings and nip them all up lightly. Turn the crankshaft to ensure it revolves freely and then start with No 1 and tighten the bolts of each cap to the specified torque.

18 After tightening each cap turn the crankshaft by hand to ensure it is not binding. A reground crank may be a little stiff but it should be possible to turn it by hand without excess effort. If any bearing binds, then something is wrong.

19 If the crank is a reground one, check the journal diameters and bearing shell sizes. Do not hope that a very tight fit will ease up later after some running. It might — but 99 times out of 100 the bearing will bind and the surface 'pick up'. Then you will have to take everything apart once more.

20 The crankshaft front seal can be renewed if necessary without engine removal. All that is required is for the drivebelt, fanbelt and crankshaft pulley wheel to be removed.

21 Ideally the seal is removed by a special threaded tube puller which bites into the internal diameter. However, if care is taken it can be dug out with a sharp pointed tool. When this is done the shaft itself must not be scored — neither should the seal housing.

22 When fitting a new seal first ensure that the housing is quite clean. Smear the seal lip with molybdenum paste or grease and the outer periphery with Silastic 732 RTV sealing compound. (Photo).

23 Carefully drive it in squarely with a flat nosed punch or drift until it is flush with crankcase and bearing cap face. (Photo).

27 Connecting rods (big-ends) - refitting to crankshaft

1 With the crankshaft replaced and all main bearing bolts tightened, the pistons replaced in the cylinders and shell bearings fitted in their rods with the locating tongues in their grooves, position the crankshaft so that the two centre or two end crankpins are conveniently placed for drawing the connecting rods up to them.

2 If not already done wipe the connecting rod bearing cap and back of the shell bearing clean, and fit the shell bearing in position ensuring that the locating tongue at the back of the bearing engages with the locating groove in the connecting rod cap.

3 Make sure the cap fits the correct rod by checking the numbers

matching marks already made and see that the spring dowel pins are intact. (Photo).

4 Generously lubricate the shell bearing and offer up the connecting rod bearing cap to the connecting rod.

5 Fit the connecting rod bolts with oiled threads and tighten them down to the specified torque. (Photo).

6 Rotate the crankshaft (it will be fairly stiff because of the drag of the piston rings in the bores — if very stiff slacken the bearing caps to ensure it is not due to a binding bearing) so that the other two crankpins are in position for the connecting rods and replace them in the same way.

7 Oil the cylinder bores generously for initial lubrication.

28 Sump - replacement

1 Before fitting the sump check that the oil pump suction pipe and strainer are correctly fitted (Section 19) and that all bearing cap bolts are tight.

2 The sump should have been thoroughly cleaned out and the flange mating surfaces of both the sump and crankcase perfectly cleaned free of all traces of old gasket. Check that the sump lies flat on the crankcase and that the flanges are not bent or damaged in any way.

3 Two specially shaped seals (included in the gasket set) are provided for the front and rear bearing caps. Ensure that the grooves and steps where the ends fit are perfectly clean and dry. Apply a smear of Silastic 732 RTV jointing compound into the groove and onto the step where the ends fit and place the seals into the grooves. (Photo).

4 Place a blob of Bostik 771 compound on top of the ends of the seal as well. (Photo).

5 Put the cork sump gaskets in position on the crankcase so that the ends bed with the compound and overlap the end seals. If the sump is being replaced with the engine in the car it is a good idea to stick the cork gasket to the crankcase with grease to hold it in place. It is not recommended that jointing compound be used. (Photo).

6 Refit the sump without disturbing the position of the gaskets and replace all the set screws (remembering the clutch cable clip on the one you marked) and tighten them evenly. Do not overtighten. (Photos).

29 Flywheel - replacement

1 The flywheel is located on two dowel pegs and can only be fitted one way because the five bolt holes are not symmetrically arranged. (Photo).

2 Locate the flywheel on the dowels and tap it home square.

3 Replace the five bolts (there are no washers) and tighten them evenly to the specified torque on clean dry threads. The flywheel may be held with a screwdriver wedged between the teeth of the wheel and the bellhousing dowel peg whilst the bolts are being tightened. (Photo).

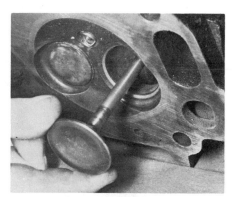
30.1 Fitting valve into guide

30.3a Replacing valve springs

30.3b Replacing valve upper collar

30.4 Compressing the valve spring and fitting the collets

31.4 Replacing the cylinder head

31.6 Tightening cylinder head bolts

31.8a Replacing exhaust manifold

31.8b Lock tabs and bolts on the exhaust manifold

31.10a Inlet manifold replacement showing two different gaskets

31.10b Tightening of the securing bolt in the thermostat housing

32.4a Lubricating camshaft bearing before reassembly

32.4b Inserting the camshaft into its bearings

32.5 Camshaft thrust washer fitted with cutout upwards

32.6 Replacing the camshaft washer and bolt

32.7 Tightening the camshaft bolt using a self-grip wrench to hold the camshaft

30 Valves and springs - reassembly to cylinder head

1   The valves and head should all be thoroughly clean before reassembly. If the same valves are being refitted they should return to the same place. It is good practice to smear the stems with a molybdenum or graphite paste before inserting them in the guides. (Photo).

2   Fit new valve stem seals and clips over the shoulders of the valve guide extension on the top of the head.

3   Replace the inner and outer coil springs and the retaining collar over them. (Photos).

4   Compress the springs using the tool until it is possible to fit the two collets around the valve stem so that they engage the groove. (Photo).

5   Release the spring compressor whilst watching to ensure that the two collets do not slip out of the groove. When released, tap the valve stem end with a mallet to 'bounce' it and ensure that everything is properly seated.

31 Cylinder head - replacement

1   Before replacing the cylinder head check that the oil transfer passageway is clear. This takes the form of a combined hollow dowel and restrictor, with an 0-ring around it.

2   The surface of both cylinder block and head must be perfectly clean and dry. Apply sealing compound to the gasket before placing in position. (Some replacement gaskets are made from re-inforced asbestos and are dark grey in colour; these gaskets must be fitted without jointing compound).

3   Place the cylinder head gasket in position on the block making quite sure that it is the correct way up — it will be fairly obvious if it is not. Make a final check that the oil transfer passage is clear.

4   Place the cylinder head squarely in position, taking care not to damage the protruding pegs before it fits over them. (Photo).

5   Replace the ten cylinder head bolts and nip them all down lightly.

6   Cylinder head bolts must be tightened down evenly and in the correct order as indicated in Fig. 1.18. Tighten all bolts down first to a torque of 45 lb ft. (6.2 kgm) in the order shown and then go round again tightening to the final specified torque. (Photo).

7   The inlet and exhaust manifolds may be replaced next or after the camshaft housing if wished.

8   The exhaust manifold requires a combined heat shield and gasket. A used gasket may be re-used provided it is not damaged or burnt. Carefully clean off any carbon traces. The bolts are replaced with a lock tab to each pair and should be tightened up moderately. Do not overdo it, and break a bolt. (Photos).

9   Bend down a tab against a convenient flat on each bolt head.

10 The inlet manifold can be replaced with the carburettor fitted or otherwise, but first of all make sure you fit the correct gaskets.

11 Check that the manifold studs in the head are tight and before placing the gaskets in position smear sealing compound round the water jacket holes on both sides.

12 Replace the bolts and the nuts — all of which have lock-washers— and tighten them evenly. The bolt which fits inside the thermostat aperture should have a new copper washer under the head. Do not forget to reconnect the water pipe from the pump.

32 Camshaft, camshaft housing and tappets - reassembly

1   The camshaft must be fitted into the housing before fitting the housing to the head.

2   Smear all the bearing surfaces of the camshaft with an oil treated with graphite or molybednum disulphide.

3   To check the endfloat, before fitting the shaft into the housing fit the thrust washer, retaining washer and original securing bolt to the rear end and check the gap between the two washers.

4   Lubricate the bearings and then insert the camshaft into the housing from the front. (Photos).

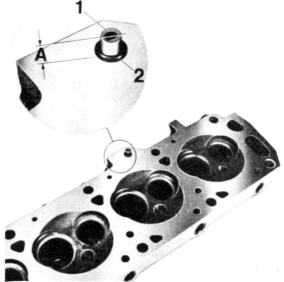

Fig. 1.16 Cylinder head - Oil transfer passage from cylinder block fitted with spring pin (1) and 'O' ring (2). Dimension 'A' is .12 ins.

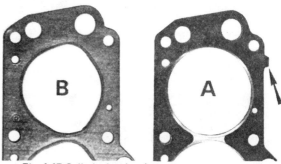

Fig. 1.17 Cylinder head gaskets

A   2279 cc engine (note arrowed identification tab)
B   1759 cc engine

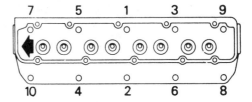

Fig. 1.18 Cylinder head. Bolt tightening sequence. Arrow points to front

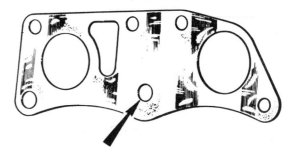

Fig. 1.19 Inlet manifold gasket (Rear gasket with additional hole)

32.8 Fitting camshaft rear end cover. Note lug (arrowed) which engages in thrust washer cut-out

32.9a Fitting a camshaft front oil seal

32.9b Tapping home the camshaft front oil seal

32.10 Replacing tappets in camshaft housing

33.2 Fitting camshaft housing gasket to cylinder head

33.3 Placing the camshaft housing assembly into position

33.4 Tightening the camshaft housing bolts

33.5 Replacing the camshaft pulley and locking bolt

34.2 Putting the auxiliary shaft together with the thrust washer into the block. Note notch which engages the peg in the bearing housing

34.3 Placing the auxiliary shaft retainer/oil seal in position

34.5 Replacing the auxiliary shaft pulley

35.2 Oil pump showing oil port 'O' rings in position

5 Fit the thrust washer so that the cut-out faces upwards where it will engage with the lug in the cover (Photo).

6 The retaining bolt is locked with a nylon insert and a new one should be used. If not, use a proprietary locking compound on the bolt threads. (Photo).

7 Grip the camshaft with self-grips whilst tightening the bolt. (Photo).

8 Using a new gasket refit the end cover so that the lug engages in the thrust washer cut-out and tighten the securing bolts. (Photo).

9 Fit a new oil seal in the front end of the housing. Smear the inner lip with molybdenum paste or grease and fit it facing inwards. Tap it home square. (Photos).

10 Lubricate the tappet bores in the housing and replace the tappets into the same locations from which they came. If you have removed the tappet adjusting screws for any reason they should be screwed in first so that the flat section faces the open end of the tappet and is approximately central across the tappet diameter. If any of the tappets look like dropping out easily under gravity use a smear of grease to hold them in position. (Photo).

33 Camshaft housing assembly - replacement

1 Make sure the cylinder head bolts are all correctly tightened down.

2 Place a new gasket in position on the cylinder head noting that the hole for the oil transfer passage should line up. (Photo).

3 Place the camshaft housing assembly in position without letting the tappets fall out of their locations in the process. Engage it over the dowels at each end of the head, and ensure the gasket position is not disturbed. (Photo).

4 The assembly will not seat right down yet because some valves will be opposite cams in the open position. Replace all the mounting bolts

and using a pattern similar to that of tightening the cylinder head, tighten them all evenly a little at a time to the specified torque.

5 Replace the pulley wheel over the key and fit the washer and bolt. The bolts may be tightened fully later after the belt has been replaced.

34 Auxiliary shaft - replacement

1 The drivebelt and pulley, fuel pump and distributor must be removed before the shaft can be refitted.

2 Lubricate the bearings with oil (treated with graphite or molybdenum disulphide) and place the shaft with the 'U' shaped thrust washer located in the shaft groove into position in the block. The small notch in the thrust washer should engage the dowel peg in the housing. (Photo). This washer is a selective fit and must be carefully chosen to ensure that the endfloat is within Specifications.

3 Lubricate the oil seal with molybdenum paste or grease and place it over the shaft open side first. (Photo).

4 Carefully tap the seal squarely into position until it stops up against the thrust washer.

5 Fit the pulley over the key and replace the washer and bolt. The bolt can be tightened after the belt is replaced. (Photo).

35 Oil pump - replacement

1 The oil pump may be refitted with or without the auxiliary shaft in position.

2 Fit new O-rings into the grooves around ports in the bottom cover and oil the ports in the cylinder block where they will press in. It is important that the O-rings are not dragged out of position when the pump is pushed into position. (Photo).

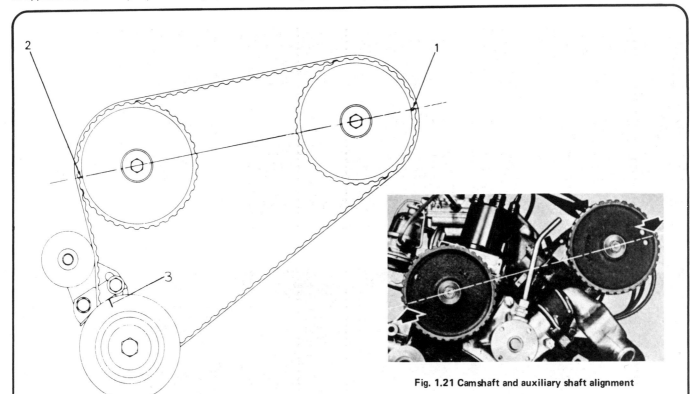

Fig. 1.20 Camshaft drive belt fitment. Alignment of camshaft pulley timing mark '1' and auxiliary shaft pulley mark '2' with crankshaft pulley mark '3' at TDC

Fig. 1.21 Camshaft and auxiliary shaft alignment

35.3 Placing oil pump gasket in position

35.4 Putting the oil pump into position

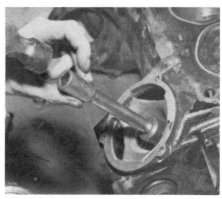
35.5 Tapping the oil pump down onto its seating using a socket and extension

36.3 Lining up the camshaft and auxiliary shaft timing marks with a straight edge

36.5 Fitting the timing belt (it is not yet round the crankshaft pulley)

36.6 Adjusting the drive belt jockey pulley

37.6 Turning the tappet with a screwdriver in the notch

37.7 Measuring tappet clearance with a feeler blade

37.9 Turning the tappet clearance adjusting screw with a hexagonal section key

37.11a Fitting a new gasket to the camshaft housing cover

37.11b Fitting the camshaft housing

3 Place a new gasket in position on the block. (Photo). On some models an adhesive type gasket is used, and this must be fitted with the adhesive side against the crankcase.

4 If the auxiliary shaft is installed hold the pump so that the opening in the body (for the gear of the auxiliary shaft) is 90° clockwise from the gear position. Put the pump into the housing and turn it anticlockwise 90° to line up the ports at the bottom. (Photo).

5 Do not press the flange of the pump body to push it down into position. Use a tube or socket of some sort in the centre of the body in order to tap it down. (Photo).

6 The pump is finally secured by the same bolts that hold the distributor in position.

36 Drivebelt replacement and valve timing

1 The drivebelt controls the valve timing and it is imperative to get it fitted in exactly the correct tooth. The auxiliary shaft and camshaft should be turned so that their timing marks and the shaft centre lines lie in a straight line, the timing marks being at the ends of the line.

2 The camshaft pulley mark is a round depression on the front face and the auxiliary pulley mark is a 'V' notch on the front face. Ignore the circular mark on the rear of the auxiliary shaft pulley.

3 Use a straight edge to line up the marks and centres. (Photo).

4 Next turn the crankshaft clockwise (use a spanner on the pulley bolt) until the timing mark in the front face of the flange is lined up with the TDC pointer (the upper one). It will be necessary to replace the belt cover temporarily as the timing marks are moulded on its front face.

5 Without disturbing the position of the pulleys, fit the drivebelt with the chalked arrow pointing in the direction of movement. There should be very little slack apparent between the auxiliary and camshaft pulleys, and camshaft and crankshaft pulleys when the teeth are engaged. There will be more between the crankshaft and auxiliary shaft pulleys as this is where the jockey pulley goes. (Photo).

6 Position and lock the jockey pulley to give moderate tension (Photo), rotate the crankshaft and stop at TDC. This will automatically put the correct tension on the section of belt between the camshaft and crankshaft pulleys because the greatest valve spring drag will be applied to the camshaft in this position. (If you inadvertently overshoot the TDC position go round again. Do not reverse!).

7 The rest of the belt tension is adjusted by movement of the jockey pulley. A 10 lb (4.5 kg) load applied midway between the auxiliary and camshaft pulleys should deflect the belt 0.30 in. (7.5 mm). It is important to remember that this tension must be checked only when the tension between camshaft and crankshaft pulleys has been set and left as described in the previous paragraph.

8 A belt set too tight will whine. A slack belt wears out quickly.

9 Tighten all pulley bolts.

37 Valve tappet clearances - adjustment

1 In order that the valves open the correct amount and to provide tolerance for thermal expansion the gap between the face of the cam and the tappet (which fits over the end of the valve stem) must be correctly set.

2 The clearances may be set with the engine in the car after removal of the camshaft housing cover.

3 Each tappet contains a screw running laterally across it with a tapered flat in the screw which bears on the end of the valve stem. The movement of the screw in or out alters the relative distance between the end of the valve stem and the tappet face.

4 Access to the end of the adjusting screw is through a hole in the side of the tappet. This hole must be aligned with the cut-out part of the housing by revolving the tappet. There are holes in the tappet at both ends of the screw and the one which has the socket head is indicated by a small notch in the top edge of the tappet. In order to identify the valve clearance requirement, early engines with the smaller

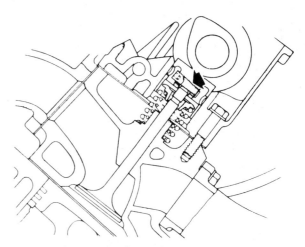

Fig. 1.22 Cylinder head/camshaft housing

Cross section to show position of valve clearance adjusting screw relative to tappet and valve stem

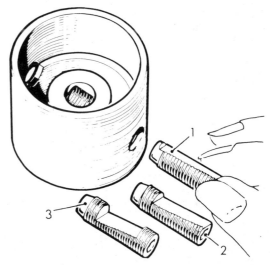

Fig. 1.23 Valve clearance adjustment. 3 types of adjusting screw

1 Standard
2 1st undersize (inadequate gap obtainable with standard screw)
3 2nd undersize (inadequate gap obtainable with 1st undersize)

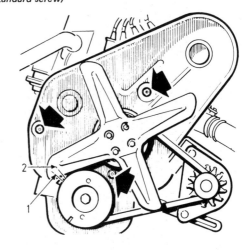

Fig. 1.24 Drive belt cover

Note securing points (arrowed) and ignition timing marks (1 and 2)

clearances can be recognised by a groove in the front end of the camshaft behind the pulley.

5   Valve clearances are set when the valve is fully closed — that is when the tappet is bearing on the lowest point of the cam — this position is easy to see — the highest point of the cam is directly opposite.

6   Turn the tappet with a screwdriver in the notch in the top edge until the screw opening is visible. (Photo).

7   Measure the gap with a feeler blade. If the engine has not been run because of overhaul and is therefore cold and the gap initially should be 0.003 in. (0.08 mm) less than specified. (Photo).

8   Having measured the gap accurately adjustment is necessary if it is not within the given range (which is inclusive).

9   The adjusting screw must be turned one complete revolution clockwise or anticlockwise to decrease or increase the gap by 0.003 in. (0.15 mm). (Photo). A measured gap of 0.006 in. (0.15 mm) will therefore be increased to 0.009 in. (0.23 mm) if the adjusting screw is given one complete anticlockwise turn.

   If a measure gap of 0.005 in. (0.13 mm) occurred on a cold engine one would decide whether 0.008 in. (0.02 mm) (+0.003 in. (0.08 mm)) fell within the range and adjust as necessary.

10 Once the cold clearances have been set they must be checked and adjusted again if necessary, when the engine is hot.

11 Refit the camshaft housing cover carefully — and preferably with a new gasket. As the gasket curves it is important to ensure that it is not dislodged during replacement. (Photos).

38 Engine - final assembly of the major overhaul

1   The ancillary components which were removed as listed in Section 6 (Engine ancillaries — removal) should be replaced as far as possible before putting the engine back in the car. Accessibility will be far better. One particular point to take care over is the fitting of the water pump inlet elbow short hose. Make sure that the joining surfaces are clean and the hose is in good condition.

   It may be worthwhile replacing the manufacturers wire type hose clips with the more positive worm screw drive type.

39 Engine - replacement in car

1   Replacement of the engine is a reversal of the removal procedure. A little trouble in getting the engine properly slung so that it takes up a suspended attitude similar to its final position will pay off when it comes to getting it set easily on the front engine mountings.

2   Refit the gearbox and propeller shaft, as described in the appropriate Chapters. Do not forget to connect the exhaust pipe to the manifold.

3   It is likely that the engine will be initially stiff to turn if new bearings and rings have been fitted and it will save a lot of irritation if the battery is well charged. After a rebore the stiffness may be more than the battery can cope with so be prepared to link another up in parallel with jumper leads.

4   The following final check list should ensure that the engine starts safely and with the minimum of delay:

   a) Fuel lines to pump and carburettors — connected and tightened.
   b) Water hoses connected and clipped.
   c) Radiator and engine drain taps closed or drain plugs fitted.
   d) Cooling system replenished.
   e) Sump drain plug fitted and tight.
   f) Oil in engine.
   g) Oil in gearbox and level plug tight.
   h) LT wires connected to distributor and coil.
   j) Oil pressures and water temperature sender units screwed tight and leads connected.
   k) Spark plugs tight.
   l) Tappet clearances set correctly.
   m) HT leads connected securely to distributor, spark plugs and coil.
   n) Rotor arm replaced in distributor.
   o) Choke and throttle cables connected.
   p) Braided earthing cable, engine to frame reconnected.
   q) Starter motor lead connected.
   r) Fan belt fitted and correctly tensioned.
   s) Alternator leads connected.
   t) Battery charged and leads connected to clean terminals.

5   Once the engine has started set the throttle stop screw to a fast tickover and let it run until fully warmed up — five minutes at least. Watch it all the time and keep an eye open for water or oil leaks.

40 Fault diagnosis - Engine

Note: When investigating starting and uneven running faults do not be tempted into a snap diagnosis. Start from the beginning of the check procedure and follow it through. It will take less time in the long run. Poor performance from an engine in terms of power and economy is not normally diagnosed quickly. In any event the ignition and fuel systems must be checked first before assuming any further investigation needs to be made.

Symptom	Reason/s	Remedy
Engine will not turn over when starter switch is operated	Flat battery Bad battery connections Bad connections at solenoid switch and/or starter motor	Check that battery is fully charged and that all connections are clean and tight.
	Starter motor jammed	Rock the car back and forth with a gear engaged. If this does not free pinion remove starter.
	Defective solenoid	Bridge the main terminals of the solenoid switch with a piece of heavy duty cable in order to operate the starter.
	Starter motor defective	Remove and overhaul starter motor.
Engine turns over normally but fails to fire and run	No spark at plugs	Check ignition system according to procedures given in Chapter 4.
	No fuel reaching engine	Check fuel system according to procedures given in Chapter 3.
	Too much fuel reaching the engine (flooding)	Check the fuel system as above.
Engine starts but runs unevenly and misfires	Ignition and/or fuel system faults	Check the ignition and fuel systems as though the engine had failed to start.
	Incorrect valve clearances	Check and reset clearances.
	Burnt out valves Blown cylinder head gasket	Remove cylinder head and examine and overhaul as necessary.
	Worn out piston rings Worn cylinder bores	Remove cylinder head and examine pistons and cylinder bores. Overhaul as necessary.
Lack of power	Ignition and/or fuel system faults	Check the ignition and fuel systems for correct ignition timing and carburettor settings.
	Incorrect valve clearances	Check and reset the clearances.
	Burnt out valves Blown cylinder head gasket	Remove cylinder head and examine and overhaul as necessary.
	Worn out piston rings Worn cylinder bores	Remove cylinder head and examine pistons and cylinder bores. Overhaul as necessary.
Excessive oil consumption	Oil leaks from crankshaft front and rear oil seals camshaft oil seal, auxiliary shaft oil seal, cambox gasket, oil filter, sump gasket or drain plug	Identify source of leak and renew seal as appropriate.
	Worn piston rings or cylinder bores resulting in oil being burnt by engine, smoky exhaust is an indication	Fit new rings or rebore cylinders and fit new pistons, depending on degree of wear.
	Worn valve guides and/or defective valve stem seals	Remove cylinder heads and recondition valve stem bores and valves and seals as necessary.
Excessive mechanical noise from engine	Wrong valve clearances	Adjust valve clearances.
	Worn crankshaft bearings Worn cylinders (piston slap)	Inspect and overhaul where necessary.
Unusual vibration	Broken engine/gearbox mounting	Renew mounting.
	Misfiring on one or more cylinders	Check ignition system.

Chapter 2 Cooling system

Contents

Antifreeze coolant solution 9	Thermostat — removal, testing and replacement 6
Cooling system — draining 2	Viscous coupling fan — general description and
Cooling system — filling 4	precautions 10
Cooling system — flushing 3	Water pump — dismantling and reassembly 8
Fan belt — removal, replacement and adjustment 11	Water pump — removal and replacement 7
Fault diagnosis — cooling system 13	Water temperature gauge — fault diagnosis and
General description 1	rectification 12
Radiator — removal, inspection, cleaning and replacement 5	

Specifications

Type of system	Pressurized, pump assisted circulation with thermostat and viscous coupling fan.
Capacity (with heater)	14 pints (Imperial)/8 litres
Radiator	Flow capacity is 5 gallons (Imp) in 22 seconds (maximum) with a constant 2 foot head through a 1¼ inch bore pipe. Leak test pressure is 20 lbs/sq in. ($1.4 kg/cm^2$) Filler cap valve opens at 15 lbs/sq in. ($1.05 kg/cm^2$) approx.
Fan belt	V-pulley drive. Tension permits depression of ¼ in. (6 mm) between generator and fan pulleys under thumb pressure.

Thermostat	Western Thomson (valve opens upwards)	AC (valve opens downwards)
Opening temperature	85° to 89° C (185° to 193°F)	80° to 84° C (176° to 183°F)
Fully open temperature	102° C	98° C
Fully open lift from flange	0.51 in. 13.3 mm (min)	0.48 in. 12.2 mm (min)

Torque wrench settings	lb/ft	kg/m
Viscous fan, centre bolt (left-hand thread)	29	4

1 General description

The engine cooling water is circulated by a thermo syphon, water pump assisted system, and the coolant is pressurised. This is both to prevent the loss of water down the overflow pipe with the radiator cap in position, and to prevent premature boiling in adverse conditions.

The radiator cap is, in effect, a safety valve designed to lift at a pressure of 15 lbs/sq in. which means that the coolant can reach a temperature above 125°C (258°F) before it lifts the cap. It then boils off, steam escaping down the overflow pipe. When the temperature/pressure decreases, the cap reseats until the temperature/pressure builds up again. In addition there is a vacuum valve in the cap which permits air to enter the system when it cools.

It is, therefore, important to check that the radiator cap fitted is of the correct specification (the relief pressure is stamped on the top) and in good condition, and that the spring behind the sealing washer has not weakened. Most garages have a device in which radiator caps can be tested.

The system functions in the following fashion: Cold water in the bottom of the radiator circulates up the lower radiator hose to the water pump, where it is pushed round the water passages in the cylinder block, helping to keep the cylinder bores and pistons cool.

The water then travels up into the cylinder head and circulates round the combustion spaces and valve seats absorbing more heat, and then, when the engine is at its proper operating temperature, travels out of the cylinder head, past the open thermostat into the upper radiator hose and so into the radiator head tank.

The water travels down the radiator where it is rapidly cooled by the inrush of cold air through the radiator core, which is created by both the fan and the forward motion of the car. The water, now cold, reaches the bottom of the radiator, whereupon the cycle is repeated.

When the engine is cold the thermostat (a valve which opens and closes according to the temperature of the water) maintains the circulation of the same water in the engine, excluding that in the radiator.

The cooling system comprises the radiator, top and bottom water hoses, heater hoses, the impeller-type water pump, (mounted on the front of the engine it carries the viscous coupling fan and is driven by the fan belt), the thermostat and the two drain taps. In later models the drain taps are replaced by drain plugs.

Only when the correct minimum operating temperature has been reached, as shown in the specification, does the thermostat begin to open, allowing water to return to the radiator.

2 Cooling system — draining

1   With the car on level ground drain the system as follows, turn the heat control lever to the Hot position to avoid air locks.
2   If the engine is cold, remove the filler cap from the radiator by turning the cap anti-clockwise. If the engine is hot, having just been run, then turn the filler cap very slightly until the pressure in the system has had time to disperse. Use a rag over the cap to protect your hand from escaping steam. If, with the engine very hot, the cap is released suddenly, the drop in pressure can result in the water boiling. With the pressure released, the cap can be removed.
3   If antifreeze is in the radiator, drain it into a clean bucket or bowl for re-use.
4   Open the two drain taps or remove the plugs. The radiator drain tap or plug is on the bottom radiator tank and the engine drain tap or plug is halfway down the rear left hand side of the cylinder block. A short length of rubber tubing over the radiator drain tap nozzle will assist draining the coolant into a container without splashing.
5   When the water has finished running, probe the drain orifices with a short piece of wire to dislodge any particles of rust or sediment which may be blocking the taps and preventing all the water draining out.
Note: Opening only the radiator tap or plug will not drain the cylinder block.

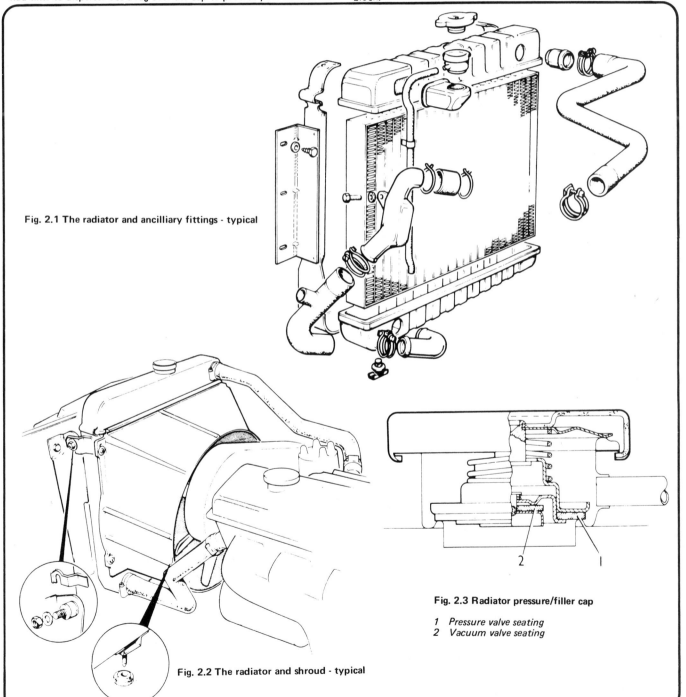

Fig. 2.1 The radiator and ancilliary fittings - typical

Fig. 2.2 The radiator and shroud - typical

Fig. 2.3 Radiator pressure/filler cap

1 *Pressure valve seating*
2 *Vacuum valve seating*

3 Cooling system — flushing

1   With time the cooling system will gradually lose its efficiency as the radiator becomes choked with rust scales, deposits from water and other sediments. To clean the system out, remove the radiator cap and the drain tap and leave a hose running in the radiator cap orifice for ten to fifteen minutes.

2   In very bad cases the radiator should be reverse flushed. This can be done with the radiator in position. The cylinder block tap is closed and a hose placed over the open radiator drain tap. Water under pressure, is then forced up through the radiator and out of the header tank filler orifice.

3   The hose is then removed and placed in the filler orifice and the radiator washed out in the usual fashion.

4 Cooling system — filling

1   Close the two drain taps or apply a non-setting gasket to the plugs and refit them.

2   Fill the system slowly to ensure that air locks are minimised. If a heater is fitted it will be necessary to disconnect the outlet hose at the connector and fill up through the pipe to force air out of the heater battery. The alternative is to turn the heat control lever to the Hot position, but this is not so foolproof as the previous method.

3   Do not fill the system higher than within ½ in. (13 mm) of the filler orifice. Overfilling will merely result in wastage, which is especially to be avoided when antifreeze is in use.

4   Only use antifreeze mixture with an ethylene glycol base. Vauxhall also use an anti-corrosion inhibitor — adding 1/8 Imperial pint (0.07 litre) each month for the first six months is recommended. Thereafter, it should be added each time the coolant is changed. If the inhibitor is used it is strongly recommended that Vauxhall or Castrol antifreeze is also used to prevent possible chemical incompatibility.

5   Replace the filler cap and turn it firmly clockwise to lock it in position.

5 Radiator — removal, inspection, cleaning and replacement

1   Drain the cooling system, as described in Section 2.

2   Undo the clip which holds the top water hose to the header tank and pull it off.

3   Unclip the hose from the bottom of the radiator where applicable, remove the radiator cowl (see Fig. 2.2).

4   Remove the bolts (three each side) which hold the side plates and radiator to the body frame.

5   Lift the radiator complete with plates from the car.

6   With the radiator removed from the car any leaks can be soldered up or repaired with a substance such as 'Cataloy'. An unfortunate fault on some models is the fragile nature of the upper and lower radiator tank sections where the hose pipe unions are soldered. With time they have been known to fracture due to the rocking motion of the flexibly mounted engine — or, of course, with rough handling when removing the flexible rubber hoses. If this occurs, remove the radiator and re-solder the joint, running in a reinforcing fillet of solder. This reduces the flexibility of the thin tank material at the joint. The obvious thing is to take great care when pulling hoses off the hose pipe unions.

Clean out the inside of the radiator by flushing as described in Section 3. When the radiator is out of the car, it is well worthwhile to invert it for reverse flushing. Clean the exterior of the radiator by hosing down the matrix (honeycomb cooling material) with a strong water jet to clear away embedded dirt and insects which will impede the air flow.

7   If it is thought that the radiator may be partially blocked it is possible to test it. Five Imperial gallons (22.73 litres) of water poured through a 1¼ in. (31.75 mm) diameter pipe from a height of 2ft (610 mm) above the filler cap should pass through the radiator in 22 seconds.

If there are obvious indications of blockage a good proprietary chemical product such as 'Radflush' should be used to clear it.

8   Inspect the radiator hoses for cracks, internal or external perishing, and damage caused by overtightening of the securing clips. Replace the hoses as necessary. Examine the radiator hose securing clips and renew them if they are rusted or distorted. The drain taps or plugs should be renewed if leaking, but ensure the leak is not caused by a faulty washer behind the tap. If the tap is suspected, try a new washer first to see if this clears the trouble.

9   Replacement is a straightforward reversal of the removal procedure.

6 Thermostat — removal, testing and replacement

1   To remove the thermostat, partially drain the cooling system (four pints is enough), loosen the upper radiator hose at the thermostat elbow on the intake manifold water jacket and withdraw from the elbow junction.

2   Unscrew the two set bolts and spring washers from the thermostat housing and lift the housing and paper gasket away. (Photo).

3   Remove the thermostat and suspend it by a piece of string in a saucepan of cold water together with a thermometer. Neither the thermostat nor the thermometer should touch the bottom of the saucepan, to ensure a false reading is not given.

4   Heat the water, stirring it gently with the thermometer to ensure temperature uniformity, and note when the thermostat begins to open. The temperature at which this should happen is given in the 'Specifications'.

5   Discard the thermostat if it opens too early. Continue heating the water until the thermostat is fully open. Then let it cool naturally. If the thermostat will not open fully in boiling water, or does not close as the water cools, then it must be exchanged for a new one. If a thermostat is unserviceable it is better to run without one rather than with one which is faulty.

6   If the thermostat is stuck open when cold, this will be apparent when removing it from the housing.

7   Replacing the thermostat is a reversal of the removal procedure. Ensure that the jiggle pin is in the highest position (in the vertical plane) in the thermostat housing. Remember to use a new paper gasket between the thermostat housing elbow and the thermostat. Renew the thermostat elbow if it is badly eaten away.

7 Water pump — removal and replacement

1   Partially drain the cooling system as described in Section 2.

2   Remove the radiator as described in Section 5.

3   Undo the clips which hold the hoses to the water pump and pull the hoses off. This involves removing the top hose first, followed by the elbow bolted to the front of the block.

4   Remove the fan belt and the *complete* viscous fan assembly. The single centre bolt has a left-hand thread.

5   Remove the drivebelt cover.

6   Undo the four bolts which hold the pump body to the cylinder block. Lift the water pump away and remove the gasket.

7   Replacement is a straightforward reversal of the removal sequence (Photo). **Note**: The fan belt tension must be correct when all is reassembled. If the belt is too tight undue strain will be placed on the water pump and alternator bearings, and if the belt is too loose it will slip and wear rapidly as well as giving rise to low electrical output from the alternator.

8 Water pump — dismantling and reassembly

1   Before dismantling check the economics of spares availability and cost against a complete new unit.

2   In order to get at the seal the rotor must be drawn off the shaft. There is no satisfactory way of doing this other than by using a puller —

5.2 Unclipping the radiator hose

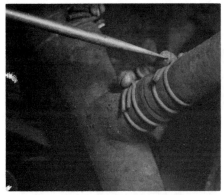

5.3 Disconnecting the heater hose from the bottom radiator hose

6.7a Replacing the thermostat

6.7b Replacing the thermostat cover

6.7c Tightening down the thermostat cover

7.3a Removing the elbow from the water pump inlet

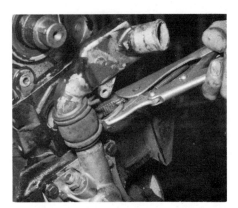

7.3b Removing the hose from the water pump inlet

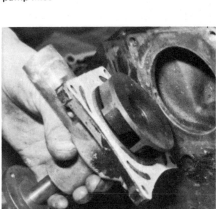

7.7 Refitting the water pump

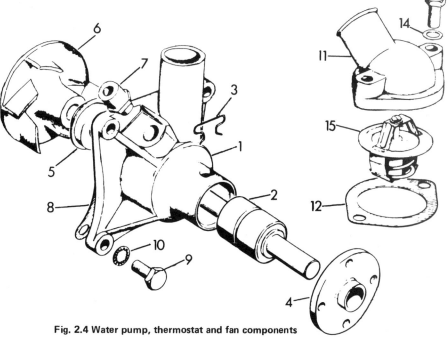

Fig. 2.4 Water pump, thermostat and fan components

1 Water pump	9 Mounting bolt
2 Shaft and bearing assembly	10 Lockwasher
3 Locking clip	11 Water outlet
4 Pulley flange	12 Gasket
5 Seal assembly	13 Bolt
6 Impeller	14 Washer
8 Connector	15 Thermostat
8 Gasket	

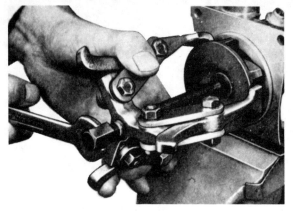

Fig. 2.5 Removing the rotor using a three-legged puller

Fig. 2.6 Removing the shaft locking clip

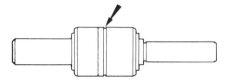

Fig. 2.7 Shaft and bearing showing the locking ring groove that must coincide with the groove in the body

Fig. 2.8 Correct method of assembling the seal

1   The grooves in the sleeve
    must line up with
2   the pip in the casing

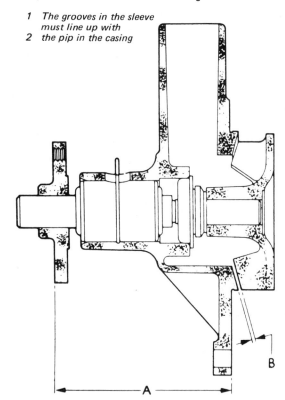

Fig. 2.9 Sectional view through pump assembly

A = 3.24 inches (82.3 mm)
B = 0.05 inches (1.27 mm)

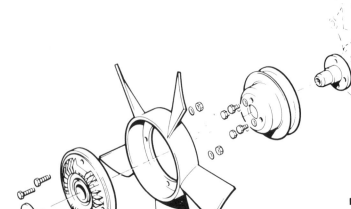

Fig. 2.10 The viscous coupling fan - exploded view

preferably one with two split claws so that the strain can be put onto the rotor astride the vanes which are the strongest part. If the rotor is a particularly tight fit any other way of attempting to remove it will probably break it.

3 With the rotor off, the seal can be withdrawn. Examine the seal on the body of the pump for damage or pitting. **Note**: On some later engines, a ceramic counter-face is installed between the rotor and water seal.

4 If the shaft/bearing assembly needs to be renewed (due to excessive play in the bearings) it can now be removed. First lift out the locking ring and then heat the body of the pump in water to $82^{o}C$ ($180^{o}F$). The shaft can then be drifted out complete with flange at the flange end of the body. When out, press or drive off the flange.

5 Reassembly sequence is in the reverse order but care must be taken to fit everything back in certain positions.

6 If the shaft assembly is being renewed, first of all press the flange on to the larger diameter of the new shaft.

7 Ensure that the flange boss is towards the end of the shaft and that the outer face of the flange is 3.24 in. (82.3 mm) from the end of the body. (See Fig. 2.9).

8 Reheat the pump body and install the shaft and bearing so that the groove in the bearing coincides with the groove in the body bore. Refit the locking ring.

9 Smear the face of the new seal and also around the body bore with the recommended grease, and install the seal. Note that the seal has a sleeve in the centre and this must be engaged properly. There are corresponding pips and grooves. Where applicable fit the counterface with the ceramic side towards the seal.

10 Press on the rotor (vanes inwards) so that the clearance between the flat face of the rotor and the pump body is 0.05 in. (1.27 mm). Fit a new gasket when replacing the pump on the block.

9 Antifreeze coolant solution

1 Where temperatures are likely to drop below freezing point, the coolant system must be adequately protected by the addition of antifreeze. Even if you keep the engine warm at night it is possible for water to freeze in the radiator with the engine running in very cold conditions — particularly if the engine cooling is being adequately dealt with by the heater radiator. The thermostat stays closed and the radiator water does not circulate.

2 It is best to drain the coolant completely and flush out the system first.

3 The table below gives the details of the antifreeze percentage to be used (on the basis of the cooling system capacity of 14 pints (8 litres).

%	Quantity	Complete protection
25	3.5 pints (2 litres)	$-11^{o}C$
35	4.9 pints (2.8 litres)	$-19^{o}C$
45	6.3 pints (3.6 litres)	$-29^{o}C$

4 Mix the required quantity of antifreeze with about 4 pints (2 litres) of water and fill the system. Top-up with water and then run the engine up to normal temperature with the heater turned on.

10 Viscous coupling fan — general description and precautions

1 The viscous coupling is filled with oil and allows direct drive to the fan at speeds up to 1000 rpm, after which it progressively begins to slip as engine speed increases. Fan noise correspondingly decreases without impairing the efficiency of the system.

2 The viscous coupling is bolted to the hub of an irregularly spaced 5-bladed fan, and the fan and coupling assembly are attached to a flange on the water pump by a single left-hand-thread bolt.

3 The fan and coupling are a balanced assembly and if they are separated it is essential that they are reconnected in their original relative positions.

4 The coupling is a sealed unit and cannot be dismantled. If there is any sign of oil leakage past the seals, the fan and coupling must both be renewed.

11 Fan belt — removal, replacement and adjustment

1 If the fan belt is worn, or has stretched unduly, it should be renewed. The most usual reason for renewal is breakage in service and every wise motorist will carry a spare.

2 Even though the belt may have broken and fallen off, go through the removal routine which is first of all to loosen the two alternator pivot bolts and the nut on the adjusting link (brace), then move the alternator inwards. Take the old belt off the three pulleys if it has not fallen off after breaking.

3 Put a new belt over the pulleys.

4 The alternator must now be used as a tensioner in effect, by pulling it away from the engine and locking it in the required position. This can call for some sustained effort unless the pivot bolts are slackened only a little so that the alternator is quite stiff to move. A lever between the alternator and block can help, but do not apply any pressure to the rear end shield or the cover may break.

5 The tension of the belt midway between the alternator and water pump pulleys should be ¼ in. (6.35 mm) under thumb pressure. If in doubt it is better to be a little slack than tight. Only slipping will occur if it is too slack. If too tight, damage can be caused by excessive strain on the pulley bearings.

6 When the adjustment is right, tighten all the mounting bolts in the following order: first the front mounting bolt nut; then the slotted brace to alternator bolt; the rear mounting bolt nut, and finally the bolt securing the slotted brace to the engine. This technique prevents side loads being imposed on the lugs.

7 With a new belt, check the tension 250 miles (400 km) after fitting.

8 Periodic checking of the belt tension is necessary and there is no hard and fast rule as to the most suitable interval, because fan belts do not necessarily stretch or wear to a pre-determined schedule. Assuming most owners check their own oil and water regularly, it is suggested as a good habit to check the fan belt tension every time the bonnet goes up. It takes only a second.

12 Water temperature gauge — fault diagnosis and rectification

1 If no reading is shown on the elctrically operated water temperature gauge when the engine is hot and the ignition switched on, either the gauge, the sender unit, or the wiring in between is at fault. Alternatively, No 2 fuse may have blown. If the fuel gauge is also not working, check that the instrument voltage stabiliser is in order as described in Chapter 10.

2 Check the fuse and, if satisfactory, pull off the wire from the sender unit in the cylinder head and connect it to earth.

3 Switch on the ignition and check if the gauge is working. The needle should rise to the 'H' (hot) or $130^{o}C$ mark which indicates that the sender unit must be renewed. To do this simply undo it and fit a replacement item.

4 If the sender unit is apparently working correctly, check the gauge and, if necessary, replace it. Details of how to remove the gauge are given in Chapter 10.

Fault diagnosis overleaf

13 Fault diagnosis — Cooling system

Symptom	Reason/s	Remedy
Loss of coolant	Leak in system	Examine all hoses, hose connections, drain taps and the radiator and heater for signs of leakage when the engine is cold, then when hot and under pressure. Tighten clips, renew hoses and repair radiator as necessary.
	Defective radiator pressure cap	Examine cap for defective seal or spring and renew if necessary.
	Overheating causing rapid evaporation due to excessive pressure in system forcing vapour past radiator cap	Check reasons for overheating.
	Blown cylinder head gasket causing excess pressure in cooling system forcing coolant past radiator cap overflow	Remove cylinder head for examination
	Cracked block or head due to freezing	Strip engine and examine. Repair as required.
Overheating	Insufficient coolant in system	Top up.
	Water pump not turning properly due to slack fan belt	Tighten fan belt.
	Kinked or collapsed water hoses causing restriction to circulation of coolant	Renew hose as required.
	Faulty thermostat (not opening properly)	Fit new thermostat.
	Engine out of tune	Check ignition setting and carburettor adjustments.
	Blocked radiator either internally or externally	Flush out cooling system and clean out cooling fins.
	Cylinder head gaskets blown forcing coolant out of system	Remove head and renew gasket.
	New engine not run-in	Adjust engine speed until run-in.
	Viscous coupling leaking.	Replace viscous coupling and fan.
Engine running too cool	Missing or faulty thermostat	Fit new thermostat.
	Viscous coupling seized	Replace viscous coupling and fan.

Chapter 3 Carburation; fuel and exhaust systems

Contents

Accelerator cable and pedal 17	Temperature controlled air cleaner — description and operating check 2
Air cleaner element — removal and refitting 3	Zenith 361 VE carburettor — adjustment 10
Exhaust manifold 19	Zenith 361 VE carburettor — description 8
Exhaust system 20	Zenith 361 VE carburettor — removal, dismantling, reassembly
Fault diagnosis — fuel system and carburation 21	and replacement 9
Fuel gauge sender unit — fault finding... 16	Zenith/Stromberg 175CD—2SET carburettor 14
Fuel pump — alternative models 7	Zenith/Stromberg 175CD—2SE carburettor — adjustment and
Fuel pump — dismantling 5	balancing 13
Fuel pump — inspection, reassembly and replacement 6	Zenith/Stromberg 175CD—2SE carburettor — description ... 11
Fuel pump — removal 4	Zenith/Stromberg 175CD—2SE carburettor — removal,
Fuel tank — removal and replacement 15	dismantling, reassembly and replacement 12
General description 1	
Intake manifold 18	

Specifications

Fuel pump

Make and type	AC, mechanical. On some models a re-circulating (3-port) pump is used

Delivery pressure

Standard pump	2 to 3½ lb/in^2 (0.14 to 0.245 kg/cm^2)
Re-circulating pump	2¾ to 4¼ lb/in^2 (0.19 to 0.3 kg/cm^2)

Air cleaner

Type	Thermostatically controlled, paper element type

Fuel tank capacity ... ... 12 gallons (Imperial)/55 litres

Fuel octane requirements

Standard 8.5:1 compression ratio	Premium grade (4-star)
Optional 7.3:1 compression ratio (1800 only)	Regular grade (2-star)

Carburettor (1800 models)

Make and type	Zenith 36IVE
Identification number	
Manual transmission	3583B
Automatic transmission	3584B
Choke tube	25mm
Main jet	115
Compensating jet	125
Pump jet	55
Part throttle air bleed screw	1.9mm
Needle valve	2mm
Needle valve washer thickness	2mm
Float position	With carburettor cover inverted and needle valve on seating, highest point of floats should be 30.5 to 31.5 mm above face of cover gasket
Engine idling speed*	725 to 775 rev/min

On cars with automatic transmission, specified idling speed to be obtained with a drive range selected

Carburettor (2300 models)

Make and type		
Manual transmission		Zenith/Stromberg 175 CD—2SE
Automatic transmission		Zenith/Stromberg 175 CD—2SET
Identification number		
Manual transmission		3599B
Automatic transmission		3600B
Metering needle		B1DC
Orifice		2.54mm
Valve spring identification colour		Blue
Fast idle cam		
Manual transmission		D
Automatic transmission		T1
Cold start needle		3mm
Needle valve		2mm
Needle valve washer thickness		1.6mm
Float position		With carburettor inverted and needle valve on seating, highest point of floats should be 16 to 17mm above the face of the main body with the gasket removed
Engine idling speed*		775 to 825 rev/min

On cars with automatic transmission, specified idling speed to be obtained with a drive range selected

1 General description

1 The system comprises a 12-gallon rear mounted fuel tank, a mechanically operated fuel pump, a single carburettor (1800 models), twin carburettors (2300 models), thermostatically controlled air cleaner and the associated interconnecting pipes.

2 The carburettor used on 1800 models is the Zenith 36IVE which is a downdraught type, incorporating an accelerator pump and diaphragm-type economy device. The carburettors used on 2300 models are two Zenith-Stromberg 175CD—2SE (manual transmission) or 175CD—2SET (automatic transmission); these are horizontal, variable choke units. The carburettors are described in separate Sections later in this Chapter.

2 Temperature controlled air cleaner — description and operating check

1 The air cleaner incorporates a temperature sensor, vacuum motor and control damper assembly.

2. The damper assembly regulates the carburettor inlet air temperature by opening and closing air ports. Hot air is generated in a shroud covering the exhaust manifold and cold air is taken from the engine compartment. It is routed to the air cleaner through hoses in proportions determined by the control damper assembly, which is in turn moved by a diaphragm type vacuum motor.

3 The vacuum motor is controlled by a temperature sensor which bleeds air into the vacuum line according to the ambient temperature.

4 Most of the time both damper ports will be partly open but when the engine is stationary, the control damper diaphragm spring closes the hot air damper and opens the cold air damper.

5 At temperatures below 10°C/50°F (ie: cold starting) the hot air port opens immediately the engine starts, and the cold air port closes. As the engine warms up, the bi-metal spring in the temperature sensor starts to bleed air into the vacuum line. The hot air port starts to close and the cold air port starts to open, thereby providing a suitable inlet air temperature for the most efficient combustion.

6 Under conditions of hard acceleration the vacuum level may fall and the cold air port will be fully open in order to allow maximum airflow for maximum acceleration.

7 Any fault in the unit is likely to result in the cold air port remaining open (rather than the hot air port remaining open), and may go unnoticed in warm weather. In cold weather where there is evidence of weak mixture, stalling, hesitancy, etc., the following basic checks will help to establish whether the system is functioning satisfactorily.

8 Check all hoses and connections for security, kinks, blockages or other damage.

9 With the engine stationary, use a mirror to observe the damper position. The cold air port should be open and the hot air port closed. If unsatisfactory, check for binding of the linkage.

10 Check the operation of the vacuum motor by removing the suction pipe on the air cleaner, and sucking (by mouth). If functioning satisfactorily, the cold air port should be closed and the hot air port opened. If unsatisfactory, check the linkage and ensure that there are no vacuum leaks.

11 If the test at paragraph 10 is satisfactory, clamp the hose to trap the vacuum in the motor assembly and check that the cold air port remains closed and the hot air port remains open. If unsatisfactory there is a leak in the diaphragm assembly.

12 The vacuum motor may be replaced by drilling out the spot welds on the retaining strap, fitting a new unit and retaining it with short self-tapping screws.

13 If the previous tests are satisfactory, a basic check of the sensor can be carried out by starting the engine at a temperature less than 10°C (50°F) and checking that immediately after starting, the cold air port is closed and the hot air port is open. As the engine warms up, the damper should start to move and the air cleaner should become warm to the hand.

14 Further checks will need the use of a thermometer which can be fitted inside the air cleaner and should be left to a Vauxhall dealer to check.

15 To renew the temperature sensor, remove the air cleaner cover, pull off the vacuum pipes and remove the retaining clip. Refitting is then straightforward.

3 Air cleaner element removal and refitting

1800 models

1 Remove the screws retaining the air cleaner top cover, carefully prise-off the cover and remove the filter element. (See Fig. 3.1).

2 The filter element can be tapped sharply on a hard surface to remove light deposits of dust, but where there is heavy contamination the element should be renewed.

3 Carefully wipe clean the interior of the air cleaner using a lint-free cloth, taking care not to allow dirt to enter the carburettor inlet.

4 Before installing the element, ensure that the drain hole in the casing is clear; also ensure that the rubber rings are correctly positioned on the top cover and air cleaner body.

5 Reassembly is the reverse of the removal procedure.

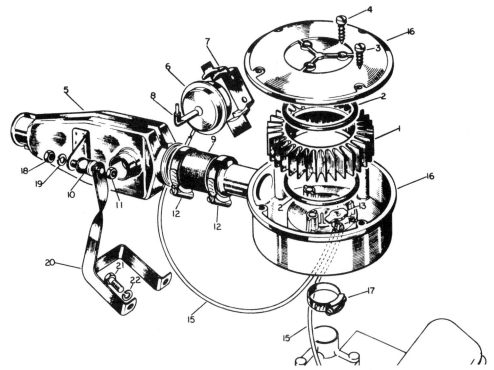

Fig. 3.1 Temperature controlled air cleaner - **1800 model**

1	Element	6	Diaphragm motor assembly	11	Nut	17	Clip
2	Gasket	7	Retainer	12	Clip	18	Nut
3	Screw	8	Tube	13	Sensor	19	Lockwasher
4	Screw	9	Hose	15	Tube	20	Bracket assembly
5	Air tube assembly	10	Mounting	16	Cover		

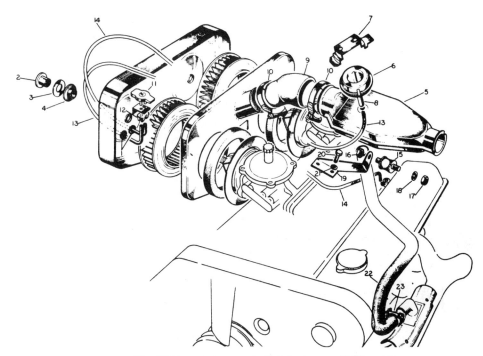

Fig. 3.2 Temperature controlled air cleaner - **2300 models**

1	Grommet	7	Retainer	13	Hose	19	Bracket
2	Nut	8	Tube	14	Hose	20	Bolt
3	Washer	9	Hose	15	Mounting	21	Lockwasher
4	Grommet	10	Clip	16	Nut	22	Hose
5	Air tube assembly	11	Sensor	17	Nut	23	Clip
6	Diaphragm motor assembly	12	Fastener	18	Lockwasher		

Fig. 3.4 Fuel pump fitted to some models: the arrow indicates the re-circulatory pipe connection

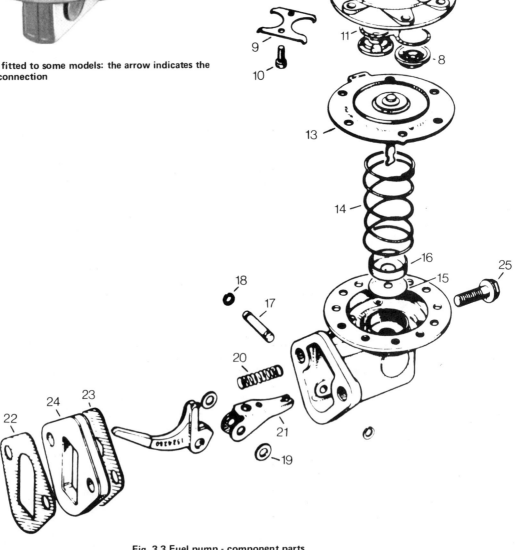

Fig. 3.3 Fuel pump - component parts

1 Upper cover screw	7 Securing stirrup	14 Spring	20 Spring
2 Upper cover screw	8 Valve	15 Oil seal	21 Link
3 Lockwasher	9 Valve retainer	16 Oil seal retainer	22 Gasket - engine pad
4 Filter screen	10 Retainer screw	17 Rocker arm pin	23 Gasket - fuel pump
5 Filter bowl	11 Valve gasket	18 Pin clip	24 Insulator
6 Gasket	13 Diaphragm	19 Spacer	25 Mounting bolt

Note: On some models item 22 is not fitted

2300 models

6   Remove the two flexible tubes on the air cleaner cover noting their respective installed positions (See Fig. 3.2).

7   Remove the two special square-headed retainers and the lower bolt.

8   Manoeuvre the cover until the two air cleaner elements can be withdrawn from inside the casing (taking care not to damage them if they are to be used again).

9   Remove the outer cover.

10 The filter elements should be tapped sharply on a hard surface to remove light deposits of dust, but where there is heavy contamination the elements should be renewed.

11 Carefully wipe clean the inside of the air cleaner using a lint-free cloth, taking care not to allow dirt to enter the carburettor inlets.

12 Reassembly is the reverse of the removal procedure, but ensure that the elements are seated correctly or the carburettor balance may be upset. Also ensure that the elements do not tilt when the cover is being fitted.

4   Fuel pump — removal

1   Disconnect the fuel lines.

2   Remove the two bolts holding the pump to the block and lift it away.

3   Recover the insulator block and gaskets.

5   Fuel pump — dismantling

1   Undo the knurled screw holding the glass bowl in position and lift off the filter screen.

2   Mark the relationship between centre and base sections of the pump body and then remove the five securing screws and lift off the centre section.

3   To release the diaphragm, depress the centre and turn it 90°. This will release the diaphragm pull rod from the stirrup in the operating link. Lift out the seal and seal retainer.

4   Do not remove the rocker arm and pivot pin from the body base unless there are signs of excessive wear — in which case it would probably be more economical to obtain an exchange pump.

5   To remove the valve assemblies from the body centre, undo the retaining plate screws and lift out each valve and the gasket behind them.

6   Fuel pump — inspection, reassembly and replacement

1   Examine the diaphragm for signs of splitting or cracking and renew it if in any doubt.

2   If the valves are suspected or malfunctioning, renew them.

3   The filter screen should be intact with no signs of enlarged holes or broken strands.

4   Renew the oil seal.

5   Clean up the recesses where the valves have been staked into the body to ensure that when replaced the valves will seat neatly.

6   To refit the valves fit a new gasket first and then locate each valve the correct way up. The inlet valve has its spring facing the bottom of the pump. Later models have the valves staked in position and these are not easily removed and replaced. Valves should be tapped or pressed into position using a sleeve with bore diameter 0.56 in. (14.22 mm) and external diameter 0.68 in. (17.27mm). Each one must lie perfectly flat and be staked securely with a flat nosed punch around the edge in six places.

7   To refit the diaphragm first put a new oil seal followed by the retainer into the body base. Put the diaphragm pull rod through the seal and the groove in the rocker arm link. Then turn the diaphragm anticlockwise 90° so that it lines up with the screw holes and the lug on the body aligns with the tab on the diaphragm.

8   Move the rocker arm until the diaphragm is level with the body flanges and hold the arm in this position. Reassemble the two halves of the pump ensuring that the previously made marks on the flanges are adjacent to each other.

9   Insert the five screws and lockwashers and tighten them down finger tight.

10 Move the rocker arm up and down several times to centralise the diaphragm, and then with the arm held down, tighten the screws securely in a diagonal sequence.

11 Replace the gauze filter in position. Fit the cover sealing ring, glass bowl and securing stirrup. Tighten the nut with the fingers only.

12 Fuel pump replacement is a straightforward reversal of the removal procedure. However, note the following points:

a) The fuel pump should be assembled to the engine block with new gaskets — one each side of the insulator block.

b) Ensure that the pump operating arm is resting on the camshaft, and not under it.

c) Do not overtighten the pump retaining bolts.

d) Test that the pump is working, by disconnecting the pipe feed at the carburettor, holding a container under it and getting someone to turn the engine. The fuel should spurt out in intermittent jets.

7   Fuel pump — alternative types

Although all of the fuel pumps are basically similar, there are one or two differences on some models that might create a few problems unless listed here, they are:

1   Not all pumps are provided with a diaphragm oil seal and retainer, or fuel drain holes in the pump body. A diaphragm oil seal and retainer must be used on pumps with fuel drain holes to prevent emission of crankcase vapours.

2   On some cars a recirculating fuel system is used. This comprises a fuel pump having an additional part with a restricted hole, in the outlet side of the pump. This part is connected by a return pipe to an additional tube in the fuel gauge tank unit. When checking delivery pressure on this type of pump, the return port must be sealed off (Fig. 3.4).

3   On later engines the gasket between the crankcase and the fuel pump heater insulator is deleted. When installing pump, assemble the single baffle gasket between the pump flange and the insulator so that the edges of centre slot project away from the pump.

8   Zenith 36IVE carburettor — description

1   The Zenith downdraught carburettor is fitted with an accelerator pump and incorporates an economy unit to correct fuel mixture at certain intermediate engine speeds. The principle of operation is as follows: At full throttle opening with the choke flap open, the depression (low pressure) in the choke tube draws a fuel/air mixture from the main discharge beak.

The fuel/air mixture has been emulsified in the emulsion tube below the discharge beak. The fuel has reached the emulsion tube, via the reserve well, from the main jet in the float chamber.

When the engine is cold and the choke flap is closed the throttle flap is automatically slightly opened by a pre-determined amount.

The choke tube depression draws principally on the discharge beak and therefore a very rich mixture reaches the engine, as air from the main air inlet has been closed off.

At idling speed, with the throttle shut, there is no depression at the main discharge beak. It is now concentrated at the idling discharge orifice on the engine side of the throttle flap. Fuel from the main reserve well is drawn via the pilot jet to this orifice, taking the requisite amount of air for the mixture through the pilot air bleed by-pass orifice. The volume of the mixture supplied is controlled by the idling mixture control screw.

As soon as the throttle is opened further, the bypass orifice is then

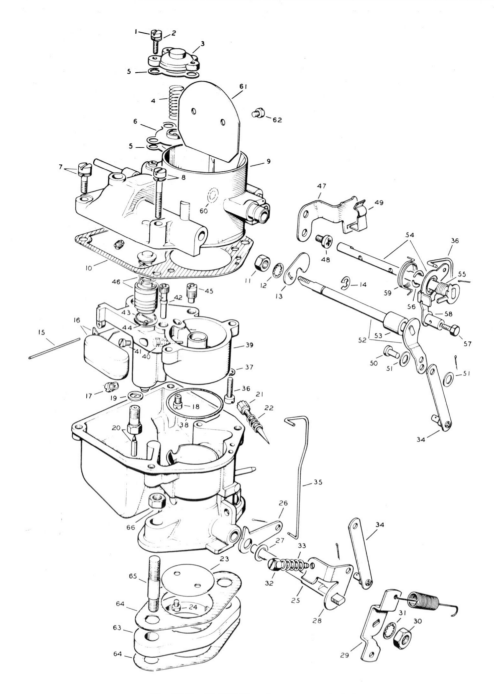

Fig. 3.5 Zenith 36IVE carburettor - exploded view

1 Screw
2 Spring washer
3 Economy valve cover
4 Spring
5 Gasket
6 Economy valve diaphragm assy
7 Screw and spring washer
8 Screw and spring washer
9 Float chamber cover
10 Gasket
11 Nut
12 Lockwasher
13 Lever
14 Retaining ring
15 Pivot
16 Float assembly
17 Main jet

18 Compensating jet
19 Washer
20 Needle and seating
21 Volume control screw
22 Spring
23 Throttle
24 Screw
25 Throttle spindle
26 Lever
27 Washer
28 Throttle stop
29 Throttle lever
30 Nut
31 Lockwasher
32 Throttle stop
33 Spring
34 Link assembly

35 Interconnection link
36 Screw
37 Spring washer
38 Sealing ring
39 Emulsion block assembly
40 Pump jet
41 Plug
42 Pump discharge valve assy.
43 Circlip
44 Ball
45 Slow running jet
46 Pump piston assembly
47 Bracket
48 Screw
49 Clip
50 Pin
51 Washer

52 Spindle and lever assembly
53 Washer
54 Spindle and lever assembly
55 Spring
56 Circlip
57 Screw
58 Lever
59 Spring
60 Washer
61 Strangler flap
62 Screw
63 Heat insulator
64 Gasket
65 Stud
66 Nut

also subject to depression so instead of feeding air in one direction to the idling discharge orifice, it now delivers fuel/air mixture in the other direction until the throttle is open sufficiently for the main discharge beak to take over.

The economy unit augments the fuel flow from the main jet automatically through the economy jet when the choke tube depression is low. At cruising speeds, when the depression is high, a diaphragm operated valve shuts off the economy jet.

There is also an accelerator pump which delivers a metered jet of neat fuel into the choke tube whenever the accelerator pedal is operated quickly. This gives the richer mixture necessary for rapid acceleration. The fuel is drawn from the float chamber into the pump chamber via a non-return valve at the bottom of the float chamber. When the pump is operated quickly (ie sudden accelerator pedal operation) the pump release valve is forced shut under pressure and the fuel passes through the injector. If the pump is operated slowly, the pressure is insufficient to close the release valve, so fuel passes through it back to the float chamber rather than out of the injector.

9 Zenith 36IVE carburettor — removal, dismantling, reassembly and replacement

1 Most of the carburettor is incorporated in the top cover so do not take the carburettor off the car unless you have to. Remove the air cleaner assembly.

2 Undo the choke cable clamp screw and disconnect the choke cable clip.

3 Slacken the throttle cable outer clamp/adjusting screw.

4 Remove the throttle spindle return spring and unhook the cable nipple from the lever.

5 Pull off the fuel feed pipe and the vacuum pipe.

6 Undo the two retaining nuts and lift the carburettor off together with the gaskets and insulator block.

7 To remove the top cover disconnect the pump linkage and choke control rod. Undo the four screws and lift the cover off carefully to avoid damaging the gasket. Take care also not to bend or damage the floats which are attached to the cover.

8 To get to the jets and accelerator pump the emulsion block must be removed from the underside of the cover. First draw out the pin on which the floats pivot and lift out the needle valve.

9 Unscrew the needle valve seat. Undo the two screws holding the emulsion block to the cover.

10 When releasing the emulsion block take care to prevent the accelerator pump and spring dropping out.

11 The economy device is held on the top cover by three screws. When these are released the cover, diaphragm and spring may be lifted out. See that the diaphragm is intact.

12 Reassembly starts with the refitting of the emulsion block to the cover. See first that the non-return ball and retaining clip of the accelerator pump are in position.

13 Fit a new gasket and ensure that the accelerator pump lever is positioned correctly (Fig. 3.7).

14 Examine the needle valve for any signs of ridging on the bevelled face and renew both the needle and the seat if in doubt.

15 Refit the floats and spindle and, holding the cover upside down, measure the distance from the bottom of the floats to the face of the cover gasket (Fig. 3.8). It should be 30.5 to 31.5 mm. Make adjustments by carefully bending the float arm centre tag which contacts the needle. This setting is important.

16 Before replacing the cover to the body check that the sealing ring around the choke tube is in good order (Fig. 3.9). A bad seal will result in fuel leaking from the float chamber.

17 Reconnect the accelerator pump linkage noting that the pin should be fitted to the upper hole in the pump lever where automatic transmission is fitted or the lower hole where manual transmission is fitted.

18 The choke control rod is not provided with any obvious adjustment. With the choke flap held shut there should be a 0.040 in gap (1mm — No 61 drill) down the side of the throttle flap. Bend the

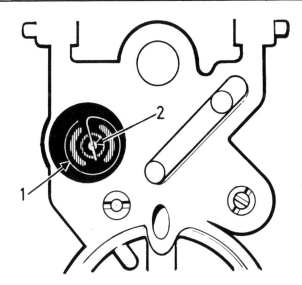

Fig. 3.6 Zenith 36IVE carburettor

Location of accelerator pump inlet ball (2) and locating clip (1) in the emulsion block

Fig. 3.7 Zenith 36IVE carburettor

Location of accelerator pump lever (A) on assembly

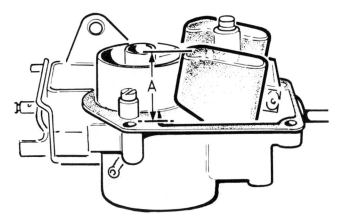

Fig. 3.8 Zenith 36IVE carburettor

Float level height - A = 30.5 to 31.5 mm

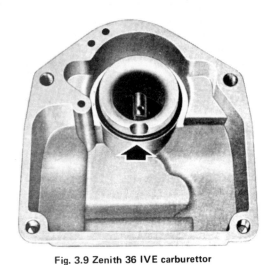

Fig. 3.9 Zenith 36 IVE carburettor

Sealing ring (arrowed) for between float chamber and cover

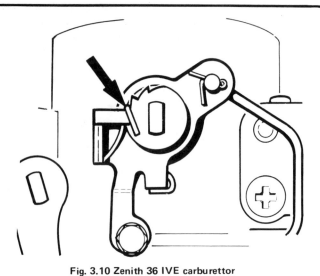

Fig. 3.10 Zenith 36 IVE carburettor

Position of choke flap spindle return spring (arrowed)

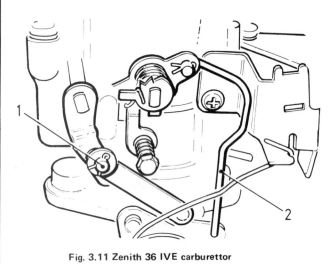

Fig. 3.11 Zenith 36 IVE carburettor

1   Pump lever link pin   2   Choke control rod
See text for position of link pin

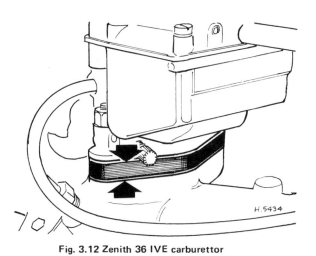

Fig. 3.12 Zenith 36 IVE carburettor

Heat insulator and gaskets (arrowed)

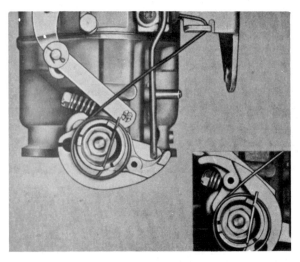

Fig. 3.13 Zenith 36 IVE carburettor

Throttle lever return spring position - (inset LHD)

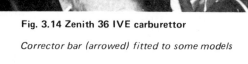

Fig. 3.14 Zenith 36 IVE carburettor

Corrector bar (arrowed) fitted to some models

Fig. 3.15a Zenith 36 IVE carburettor

1   *Volume control screw*   2   *Throttle stop screw*

control rod if necessary to get this setting.

19 The choke flap spindle return spring should engage the first notch on the lever.

20 When refitting the carburettor to the inlet manifold use two new gaskets one each side of the heat insulator.

21 If a corrector bar is fitted to your particular engine, ensure that the ends of the bar (Fig. 3.14) are located in the cut-outs in the gasket.

22 When reconnecting the throttle cable and return spring locate the return spring correctly.

23 It is important that the outer cable of the throttle is adjusted so that when the accelerator pedal is down as far as it will go the throttle flap is just fully open. The throttle should not open fully before the pedal is right down otherwise further pressure will impart a very severe strain on the throttle spindle.

24 Make sure that the choke cable operates correctly also and that the outer sleeve is clipped far enough back to allow full travel of the choke spindle lever.

10 Zenith 36 IVE carburettor — adjustment

1   If it is known that the reason for adjustment is something more than just slow running then check the settings as described in the previous Section on assembly.

2   Slow running adjustment is carried out by the throttle stop screw and volume control screw together.

3   First get the engine up to running temperature and set the volume control screw 1¼ turns out from closed. Then set the throttle stop screw so that the engine runs fast enough not to stall. Adjust the volume control screw one way or the other so the engine speed increases and then reduce speed using the throttle stop screw. Keep doing this in stages until the tickover speed is even, and is at 725 to 775 rev/min.

4   With automatic transmission the adjustment is made with drive or reverse engaged and the handbrake on, otherwise the procedure is the same.

11 Zenith/Stromberg 175CD—2SE carburettor — description

This carburettor has a single horizontal variable choke and is quite different in principle of operation to the fixed choked Zenith. The air intake is choked by a cylindrical air valve which moves vertically (Fig. 3.15B).

1   To the base of the air valve a tapered needle is fitted which runs in and out of a jet orifice through which fuel is drawn from the float chamber which is underneath the main body. Suction from the engine inlet manifold passes through a hole in the base of the air valve to the suction chamber. This suction acts on the diaphragm, to which the air

valve and metering needle are attached, and raises them. This increases the air flow through the choke tube and the fuel flow through the jet as the tapered needle withdraws. As the air valve rises to the concentration of suction through the valve hole is reduced and the valve reaches a point of equilibrium, balanced against throttle opening and air valve height.

2   Sudden acceleration demands would apparently cause the air valve to rise sharply, thus tending to weaken the mixture. In fact the rise of the valve is damped by an oil controlled piston. Thus when the throttle is opened suddenly the initial suction is concentrated at the fuel jet and the quantity of air let through to reduce the mixture richness to normal occurs slightly later as the piston rises. The taper of the metering needle is obviously the main controlling feature of the carburettor's performance and this controls the fuel/air mixture at all heights of the valve. At the same time the height of the air valve is nicely balanced, according to throttle opening, in conjunction with the metering needle. The jet itself is adjustable by raising or lowering, thus altering the position of the jet orifice in relation to the taper of the needle.

3   For cold starts there is a device mounted on the side of the front carburettor consisting of a rotating disc with a number of holes drilled in it. When the disc is moved by the control lever a passageway is opened up. Depending on the number of holes uncovered so the flow is restricted. The fuel from the float chamber can then be drawn directly into the choke tube supplementing that from the main jet.

4   The carburettor incorporates a temperature compensator to control minor mixture strength variations caused by heat transfer from the engine to the carburettor body (see Fig. 3.18). The assembly is preset and cannot be adjusted.

12 Zenith/Stromberg 175CD—2SE carburettor — removal, dismantling, reassembly and replacement

1   Remove the air cleaner then disconnect the accelerator cable at the carburettor.

2   Disconnect the choke cable.

3   Disconnect the throttle coupling linkage.

4   Detach the carburettor interconnecting pipes.

5   Undo and remove the carburettor mounting nuts and bolts. Lift off the carburettor(s) complete with gasket(s).

6   With the carburettor on the bench, undo and remove the damper cap and plunger. Mark the relative positions of the suction chamber cover and main body and then undo and remove the four screws and spring washers which hold the suction chamber cover in place. Lift away the cover.

7   The air valve complete with needle and diaphragm may now be lifted away. Handle the assembly with the greatest of care as it is very easy to damage the needle accidently.

8   The bottom of the float chamber may next be removed. Undo and remove the six retaining screws and spring washers noting that they are of different lengths. Lift away the float chamber and gasket. **Note:** It may be necessary to rotate the adjuster slightly to break the O-ring seal on the jet assembly.

9   Withdraw the pin that acts as a pivot/retainer from the float assembly. Lift away the float assembly, then unscrew the fuel level needle valve. Do not attempt to remove the filter gauze.

10 If desired, the needle may be removed from the air valve by slackening the small grub screw in the side of the piston.

11 To remove the diaphragm from the piston, simply undo the four screws and washers which hold the diaphragm retaining ring in place.

12 From the carburettor body, unscrew the jet adjuster.

13 Undo and remove the two screws and spring washers that secure the cold start device to the side of the main body.

14 Remove the cover from the temperature compensator to check that all is clean and in order. Do not attempt to dismantle it.

15 On reassembly there are several points which should be noted particularly. The first is that if fitting a new needle to the piston ensure it has the same markings stamped on it as the old one. Fit it

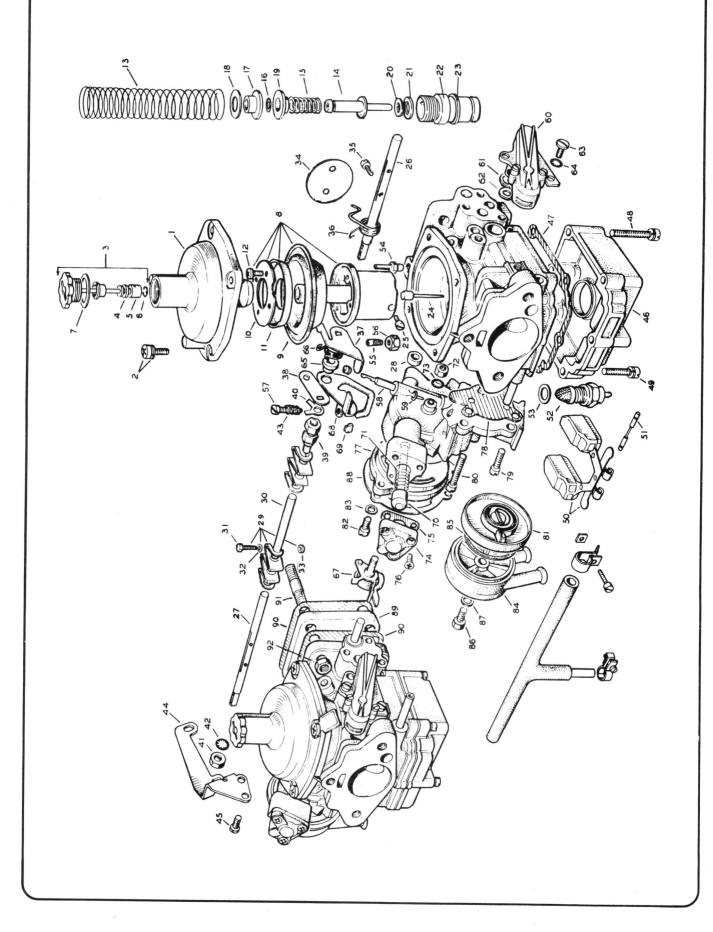

Fig. 3.15b Zenith Stromberg 175CD-2SET carburettor - exploded view
Note: The 175CD-2SE is similar. See Fig. 3.20 which shows the linkage and cable connections

1 Cover
2 Screw and spring washer
3 Damper assembly
4 Washer
5 Bushing
6 Retaining ring
7 Washer
8 Air valve
9 Diaphragm
10 Retaining washer
11 Sealing ring
12 Screw
13 Spring
14 Jet and 'O' ring
15 Spring
16 'O' ring
17 Bushing
18 Washer
19 Washer

20 Nylon washer
21 Plain washer
22 Jet adjuster
23 'O' ring
24 Needle
25 Screw
26 Throttle spindle
27 Throttle spindle
28 Seal
29 Coupling assembly
30 Coupling spindle
31 Bolt
32 Washer
33 Nut
34 Throttle
35 Screw
36 Throttle return
37 Throttle stop lever
38 Throttle lever

39 Nut
40 Tab washer
41 Nut
42 Shake proof washer
43 Spring
44 Detent bracket
45 Screw
46 Floatchamber
47 Gasket
48 Screw and washer assembly
49 Screw and washer assembly
50 Float and arm assembly
51 Pivot
52 Needle valve and filter assy
53 Washer
54 Adaptor
55 Throttle stop screw
56 Lock nut
57 Fast idle screw

58 Needle assembly
59 'O' ring
60 Temperature compensator assembly
61 Sealing washer outer
62 Sealing washer inner
63 Screw
64 Shake proof washer
65 Bush
66 Spring
67 Fast idle cam
68 Fast idle lever
69 Cover
70 Vacuum kick piston assembly
71 Spring
72 Nut
73 Shake proof washer
74 Cover
75 Gasket
76 Screw

77 Insulator
78 Gasket
79 Screw
80 Screw
81 Heat mass assembly
82 Washer
83 Cover
84 Cover
85 Washer
86 Screw
87 Washer
88 Clamping ring
89 Heat insulator
90 Gasket
91 Stud
92 Nut

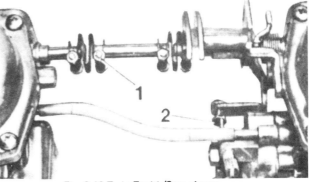

Fig. 3.16 Twin Zenith/Strombergs

1 Throttle coupling clamp bolt 2 Stop screw

Fig. 3.17 Zenith/Stromberg 175D-2SE carburettor

Float level setting A = 16 to 17 mm

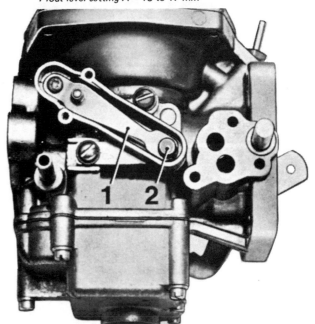

Fig. 3.18 Zenith/Stromberg 175CD-2SE carburettor
Temperature compensation (cover removed)
1 Be-metal strip 2 Tapered plug

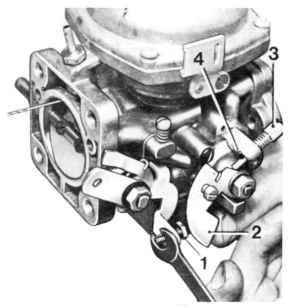

Fig. 3.19 Zenith/Stromberg 175CD-2SE carburettor

Fast idle setting

1 Stop screw
2 Fast idle cam
3 Cold start stop pin

4 Stop pin cross piece in
vertical position

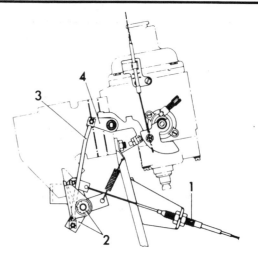

Fig. 3.20 Zenith/Stromberg 175CD-2SE carburettor

1 Threaded sleeve
2 Relay lever and shaft

3 Link
4 Throttle lever

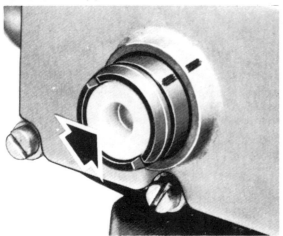

Fig. 3.21 Zenith/Stromberg 175CD-2SE carburettor

The nylon plug in the jet adjuster

Fig. 3.22 Zenith/Stromberg 175CD-2SE carburettor

The float needle valve and filter assembly

Fig. 3.23. Zenith/Stromberg 175CD - 2SE carburettor

The component parts of the jet and adjuster

Fig. 3.24 Zenith/Stromberg 175CD-2SE carburettor

Installing the needle

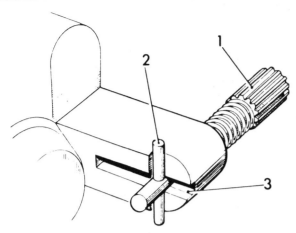

Fig. 3.25 Zenith/Stromberg 175CD-2SE carburettor

1 Spring loaded stop   3 Groove
2 Pin

Fig. 3.26 Zenith/Stromberg 175CD-2SET carburettor

1 Thermostat lever peg   3 Vacuum kick rod
2 Thermostat lever spade

Automatic cold start device

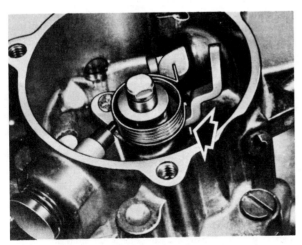

Fig. 3.27 Zenith/Stromberg 175CD-2SET carburettor

Automatic cold start device
Arrow shoes spring hooked over thermostat lever

so that the nylon washer is perfectly flush with the base of the piston. This can be done by placing a metal rule across the base of the valve and pulling the needle out until it abuts the rule. The needle must be installed so that the ground flat aligns with the securing screw to ensure that the needle leans away from the depression holes in the valve face. Do not overtighten the screw.

16 Thoroughly clean the piston and its cylinder in paraffin. Do not use any abrasive material.

17 Assemble the jet in the order shown in Fig. 3.23 and screw it fully into the carburettor body.

18 Assembly is now a straightworward reversal of the removal procedure but make sure that the holes in the diaphragm line up with the screw holes in the piston and retaining ring, and that the diaphragm is correctly positioned with the upper and lower tongues engaged in the slots in piston and body, after the piston has been fitted and checked for freedom of movement.

19 After fitting the float chamber, screw the jet down two complete turns.

20 The cold start device can be set to operate in two positions. The two position stop can be set to control the maximum amount to which the unit may rotate. With the cross pin in the slot the device may rotate to its full extent but this is not usually needed unless the temperature drops below -18°C (0°F). The fast idle cam operates against the throttle lever via an adjusting screw which may be set to ensure a suitably fast idling speed under cold start conditions.

21 To adjust the fast idle, the cold start cam must be set correctly in relation to the throttle flap. To do this put the cold start setting pin in the normal (vertical) position and press the cam against the end of the pin. Then move the adjusting screw on the throttle control lever against the cam until there is a gap between the throttle flap and carburettor body of 1/32 in (0.8mm). Use a number 68 drill to assist in obtaining accuracy.

22 The carburettor(s) can now be refitted to the engine by following the reverse procedure to removal, but ensure that new gaskets are used. Also check that the coupling clamps are as shown in Fig. 3.16 (ie; at 90° to each other) and ensure that all slack is taken up at the cable adjustments. Do not fit the air cleaner until the carburettors have been adjusted and balanced.

23 Remove the damper plastic cap then lift the air valve by inserting a finger in the air intake. The oil level should be topped-up in the hollow guide rod using 10W/30 engine oil until it is ¼in (6mm) below the top of the guide rod. Allow the air valve to close then refit the plastic cap, raise the air valve again until the collar on the hydraulic damper is pressed back into the hollow guide rod. To check that it is pressed right in, lift the air valve again and remove the plastic cap just enough to look into the guide rod.

13 Zenith/Stromberg 175CD—2SE carburettor — adjustment and balancing

NOTE: Where European Exhaust Emission Control Regulations apply, no mixture adjustment should be carried out without the use of a carbon monoxide (CO) meter. The percentage of CO in the exhaust gas, at normal operating temperature, is 2.5 to 3.5%.

1 As there is no separate idling jet, the mixture for all conditions is supplied by the main jet and variable choke. Thus the strength of the mixture throughout the range depends on the height of the jet in the carburettor body and when the idling mixture is correct, the mixture will be correct throughout the range. Adjustment is by means of the adjusting screw which protrudes through the base of the float chamber. Turning the screw clockwise raises the jet and weakens the mixture. Turning the screw anticlockwise enriches the mixture. The idling speed is controlled by the throttle stop screw.

2 To adjust a Stromberg carburettor from scratch it is assumed that the fast idle cam has already been correctly set as described in the reassembly procedure, that the jet has been screwed down two full turns from the fully home position and that the damper oil level is correct. (Section 12).

3 To commence the adjustment and balancing procedure, remove

Fig. 3.28 Zenith/Stromberg 175CD-2SET carburettor

Automatic cold start device
Plunger to cam clearance (A)

Fig. 3.29 Zenith/Stromberg 175CD-2SET carburettor

Automatic cold start device
Housing, insulator and body line up marks

Fig. 3.30 Zenith/Stromberg 175CD-2SET carburettor

1 *Idling speed adjusting screw*
2 *Fast idle screw (not to be adjusted independently)*

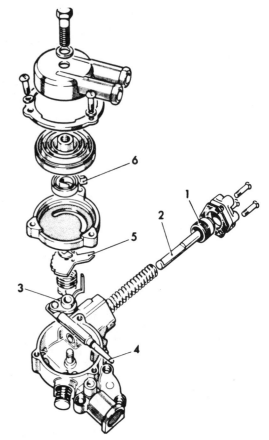

Fig. 3.31 Zenith/Stromberg 175CD-2SET carburettor - cold start device

1 *Vacuum piston*	4 *Tapered fuel needle*
2 *Vacuum kick rod*	5 *Fast idle cam*
3 *Thermostat lever*	6 *Bi-metal thermostat*

the air cleaner then slacken the throttle coupling rear clamp bolt to ensure that the throttle spindles rotate without binding.

4 Tighten the clamp bolt then run the engine to attain the normal operating temperature. Slacken the clamp bolt again and adjust the idle screw on each carburettor to obtain the specified idle speed. Use a piece of flexible tubing to listen to the air hiss at the carburettor air intake to assist in the setting. An even hiss should be heard at each carburettor when balanced. Slight adjustment of the mixture screw is permissible provided that this does not exceed ½ turn either way from the original setting.

5 Check the adjustment by lifting the air valve approximately 0.4in (10mm) using a screwdriver. A momentary increase in speed should result then it should slow down again. If the engine speed continues to rise the mixture is too rich; if the engine stalls, the mixture is too weak.

6 Finally tighten the clamp bolt, ensure that the damper oil level is correct (Section 12) then refit the air cleaner.

14 Zenith/Stromberg 175CD—2SET carburettor

1 The 175CD—2SET carburettor is the same as the 175CD—2SE except that a hot water controlled automatic cold start device is fitted (Fig. 3.31).

This device is controlled by the temperature of the engine coolant. A bi-metal spring thermostat controls a tapered needle which regulates fuel flowing into a mixture chamber. In addition a pushrod and piston controlled by inlet manifold vacuum over-ride the action of the thermostat under certain engine speed conditions.

2 It is not recommended that this item is tampered with but in the

event of the owner deciding to investigate because of malfunction the following points should be noted on reassembly.

3   When replacing the fast idle cam and thermostat lever, the lever peg should engage in the taper needle slot and the spade in the flat in the vacuum kick rod (Fig. 3.26).

4   The interconnecting spring should be fitted so that the inner end goes over the long arm of the thermostat lever and the other end hooks into the hole in the fast idle cam afterwards.

5   The clearance between the fast idle screw and cam (on the base circle) should be 0.035in (0.9mm) when the thermostat lever is rotated fully anticlockwise. The fast idle screw can be adjusted as required and re-secured using 'Loctite' (AA Grade).

6   When fitting the water jacket and cover make sure that the square loop on the thermostat spring enagages the peg on the thermostat lever.

7   Correct positioning of the thermostat after reassembly is indicated by line up marks on the housing and rims. No variations should be made (Fig. 3.29).

8   The only adjustment after assembly is to the idling screw which is set when the engine has reached normal running temperature.

Adjustment should never be made to the fast idle screw except as described in paragraph 5.

9   If the fast idle cam should stick in the open position for some reason it can be moved back manually. Remove the plug in the housing and insert a piece of 3/16 in (4.8 mm) rod and push it back. It is essential that the end of the rod is flat. If the rod end is tapered it may pass behind the cam and jam between the cam and thermostat housing.

15 Fuel tank — removal and replacement

1   Remove the battery from the car as a safety measure, also ensure there are no open flames in the vicinity. **Do not** smoke during removal and replacement of the tank.

2   The tank outlet pipe and fuel gauge unit are on the front of the tank and will need to be disconnected.

3   The tank can be removed by unscrewing the bracket bolts on the rear longitudinal members. On some models a shield is fitted at the front of the tank.

4   Replacement is the reverse of the removal procedure.

5   Repairs to the fuel tank to stop leaks are best carried out using resin adhesives and hardeners as supplied in most accessory shops. In cases of repairs being done to large holes, fibre glass mats or perforated zinc sheet may be required to give area support. If any soldering, welding or brazing is contemplated, the tank must be steamed out to remove any traces of petroleum vapour. It is dangerous to use naked flames on a fuel tank without this, even though it may have been lying empty for a considerable period.

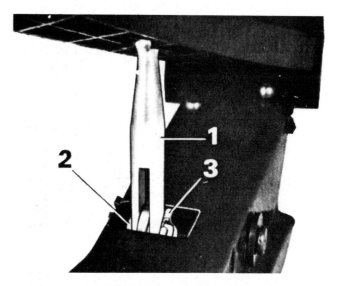

Fig. 3.33 Accelerator pedal assembly

1   Non-adjustable link
2   Clevis pin
3   Clip

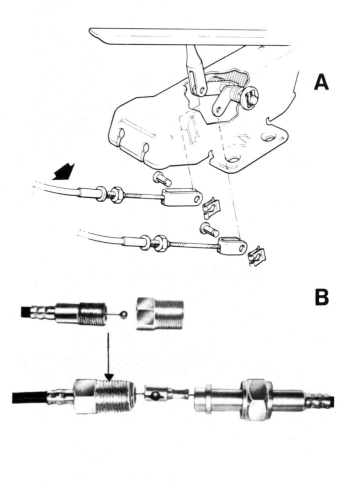

Fig. 3.34 Automatic transmission detent valve operating cable

A   Connections at accelerator pedal

B   Method of connecting the two-part cable

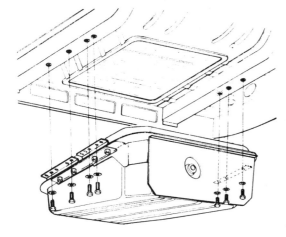

Fig. 3.32 Fuel tank installation (and shield - where applicable)

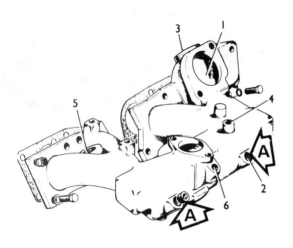

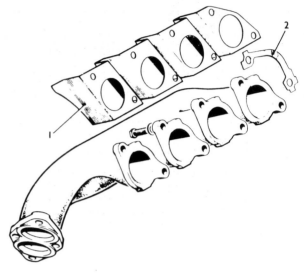

Fig. 3.35 Inlet manifold details

A Manifold tapping points
1 Thermostat housing
2 Temperature gauge tapping
3 Heater hose connection
4 Brake servo tapping
5 Water pump hose connection
6 Breather pipe
B Nut and copper washer inside thermostat housing

Fig. 3.36 Exhaust manifold

1 Spark plug heat shield
2 Lock plates

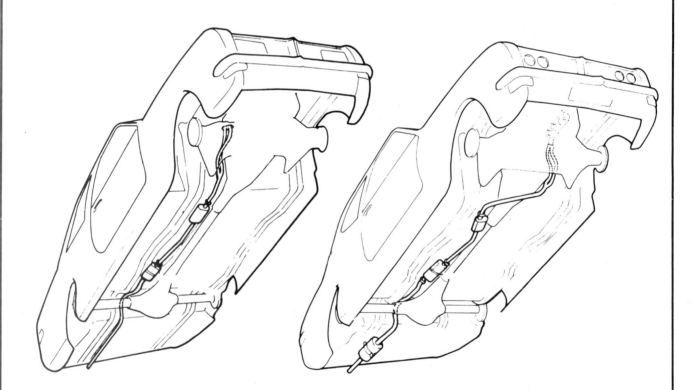

Fig. 3.37 Exhaust layout - 1800 models

Fig. 3.38 Exhaust layout - 2300 models

16 Fuel gauge sender unit – fault finding

1 If the fuel gauge does not work correctly, the fault is either in the sender unit in the fuel tank, the gauge in the instrument panel, or the wiring.

2 To check the sender unit, first disconnect the green/black wire from the unit at the connector on the tank. With the ignition on, the gauge should read 'full'. With the same lead connected to earth the gauge should read 'empty'. If *both* of these situations are correct then the fault (if any) lies in the sender unit.

3 If the gauge does not read 'full' with the wire disconnected from the sender unit, the wire should then be disconnected from the gauge unit (having removed the instrument panel as described in Chapter 10). If the gauge now reads 'full' then the fault lies in the wire from the gauge to the sender unit.

4 If not, the gauge is faulty and should be replaced (for details see Chapter 10).

5 With the wire disconnected from the sender unit and earthed, if the gauge reads anything other than 'empty', check the rest of the circuit as described in Chapter 10.

6 Removal of the gauge sender unit is referred to in the previous Section.

17 Accelerator cable and pedal

Manual transmission

1 Should the accelerator cable break, it may be removed by first removing the whole pedal assembly from the floor of the car. The clevis pin can then be taken out of the cable end. The other end of the cable is detached from the carburettor. The cable outer is removed by undoing the clamping nuts at each end and detaching it from its mountings.

Automatic transmission

2 On models with automatic transmission, a detent valve operating cable is connected by a yoke to the accelerator pedal linkage. The outer cable is secured to the housing by a locknut.

3 The cable is in two parts connected by an adjuster. To adjust the cable, unscrew the adjuster locknut (6) and screw adjuster (1) on to the front cable casing (2) until the threaded portion of the casing protrudes through the adjuster. Ensure that the two inner cables (3) and (4) are connected. With the accelerator pedal held at full throttle, tension the inner cable by pulling the outer casings apart until the detent valve is felt to bottom against the stop. Maintaining tension, rotate the adjuster until the flange (5) on the rear casing is in contact with the adjuster; back off the adjuster half a turn and lock with the locknut (6). (Fig. 3.34 refers).

18 Intake manifold

1 The intake manifold is separate from the exhaust manifold and incorporates a hot water jacket to assist fuel vapourisation. A cooling system thermostat is located in the water jacket aperture (1). The manifold also includes tappings for a water temperature gauge unit (2), heater water hose connector (3), brake servo (4), water pipe to water pump connection (5) and breather pipe (6). (Refer to Fig. 3.35).

2 Before removing manifold, drain the cooling system and withdraw thermostat to gain access to nut and copper washer situated inside manifold.

3 Before installing manifold gaskets, smear sealing compound on both sides of gaskets around the two holes corresponding with water passage between the cylinder head and manifold. Use a new copper washer on the stud inside the manifold, and smear the stud, washer and nut with sealing compound.

19 Exhaust manifold

1 A spark plug heat shield (1) of insulating material is fitted between the exhaust manifold and the cylinder head. The manifold attaching bolts are secured by lockplates (2). Access to manifold lower bolts can be gained from beneath the car. (Refer to Fig. 3.36).

2 Before removing manifold, remove nut from engine left hand mounting bracket. Raise the left hand side of engine sufficiently to enable manifold to be withdrawn.

3 When installing the manifold, tighten the centre nuts of exhaust pipe flange evenly, then the other two nuts. Finally, check the tightness of the centre nuts.

20 Exhaust system

1800 models

1 The exhaust system comprises twin front pipes, a silencer and a resonator. The layout of the system is shown in Fig. 3.37 and 3.39.

2300 models

2 The exhaust system for these models, comprises twin front pipes, a silencer and two resonators. The layout of the system is shown in Figs. 3.38 and 3.39.

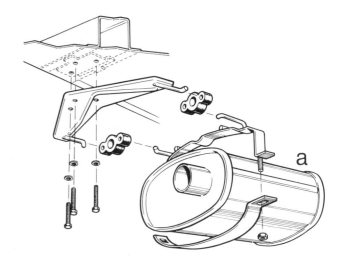

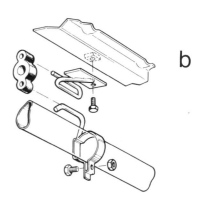

Fig. 3.39 Exhaust details - all models

a   *Silencer mounting*
b   *Tail pipe mounting*

Note: On any exhaust system, ensure that a minimum of 1 inch (25 mm) clearance exists between silencers and floor panelling

2   Fault diagnosis — fuel system and carburation

Unsatisfactory engine performance and excessive fuel consumption are not necessarily the fault of the fuel system or carburettor. In fact they more commonly occur as a result of ignition and timing faults. Before acting on the following it is necessary to check the ignition system first. Even though a fault may lie in the fuel system it will be difficult to trace unless the ignition is correct. The faults below, therefore, assume that this has been attended to first (where appropriate). It is also assumed that the engine is not significantly worn.

Symptom	Reason/s	Remedy
Smell of petrol when engine is stopped	Leaking fuel lines or unions Leaking fuel tank	Repair or renew as necessary. Fill fuel tank to capacity and examine carefully at seams, unions and filler pipe connections. Repair as necessary.
Smell of petrol when engine is idling	Leaking fuel line unions between pump and carburettor Overflow of fuel from float chamber due to wrong level setting, ineffective needle valve or punctured float	Check line and unions and tighten or repair. Check fuel level setting and condition of float and needle valve, and renew if necessary.
Excessive fuel consumption for reasons not covered by leaks or float chamber faults	Worn jets (Zenith) Over-rich jet setting (Stromberg) Sticking strangler flap (Zenith)	Renew jets. Adjust jet. Check correct movement of strangler flap.
Difficult starting, uneven running, lack of power, cutting out	One or more jets blocked or restricted (Zenith) Float chamber fuel level too low or needle valve sticking Fuel pump not delivering sufficient fuel Air valve piston not operating correctly (Stromberg)	Dismantle and clean out float chamber and jets. Dismantle and check fuel level and needle valve. Check pump delivery and clean or repair as required. Dismantle and examine. Clean and repair as required.

Chapter 4 Ignition system

Contents

Condenser — removal and replacement 5	Fault diagnosis — ignition system (general) 10
Contact breaker points — adjustment 3	Fault diagnosis — ignition system (misfiring) 11
Contact breaker points — removal and replacement 4	General description 1
Distributor — dismantling and reassembly 7	Ignition timing 8
Distributor — removal and replacement 6	Spark plugs and HT leads 9
Distributor rotor — removal and replacement.. 2	

Specifications

Spark plugs

Type:

1800 ... ... AC R41TS

2300 ... ... AC R42TS

Electrode gap ... ... 0.030 in (0.75mm)

Coil

Make ... ... Delco-Remy

Type ... ... Oil-filled, LT resistor in circuit, by-passed for addition starting voltage

Distributor

Make ... ... Delco-Remy

Rotation ... ... Anti-clockwise

Firing order ... ... 1—3—4—2

Contact points gap ... ... 0.020 in (0.50mm)

Contact arm spring tension ... ... 22 to 26 ozs.

Cam dwell angle ... ... 35 to 37°

Mainshaft clearance in bushes ... ... 0.001 to 0.0011 in (0.0254 to 0.0279mm)

Mainshaft endfloat ... ... 0.085 to 0.175 in (2.16 to 4.445mm)

Ignition timing (static) ... ... 9° B.T.D.C.

Vacuum advance data

1800 (all models) and 2300 (1974 onwards):

Vacuum (in Hg)	Distributor Degrees
4	0
6	0 to 2½
7 and above	1½ to 3½

2300 (pre-1974 models):

4	0
6	0 to 1
8	1 to 3
11 and above	4 to 6

Centrifugal advance data (1800)

Cut-in speed ... ... 350—550 rev/min

Distributor rev/min	Distributor Degrees
350	0
550	0—4½
750	4½—8
1000	7—9
1500	9—11½
2000	11½—13½
2500 and over	12½—14½

Centrifugal advance data (2300)

Cut-in speed ...   .   375—525 rev/min

Distributor rev/min	Distributor Degrees
375	0
525	0—2
600	1—3
900	4½—7
1250	6½—9
2000	9—11
2500	10½—12½
2750 and over	11—13½

Torque wrench settings*

	16 ft	kg in
Spark plugs	15	2.07

*Clean dry threads

1 General description

In order that the engine can run correctly it is necessary for an electrical spark to ignite the fuel/air mixture in the combustion chamber at exactly the right moment in relation to engine speed and load. The ignition system is based on feeding low tension voltage from the battery to the coil where in conjunction with the distributor, it is converted to high tension voltage. The high tension voltage is powerful enough to jump the sparking plug gap in the cylinders many times a second under high compression pressures, providing that the system is in good condition and that all adjustments are correct.

The ignition system is divided into two circuits. The low tension circuit and the high tension circuit.

The low tension (sometimes known as the primary) circuit consists of the battery, lead to the ignition switch, lead from the ignition switch to the low tension or primary coil windings (terminal +), and the lead from the low tension coil windings (terminal —) to the contact breaker points and condenser in the distributor.

The high tension circuit consists of the high tension or secondary coil windings, the heavy ignition lead from the centre of the coil to the centre of the distributor cap, the rotor arm, and the spark plug leads and spark plugs.

The system functions in the following manner: High tension voltage is generated in the coil by the interruption of the low tension circuit. The interruption is effected by the opening of the contact breaker points in this low tension circuit.

High tension voltage is fed via the carbon brush in the centre of the distributor cap to the rotor arm of the distributor.

The rotor arm revolves anticlockwise at half engine speed inside the distributor cap, and each time it comes in line with one of the four metal segments in the cap, which are connected to the spark plug leads, the opening and closing of the contact breaker points causes the high tension voltage to build up, jump the gap from the rotor arm to the appropriate metal segment and so via the spark plug lead to the spark plug, where it finally jumps the spark plug gap before going to earth.

The distributor incorporates a centrifugal advance mechanism located above the circuit breaker contacts. A one-piece circuit breaker plate pivots on the mainshaft upper bush and is retained on the bush by a circlip. A vacuum control unit support bracket and operating arm is located underneath the circuit breaker plate. The mainshaft bushes are lubricated by a felt ring in the base. On later models, a renewable plastic foam lubricator pad is incorporated for lubrication of the cam.

The detachable rotor is located on the cam assembly by dowels and secured by two screws. The drive gear is secured to the mainshaft by a spring pin.

Elongated bolt holes in the distributor base flange provide a means of varying the radial position of the distributor relative to the mounting on the engine, for adjustment of ignition timing. (Fig. 4.7).

The ignition is advanced and retarded automatically, to ensure the spark occurs at just the right instant for the particular load at the prevailing engine speed.

The ignition advance is controlled both mechanically and by a vacuum operated system. The mechanical governor mechanism comprises two weights, which move out from the distributor shaft as the engine speed rises, due to centrifugal force. As they move outwards they rotate the cam relative to the distributor shaft, and so advance the spark. The weights are held in position by two light springs and it is the tension of the springs which is largely responsible for correct spark advancement.

The vacuum control consists of a diaphragm, one side of which is connected via a small bore tube to the carburettor, which varies with engine speed and throttle opening, causes the diaphragm to move, so moving the contact breaker plate, and advancing or retarding the spark. A fine degree of control is achieved by a spring in the vacuum assembly.

2 Distributor rotor — removal and replacement

1 Having removed the distributor cap by undoing the two spring clips, remove the rotor by undoing the two securing screws in the top.
2 Lift off the rotor.
3 It will be seen that on the underside of the rotor there are two locating pegs. One is round and the other square. These must fit into the corresponding holes in the mainshaft and cam assembly when the rotor is replaced.
4 The contact spring on the rotor should not be bent or damaged in any way. The height of the spring should be set 1.38 — 1.44 inch (35 to 37 mm) above the base of the rotor (Fig. 4.1).
5 Tighten the screws firmly on replacement, but do not overtighten.

3 Contact breaker points — adjustment

1 To adjust the contact breaker points to the correct gap, first pull off the two clips securing the distributor cap to the distributor body, and lift away the cap. Clean the cap inside and out with a dry cloth. It is unlikely that the four segments will be badly burned or scored, but if they are, the cap will have to be renewed.
2 Check the carbon brush located in the top of the cap to make sure that it is not broken or missing.
3 Access to the contact points is better if the rotor is removed.
4 Gently prise the contact breaker points open to examine the condition of their faces. If they are rough, pitted or dirty, it will be necessary to remove them for resurfacing, or for replacement points to be fitted.
5 Assuming the points are satisfactory, or that they have been cleaned and replaced, measure the gap between the points by turning the engine over until the contact breaker arm is on the peak of one of the four cam lobes.
6 A 0.020 inch (0.50mm) feeler gauge should now just fit between the points.

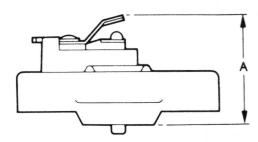

Fig. 4.1 Distributor rotor - contact spring height

A = 1.38 to 1.44 inches (35 to 37 mm)

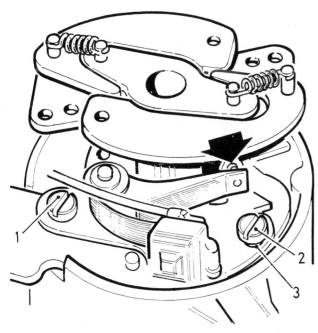

Fig. 4.2 Contact breaker points - rotor removed

1 *Fixing screw*   3 *Adjusting slot*
2 *Fixing screw*

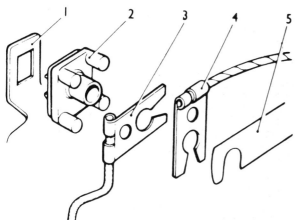

Fig. 4.3 Contact points and condenser lead fixing

1 *Base plate lug*   4 *LT wire from coil*
2 *Insulator/connector*   5 *Contact point spring*
3 *Condenser wire*

7 If the gap varies from this amount, slacken the two securing screws.
8 Adjust the contact gap by inserting a screwdriver in the slot in the fixed plate and levering it. It is best to do this with the securing screws holding the plate enough to prevent inadvertent movement.
9 Always check the gap again after tightening the screws. Sometimes the final tightening moves the points from their original setting.

4 Contact breaker points — removal and replacement

1 Remove the distributor cap.
2 Remove the rotor arm. Do not pull it by the contact spring.
3 Remove the contact points holding screws.
4 Ease the end of the moving contact spring out of the insulator.
5 Lift the complete contact set assembly off the pivot pin of the mounting plate.
6 If the condition of the points is not too bad they can be reconditioned by rubbing the contacts clean with fine emery cloth or a fine carborundum stone. It is important that the faces are rubbed flat and parallel to each other so that there will be complete face to face contact when the points are closed. One of the points will be pitted and the other will have deposits on it.
7 It is necessary to remove completely the built-up deposits, but not necessary to rub the pitted point right down to the stage where all the pitting has disappeared, although obviously if this is done it will prolong the time before the operation of refacing the points has to be repeated.
8 Thoroughly clean the points before refitting them. Locate the fixed contact plate over the base of the pivot pin and then fix the moving contact into position so that the end of the spring fits over the centre boss of the nylon lug. Replace the fixing screws. Press in the condenser and coil lead tags to the nylon lug behind the spring.
9 Adjust the gap as described in Section 3.
10 Check the ignition timing as described in Section 8. The reason for this is because slight wear on the heel of the moving contact, or manufacturing tolerances on new contacts, can affect the point at which the contacts open and close.

5 Condenser — removal and replacement

1 The purpose of the condenser (sometimes known as capacitor) is to ensure that when the contact breaker points open there is no sparking across them which would waste voltage and cause rapid deterioration of the points. It also boosts the spark across the plugs.
2 The condenser is fitted in parallel with the contact breaker points. If it develops a short circuit, it will cause ignition failure as the points will be prevented from interrupting the low tension circuit.
3 If the engine becomes very difficult to start or begins to misfire whilst running and the breaker points show signs of excessive burning, then the condition of the condenser must be suspect. A further test can be made by separating the points by hand with the ignition switched on. If this is accompanied by a bright spark at the contact points it is indicative that the condenser has failed.
4 Without special test equipment the only sure way to diagnose condenser trouble is to replace a suspected unit with a new one and note if there is any improvement.
5 To remove the condenser from the distributor, remove the distributor cap and the rotor arm.
6 Pull out the condenser lead clip from the nylon insulator where it fits behind the spring.
7 Undo the mounting bracket screw and remove the condenser.
8 Replacement is simply a reversal of the removal process. Take particular care that the condenser wire cannot short circuit against any portion of the breaker plate.

Fig. 4.4 Distributor installation

*Showing the oil pump tongue ready to line up with the slot
in the distributor shaft*

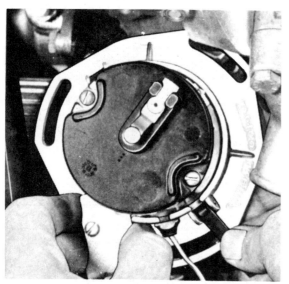

Fig. 4.5 Distributor installation

*To allow for the helix on the gears turn the rotor anti-clockwise
as shown, then insert the distributor*

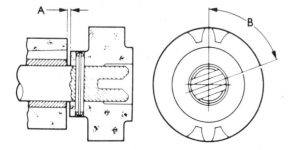

Fig. 4.6 Distributor - mainshaft drive gear pinned position

A   Endfloat = 0.085 to 0.175 inch
*B   Angle between centre line of any tooth and centre line of
     drive slot is 70 degrees*

Fig. 4.7 Distributor installation

*When distributor is subsequently installed, rotor should be in
position show, and vacuum control towards fuel pump and
securing bolts approximately central in slots*

6   Distributor — removal and replacement

1   To remove the distributor complete with cap from the engine,
begin by pulling the plug lead terminals off the four spark plugs. Free
the HT lead from the coil. In each case it is good policy to take a note
of every lead that is disconnected, this will prevent problems when
reconnecting.
2   Pull off the vacuum advance.
3   Disconnect the low tension wire from the coil.
4   It is not possible to remove and replace the distributor without
having to reset the ignition timing. Removal and replacement therefore
is dealt with under the 'Ignition timing' section.
5   The distributor is held in place by three bolts through slotted holes
in the base flange. When the bolts are removed the distributor can be
lifted straight out.
6   Replacement of the distributor must follow the procedure as
described under 'Ignition timing'.

7   Distributor — dismantling and reassembly

1   Before deciding to dismantle the distributor bear in mind the
following:
   *a) Shaft bushes, if worn, are not supplied separately (by Vauxhall).
   A complete base assembly must be acquired.*
   *b) With the exception of the rotor and contact points other parts
   may not be readily obtainable. It is very important to be quite sure
   of the type of distributor fitted before changing weights, springs or
   mainshaft cam.*
   *c) If the distributor is seriously worn it may be more satisfactory
   in the long run to change the whole unit.*
2   Begin dismantling by removing the rotor, condenser and contact
breaker points as previously described.
3   The contact breaker points mounting plate may be detached after
removing the circlip at the top end of the mainshaft.
4   To remove the mainshaft involves driving out the spring pin which
holds the gear to the shaft — use a flat nosed punch.
5   If items are being replaced take care to note the numbers stamped
on them which identify the type for each engine.
6   Some later mainshafts were revised and incorporated an oil return
scroll at the upper end. They also had a wider slot in the end which
drives the oil pump and in such instances the oil pump driveshaft
should be changed to suit.
7   When reassembling the distributor make sure the felt oil retainer

Fig. 4.8 Distributor components

1 Distributor cap
2 Rotor
3 Rotor securing screw
4 Lockwasher
5 Mainshaft
6 Mainshaft
7 Bob weights
8 Bob weights
9 Bob weight spring
10 Bob weight spring
11 Cam assembly
12 Cam assembly
13 Retainer clip
14 Contact points
15 Insulator clip
16 Contacts locking screw
17 Condenser bracket
18 Condenser fixing screw
19 LT lead and grommet
20 Earth lead
21 Contact breaker plate
22 Felt washer
23 Vacuum advance unit
24 Screw
25 Base
26 Cap clip
27 Spring pin
28 Drive gear
29 Gear retainer pin
30 Suction pipe
31 Gasket (not fitted later)
32 Securing screw (oil pump also)

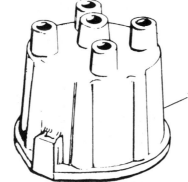

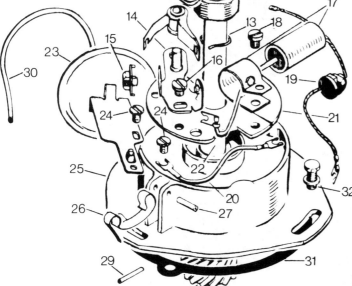

Refer to Figs. 4.12 and 4.13 for the lubrication pad fitted to later distributors

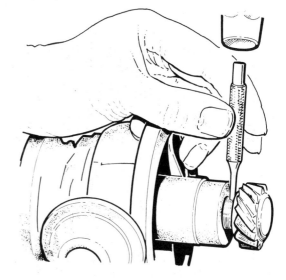

Fig. 4.9 Distributor

Driving out the spring pin securing the drive gear to the mainshaft

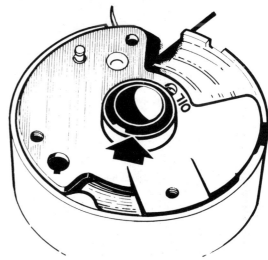

Fig. 4.10 Distributor

Circlip (arrowed) retaining the contact points mounting plate

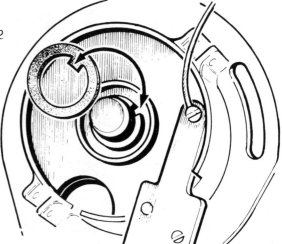

Fig. 4.11 Distributor

Positioning felt lubricator in slotted base

Fig. 4.13 Removing the cam lubricator with pliers

Fig. 4.12 The cam lubricator

(a) Installed position
(b) Component parts

Fig. 4.14 Ignition timing marks - early models

1   Pulley marking   2   9⁰ BTDC marking

Fig. 4.15 Ignition timing - later models

These are similar markings to the early models except that the pulley carries a pointer on its rear flange

engages properly in the slot in the main base before installing the circuit breaker plate.

8   If a new driveshaft is fitted the gear pin hole will need to be drilled (1/8 inch). This hole must be positioned to allow the correct endfloat. It should also be arranged so that the angle between the centre line of any gear tooth and the centre line of the drive slot is 70°.

9   Note that later model distributors have a renewable plastic foam wick for lubrication of the distributor cam. The only permitted lubricant is a trace of general purpose lithium based grease which should be worked well in with the fingers.

8   Ignition timing

1   Refer to Figs. 4.14 and 4.15 which show the ignition timing marks on the crankshaft pulley and drive belt cover.

2   The procedure for setting the timing is detailed from the point of installing the distributor. If the distributor is not removed and the timing is known to be in need only of fine adjustment then the procedures leading up to this stage can be ignored. Only the final setting of the opening of the points gap is necessary.

3   With the distributor removed, turn the engine so that the crankshaft pulley mark is on the 9° A (Advance) mark. At the same time the No. 1 piston should be on the compression stroke. This can be verified by removing the plug and placing a finger over the plug hole. Pressure should be felt as the piston rises and the inlet and outlet valves should both be closed.

4   Prepare the mating faces of the distributor body flange and the oil pump flange by cleaning them thoroughly and applying a thin coat of 'Hylomar'. In early models a gasket was provided and this should be fitted with the adhesive side to the oil pump. Do not use 'Hylomar' when a gasket is provided.

5   Hold the distributor over the installation position with the vacuum advance unit facing towards the fuel pump and the rotor contact at about 11 o'clock as you look down on the distributor from the side of the engine.

6   Line up the oil pump shaft tongue with the slot in the bottom of the distributor drive shaft.

7   Put the distributor down into position. If you have everything correctly lined up the rotor tip should have moved clockwise to 12 o'clock and the mounting bolt holes should be in the centre of the flange slots.

8   If you make an error lift the distributor out and repeat the procedure. If the body does not go right down easily it will be because the oil pump drive shaft is not properly aligned.

9   Replace the three distributor securing bolts but do not tighten them. Set the contact breaker points gap if not already done.

10 Turn the body of the distributor anticlockwise until the points are closed.

11 Now turn the distributor body clockwise until the contact points are just about to open. This can be accurately gauged if a 12 volt 6 watt bulb is wired in parallel with the contact points. Switch on the ignition and when the points open the bulb should light.

12 Tighten the distributor clamp bolts.

13 If a stroboscopic light is used for a final static ignition timing check, remove the lead from No. 1 plug and then connect the strobe, one wire to the plug and the other to the plug lead. With the engine idling as slowly as possible shine the strobe light on to the timing case marker when the pulley pointer should appear stationary on the lower marker (9° advance).

14 If the engine speed is increased, then the effect of the vacuum and the centrifugal advance controls can be seen and in fact, measured to some extent, in so far as the distance between the two crankcase timing markers represents 9° of crankshaft revolution.

9   Spark plugs and HT leads

1   The correct functioning of the spark plugs is vital for the correct running and efficiency of the engine. The plugs fitted as standard are listed in the specifications at the beginning of the Chapter.

2   At intervals of 6000 miles the plugs should be removed, examined and cleaned. If worn excessively, they should be renewed. The condition of the spark plug will also tell much about the overall condition of the engine.

3   If the insulator nose of the spark plug is clean and white, with no

White deposits and damaged porcelain insulation indicating overheating

Broken porcelain insulation due to bent central electrode

Electrodes burnt away due to wrong heat value or chronic pre-ignition (pinking)

Excessive black deposits caused by over-rich mixture or wrong heat value

Mild white deposits and electrode burnt indicating too weak a fuel mixture

Plug in sound condition with light greyish brown deposits

Fig. 4.16 Various spark plug conditions

deposits, this is indicative of a weak mixture, or too hot a plug. (A hot plug transfers heat away from the electrode slowly — a cold plug transfers it away quickly).

4   If the tip and insulator nose is covered with sooty black deposits, then this is indicative that the mixture is too rich. Should the plug be black and oily, then it is likely that the engine is fairly worn, as well as the mixture being rich.

5   If the insulator nose is covered with light tan to greyish brown deposits, then the mixture is correct and it is likely that the engine is in good condition.

6   If there are any traces of long brown tapering stains on the outside of the white portion of the plug, then the plug will have to be renewed, as this shows that there is a faulty joint between the plug body and the insulator, and compression is being allowed to leak away.

7   Plugs should be cleaned by a sand blasting machine, which will free them from carbon more thoroughly than cleaning by hand. The machine will also test the condition of the plugs under compression. Any plug that fails to spark at the recommended pressure should be renewed.

8   The spark plug gap is of considerable importance; if it is too large or too small the size of the spark and its efficiency will be seriously impaired. The spark plug gap should be set to 0.030 inch (0.75mm) for the best results.

9   To set it, measure the gap with a feeler gauge, and then bend open, or closed, the outer plug electrode until the correct gap is achieved. The centre electrode should never be bent as this may crack the insulation and cause plug failure, if nothing worse.

10   When replacing the plugs it is important that the tapered contact seats of the plugs and cylinder head are clean and undamaged.

11   Plugs must not be overtightened. As they are a different size (5/8 in AF) from most other plugs it is worthwhile obtaining the proper socket and extension to fit a torque wrench.

10 Fault diagnosis — ignition system (general)

1   By far the majority of breakdown and running troubles are caused by faults in the ignition system, either in the low tension or high tension circuits.

2   There are two main symptoms indicating ignition faults. Either the engine will not start or fire, or the engine is difficult to start and mis-fires. If it is a regular misfire (ie: the engine is only running on two or three cylinders) the fault it is almost sure to be in the secondary, or high tension, circuit. If the misfiring is intermittent, the fault could be in either the high or low tension circuits. If the car stops suddenly, or will not start at all, it is likely that the fault is in the low tension circuit. Loss of power and overheating, apart from faulty carburation settings, are normally due to faults in the distributor, or incorrect ignition timing.

3   If the engine fails to start and the car was running normally when it was last used, first check there is fuel in the petrol tank. If the engine turns over normally on the starter motor and the battery is evidently well charged, then the fault may be in either the high or low tension circuits. First check the HT circuit.
Note: If the battery is known to be fully charged, the ignition light comes on, and the starter motor fails to turn the engine check the tightness of the leads on the battery terminals and the security of the earth connection to the body. It is quite common for the leads to have worked loose, even if they look and feel secure. If one of the battery terminal posts gets hot when trying to work the starter motor this is a sure indication of a faulty connection to that terminal.

4   One of the common reasons for bad starting is wet or damp plug leads and distributor. Remove the distributor cap. If condensation is visible internally, dry the cap with a rag and also wipe over the leads. Replace the cap.

5   If the engine still fails to start, check that current is reaching the plugs, by disconnecting each plug lead in turn at the spark plug end, and hold the end of the cable about 3/16 inch (4mm) away from the cylinder block. Spin the engine on the starter motor.

6   Sparking between the end of the cable and the block should be

fairly strong with a regular blue spark. (Hold the lead with rubber to avoid electric shocks). If current is reaching the plugs, then remove them, and clean and regap them. The engine should now start.

7   If there is no spark at the plug leads take off the HT lead from the centre of the distributor cap and hold it to the block as before. Spin the engine on the starter once more. A rapid succession of blue sparks between the end of the lead and the block indicate that the coil is in order and that the distributor cap is cracked, the rotor arm faulty, or the carbon brush in the top of the distributor cap is not making good contact with the spring on the rotor arm. Possibly the points are in bad condition. Clean and reset them as described earlier in this Chapter.

8   If there are no sparks from the end of the lead from the coil, check the connections at the coil end of the lead. If it is in order start checking the low tension circuit.

9   Use a 12V voltmeter or a 12V bulb and two lengths of wire. With the ignition switch on and the points open, test between the low tension wire to the coil (it is marked +) and earth. No reading indicates a break in the supply from the ignition switch. Check the connections at the switch to see if any are loose. Refit them. A reading shows a faulty coil or condenser, or broken lead between the coil and the distributor.

10   Take the condenser wire off the points assembly and with the points open, test between the moving point and earth. If there now is a reading, then the fault is in the condenser. Fit a new one.

11   With no reading from the moving point to earth, take a reading between earth and the — terminal of the coil. A reading here shows a broken wire which will need to be replaced between the coil and the distributor. No reading confirms that the coil has failed and must be renewed. Remember to refit the condenser wire to the points assembly. For these tests it is sufficient to separate the points with a piece of dry paper while testing with the points open.

12   The system is fitted with a device which boosts the output from the coil when the starter is operated. (When the starter is used battery voltage tends to drop due to the load placed upon it). Quite simply, the coil is rated for a continuous 6 volts supply. As the vehicle system is 12 volt a resistance wire is fitted into the LT supply to the coil so that under normal running conditions the coil only receives a 6 volt supply. When the starter is operated the system voltage drops; this is usual. In addition to the normal LT feed to the coil therefore, an additional feed is taken from the starter solenoid switch direct to the coil. This feed only operates when the solenoid starter terminals are closed, ie: when the starter is turning. Consequently, for the brief time when the voltage drops from 12 to about 8 volts is fed direct to the 6 volt coil providing a temporary starting boost.

Certain checks are necessary to ensure that:
A) The starter feed is functioning properly — otherwise only about 2 volts would reach the coil on starting.
B) The resistor cable is in good order — otherwise 12 volts or no volts may reach the 6 volt coil.

AI   To check the current supply to the coil through the resistor wire, disconnect the resistor wire and connect it to earth via a volt-meter. With contact points closed and ignition switched on the reading should be 5 volts (approx.). If not then there is a fault in the wire, the ignition switch, or the feed to the ignition switch.

AII   With the connections still made, operate the starter motor. The voltage should jump to 8V (approx.) whilst the starter is turning. If the wire is not faulty and voltage does not rise, then the starter solenoid switch must be faulty and will need renewal.

BI   To check the primary (LT) coil winding, points and condenser, connect the voltmeter to the — terminal of the coil leaving both coil wires connected. Switch on the ignition with the contact points *open*. The voltage should be 12V (approx.). If the reading is low or zero, then there is a fault in the coil primary winding or a short circuit at the contact points or condenser.

BII   With the same connections, close the contact breaker points. With the ignition still on the reading should be 0 — 0.2 volts. If the voltage is greater then the contact points are dirty, the wire from the '—' coil terminal is broken, or the distributor body to earth resistance is very high.

13 Should indications be that the resistance in the wiring harness is faulty the whole harness may need renewal as this particular resistance wire is not supplied or serviced separately. However, if the wiring harness is removed and the wires separated a competent electrician might succeed in fitting a new resistance wire.

11 Fault diagnosis — ignition system (misfiring)

1 If the engine misfires regularly run it at a fast idling speed. Pull off each of the plug caps in turn and listen to the note of the engine. Hold the plug cap in a dry cloth or with a rubber glove as additional protection against a shock from the HT supply.

2 No difference in engine running will be noticed when the lead from the defective circuit is removed. Removing the lead from one of the good cylinders will accentuate the misfire.

3 Remove the plug lead from the end of the defective plug and hold it about 3/16 inch (4mm) away from the block. Restart the engine. If the sparking is fairly strong and regular the fault must lie in the spark plug.

4 The plug may be loose, the insulation may be cracked, or the points may have burnt away giving too wide a gap for the spark to jump. Worse still, one of the points may have broken off. Either renew the plug, or clean it, reset the gap, and then test it.

5 If there is no spark at the end of the plug lead, or if it is weak and intermittent, check the ignition lead from the distributor to the plug. If the insulation is cracked or perished, renew the lead. Check the connections at the distributor cap.

6 If there is still no spark, examine the distributor cap carefully for tracking. This can be recognised by a very thin black line running between two or more electrodes, or between an electrode and some other part of the distributor. These lines are paths which now conduct electricity across the cap thus letting it run to earth. The only answer is a new distributor cap.

7 Apart from the ignition timing being incorrect, other causes of misfiring have already been dealt with under the Section dealing with the failure of the engine to start. To recap — these are that:

  a) *The coil may be faulty giving an intermittent misfire.*

  b) *There may be a damaged wire or loose connection in the low tension circuit.*

  c) *The condenser may be short circuiting.*

  d) *There may be a mechanical fault in the distributor — a broken driving spindle or contact breaker spring.*

8 If the ignition timing is too far retarded, it should be noted that the engine will tend to overheat, and there will be a quite noticeable drop in power. Backfiring in the exhaust is usually evident with retarded ignition also. If the engine is overheating and the power is down, and the ignition timing is correct, then the carburettor should be checked, followed by valves.

Chapter 5 Clutch

Contents

Clutch adjustment 3	Clutch assembly — replacement 6
Clutch actuating lever and thrust release bearing — removal, inspection and replacement 7	Clutch cable — removal and replacement 2
	Clutch pilot bearing — renewal 8
Clutch and brake pedals, and shaft — renewal of bushes 4	Fault diagnosis — clutch 9
Clutch assembly — removal and inspection 5	General description 1

Specifications

	1800	2300
Make	Borg and Beck	Laycock
Type	Diaphragm spring	Diaphragm spring
Clutch size	8.5 in (216mm)	8.5 in (216mm)
Disc size	8.0 in (203mm)	8.5in (216mm)
Operating fork free-travel	0.2 in (5.1mm)	0.2in (5.1mm)

Torque wrench settings	lb/ft	kg/m
Clutch to flywheel bolts	14	19.4

1 General description

The clutch consists of an integral pressure plate and diaphragm spring assembly with a single dry plate friction disc between the pressure plate assembly and the flywheel.

The bellhousing on the gearbox encloses the whole unit but only the top half of the bellhousing bolts to the engine. Consequently, there is a semi-circular steel plate bolted to the lower half of the bellhousing to act as a cover.

The clutch is operated mechanically by a Bowden cable direct from the clutch pedal. This actuates a clutch release lever and thrust bearing, the lever pivoting on a ball pin inside the bellhousing and projecting through an aperture in the bellhousing opposite to the pin. Adjustment of free-play is effected by a threaded ball joint at the end of the cable where it is attached to the clutch operating lever.

2 Clutch cable — removal and replacement

1 Slacken the locknut at the clutch operating lever end of the cable and remove it and the adjusting nut completely from the thread, together with the pressure pad and insulator. Remove the sump screw which holds the cable clip locating the outer cable to the side of the engine where the sump joins the crankcase (where applicable), then draw the cable through the hole in the bellhousing.
2 Withdraw the panel covering the pedal mounting assembly.
3 Pull the clip off the end of the pedal shaft and then draw it to one side far enough to allow the pedal arm to drop. The end of the cable may then be detached by removing the clevis pin.
4 Unscrew the outer cable locknut and remove the washer.

5 The cable assembly may then be drawn out through the bulkhead. Note the washer fitted on the engine compartment side also.
6 Replacement of the cable is an exact reversal of the removal procedure.
7 If there are signs that the pedal shaft bushes are worn this is a good opportunity to renew them. They can easily be prised out of their locations if the pedal shaft is fully withdrawn. New ones are simply pressed into position.
8 Reset the clutch fork free-travel as described in Section 3.

3 Clutch — adjustment

1 The free-play in the clutch pedal cannot be determined accurately from the pedal itself. It is necessary to check the gap between the adjusting nut and actuating arm.
2 To measure the gap first unhook the return spring from the arm. Then prop, or get someone to hold, the pedal in the fully up position.
3 Move the actuating arm until it can be felt to be up against the clutch and pull the cable to eliminate any endplay there may be. Adjust the nut as necessary to obtain the specified gap between the arm and adjuster.
4 Too little, or no gap, will wear out the thrust race prematurely. If very badly adjusted, clutch slip will occur. Too much gap will result in excessive pedal movement before the clutch disengages.
5 Do not forget to refit the return spring. If the spring is broken or disconnected it will immediately be apparent by looseness in the pedal at the top end of its travel. The clutch will work still but the actuating arm will rattle and cause wear on the thrust bearing.
6 Do not forget to tighten the locknut after adjustment is complete.

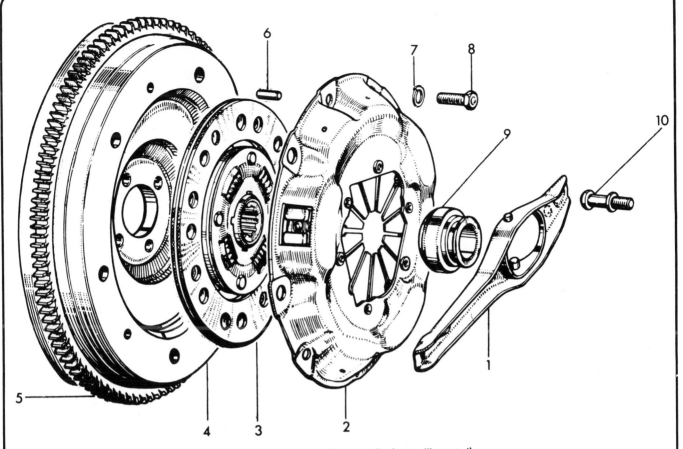

Fig. 5.1 Clutch components (Borg and Beck type illustrated)

1 Operating lever
2 Cover and diaphragm spring
   assembly

3 Driven plate assembly
4 Flywheel
5 Starter ring gear

6 Dowel pin
7 Split washer
8 Clutch cover bolt

9   Thrust bearing
10 Operating lever pivot pin

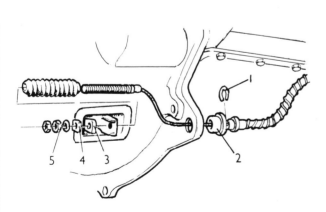

Fig. 5.2 Clutch operating cable - components

1 Horse-shoe washer
2 Insulator
3 Insulator

4 Pressure pad
5 Plain nut

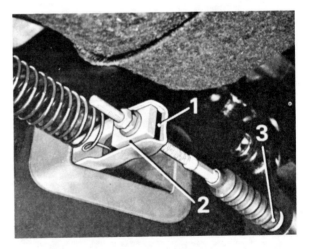

Fig. 5.3 Clutch operating cable - assembled

1 Insulator
2 Pressure pad
3 Protective rubber boot

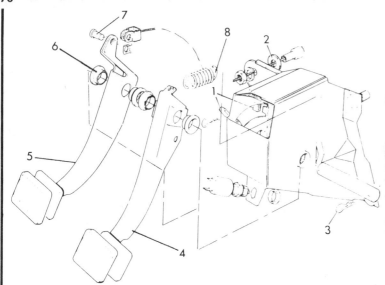

Fig. 5.4 Pedal assembly - components

1	Rubber stops	5	Clutch pedal
2	Washer	6	Bushes (4)
3	Spring pin	7	Clevis pin
4	Brake pedal	8	Return spring

Fig. 5.5 Removing the bellhousing-to-transmission lower bolts using special Vauxhall tool

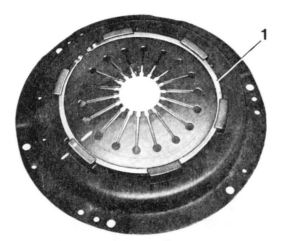

Fig. 5.6 Laycock clutch

1 Diaphragm spring retaining ring
2 Anti-rattle springs

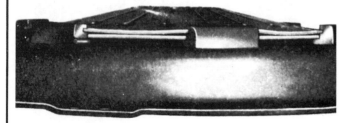

Fig. 5.7 Location of spring retaining ring on a Laycock clutch

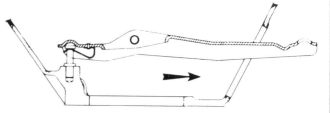

Fig. 5.8 Clutch actuating arm. Cross section showing pivot pin and clip. Pull in direction of arrows to remove the arm

4 Clutch and brake pedals, and shaft — renewal of bushes

1   Should excessive play develop in the movement of the pedals on the shaft, the bushes may be renewed. The shaft can be withdrawn after removing the spring clips at the ends. (Fig. 5.4).

2   The pedals can be lowered and the nylon bushes pressed out and new ones fitted.

3   When replacing the shaft use the special grease for lubrication of the nylon bearings such as Duckhams Keenol.

4   Make sure the spring clips are properly located on the ends of the shaft so that they also lock into the mounting plate to prevent the shaft rotating.

5 Clutch assembly — removal and inspection

1   Remove the gearbox (see Chapter 6).

2   To remove the clutch bellhousing, the engine may have to be lowered and moved to one side. This is to get access to the two top bolts on the left-hand side. A special shaped tool is necessary to remove these bolts if the engine is not lowered. This tool is usually only obtainable from a Vauxhall agent.

3   If the engine is not being removed then disconnect the clutch operating cable and pull out the actuating arm from its ball pin support. When the clutch operating cable is disconnected, carefully note and retain the insulator and pressure pad between the washer and the arm.

4   The right hand engine mounting bracket has to be unbolted from the engine so the engine must be supported — preferably by a sling from above. If supported from underneath remember that it has to be lowered and swung to one side.

5   Undo the bellhousing bolts and take off the bellhousing. Once again it is difficult to remove the two bolts inside the lower half of the bellhousing, (that mate up with the transmission) unless a specially-shaped spanner is obtained from the Vauxhall agent in your area. Access to these bolts is through the clutch fork slots (Fig. 5.5). These bolts can be removed using a standard spanner or socket — but a great deal of patience and dexterity is necessary. You must also remember that the starter motor bolts are used to secure the clutch housing to the crankcase; so these too must be removed.

6   Mark the position of the clutch cover relative the flywheel.

7   Slacken off the bolts holding the clutch cover to the flywheel in a diagonal sequence, undoing each bolt a little at a time. This keeps the pressure even all round the diaphragm spring and prevents distortion. When all the pressure on the bolts is released remove them, lift the cover off the dowel pegs and take off together with the friction disc which is between it and the flywheel.

8   Examine the diaphragm spring for signs of distortion or fracture.

9   Examine the pressure plate for signs of scoring or abnormal wear.

10 If either the spring or the plate is defective it will be necessary to replace the complete assembly with an exchange unit. The assembly can only be taken to pieces with special equipment and in any case individual parts of the assembly are not obtainable as regular spares.

Note: 2300cc models are fitted with the Laycock clutch assembly. On these versions the diaphragm spring, driving plate and pressure plate can be separated as they are simply held together by a large retaining ring and no rivets are used. The relative position of the three items should be marked. The retaining ring and anti-rattle springs can then be detached and the assembly comes apart. On assembly the pressure points should be greased sparingly with a general purpose molybdenum disulphide grease. Make sure the retaining ring is replaced with the flat sections under the pressure plate lugs and the curved sections against the edge of the diaphragm spring. (Fig. 5.6 and 5.7).

11 Examine the friction disc for indications of uneven wear and scoring of the friction surfaces. Contamination by oil will also show as hard and blackened areas which can cause defective operation. If the clearance between the heads of the securing rivets and the face of the friction lining material is less than .025 in (0.6mm), it would be

worthwhile to fit a new disc. Around the hub of the friction disc are four springs acting as shock absorbers between the hub and the friction area. These should be intact and tightly in position.

12 The face of the flywheel should be examined for signs of scoring or uneven wear and if necessary it will have to be renewed or reconditioned. See Chapter 1, for details of flywheel removal.

6 Clutch assembly — replacement

1   Replacement of the clutch cover and friction plate is the reverse of the removal procedure but not quite so straightforward, as the following paragraphs will indicate.

2   If the clutch assembly has been removed from the engine with the engine out of the car, it is a relatively easy matter to line up the hub of the friction disc with the centre of the cover and flywheel. The cover and friction plate are replaced onto the flywheel with the holes in the cover fitting over the three dowels on the flywheel. The friction plate is supported with a finger while this is being done.

3   Note that the friction plate is mounted with the longer hub of the boss towards the flywheel. Usually the replacement disc is marked 'flywheel side' to prevent a mistake being made.

4   Replace the cover mounting bolt finger tight sufficiently to just grip the friction plate. Then set the friction plate in position so that the hub is exactly concentric with the centre of the flywheel and the cover assembly. An easy way of doing this is to make a temporary mandrel using a bar from a socket set which should fit fairly closely in the flywheel bush. Wrap a few turns of adhesive tape round the bar near the end which will make a snug fit inside the splined boss of the friction plate. Use this as a centring device. It is most important to get this right when replacing the clutch to an engine which is still in the car. Otherwise, difficulty and possibly damage could occur when refitting the gearbox.

5   Tighten the cover bolts one turn at a time in a diagonal sequence to maintain an even pressure. Finally tighten to the specified torque.

6   Replace the bellhousing. Position the engine back onto the right hand mounting bracket. Then replace the gearbox and propeller shaft.

7 Clutch actuating lever and thrust release bearing — removal, inspection and replacement

1   Remove the gearbox as described in Chapter 6, 'Gearbox removal'.

2   Move the lever sideways so that the end over the ball pivot pin is freed by springing back the retaining clip.

3   The lever jaw pins can then be disengaged from the groove in the thrust release bearing and the lever taken off over the end of the input shaft.

4   The clutch release bearing may then be taken off the input shaft.

5   Inspect the pivot pin ball for signs of wear and flats. If necessary it can be removed by driving it out of the bellhousing with a drift. A new one can be driven in with a soft headed hammer.

6   If the release bearing is obviously worn and is noisy it should be renewed. Do not clean the release bearing in any solvent as the ball races have been prepacked with grease and such cleaning would wash it out.

7   Replace the operating lever and release bearing in the reverse order of dismantling. Note that the grooved side of the thrust bearing goes towards the gearbox.

8   Ensure that the spring retaining clip on the end of the lever fastens securely over the mushroom head of the ball pivot pin.

9   Replace the gearbox as described in Chapter 6, 'Gearbox replacement'.

8 Clutch pilot bearing — renewal

1   In the centre of the flywheel is a pilot bearing in which the gearbox

input shaft runs. If the bearing is badly worn the clutch operation will be unsatisfactory and out of balance.

2   The bearing is of the caged needle-roller type and can be withdrawn from the flywheel by using a suitable extractor.

3   The new bearing can be pressed in using a suitable mandrel, but ensure that the side with the seal is towards the gearbox. Lubricate the bearing with a general purpose grease.

9   Fault diagnosis — clutch

Symptom	Reason/s	Remedy
Judder when taking up drive	Loose engine or gearbox mountings or over flexible mountings	Check and tighten all mounting bolts and replace any 'soft' or broken mountings.
	Badly worn friction surfaces or friction plate contaminated with oil carbon deposit	Remove clutch assembly and replace parts as required. Rectify any oil leakage points which may have caused contamination.
	Worn splines in the friction plate hub or on the gearbox input shaft	Renew friction plate and/or input shaft.
	Badly worn bush in flywheel centre for input shaft spigot	Renew bush in flywheel.
Clutch spin (or failure to disengage) so that gears cannot be engaged	Clutch actuating cable clearance from fork too great	Adjust clearance.
	Clutch friction disc sticking to pressure surface because of oil contamination (usually apparent after standing idle for some length of time)	As temporary remedy engage top gear, apply handbrake, depress clutch and start engine. (If very badly stuck engine will not turn). When running rev up engine and slip clutch until disengagement is normally possible. Renew friction plate at earliest opportunity.
	Damaged or misaligned pressure plate assembly	Replace pressure plate assembly.
Clutch slip — (increase in engine speed does not result in increase in car speed — especially on hills)	Clutch actuating cable clearance from fork too little resulting in partially disengaged clutch at all times	Adjust clearance.
	Clutch friction surfaces worn out (beyond further adjustment of operating cable) or clutch surfaces oil soaked	Replace friction plate and remedy source of oil leakage.

Chapter 6 Manual gearbox and automatic transmission

Contents

Automatic transmission — adjustments and attention ...	18
Automatic transmission — description	16
Automatic transmission — fluid level	17
Automatic transmission — removal and replacement ...	19
Extension housing oil seal — removal and refitting ...	13
Fault diagnosis — manual gearbox	15
Gearbox components — inspection	8
Gearbox — dismantling	3
Gearbox — mechanism	14
Gearbox — reassembly	11
Gearbox — removal	2
Gearbox — replacement	12
General description	1
Input shaft — dismantling	5
Input shaft — reassembly	9
Mainshaft — dismantling	4
Mainshaft — reassembly	10
Synchro hubs — dismantling and inspection	6
Synchro hubs — reassembly	7

Specifications

Manual gearbox

General

No of gears	4 forward, 1 reverse
Type	Helical-cut constant-mesh with straight-cut reverse gears. Synchromesh on all forward speeds
Change mechanism	Floor-mounted remote lever
Oil capacity	2.4 pints (Imperial)/1.36 litres.
Oil type	SAE 90EP

Ratios:

First	3.3 : 1
Second	2.145 : 1
Third	1.414 : 1
Fourth	Direct
Reverse	3.063 : 1

Mainshaft

Diameter	1.4738—1.4744
Gear to shaft clearance	0.0016—0.0032
1st gear sleeve diameter	1.3484—1.3490 in
1st gear clearance on sleeve	0.0020—0.0041 in

Laygear

Length	7.141—7.144 in
Thrust washer thickness	0.0615—0.0635 in
Endfloat in casing	0.0048—0.0177 in

Reverse pinion

Shaft diameter	0.779—0.7795 in
Pinion clearance on shaft	0.0025—0.0040 in

Speedometer gears

Driving gear on mainshaft	5 starts (worm)
Driven gears:	

	Number of teeth
1800	16
2300	15

Circlips and shims — available thicknesses

Circlips	0.059—0.061 in
	0.062—0.064 in
	0.065—0.067 in
	0.068—0.070 in
	0.071—0.073 in
	0.074—0.076 in
	0.077—0.079 in
Shims	0.003 in
	0.005 in
	0.010 in

Automatic transmission

Gear ratios

1st	2.4 : 1
2nd	1.48 : 1
3rd	1 : 1
Reverse	1.92 : 1

Oil capacity (dry)	9 pints (Imperial)/5.1 litres
Oil capacity (refill)	4.5 pints (Imperial)/2.6 litres
Oil type	Dexron type ATF fluid
Stall speed	2100 to 2150 rpm

Approximate change speeds in 'D' range

		Change	Speed
Minimum throttle		1—2	10 mph
		2—3	12 mph
Closed throttle		3—2	10 mph
		2—1	8 mph
90% throttle		1—2	32 mph
		2—3	43 mph
Full throttle		1—2	35 mph
		2—3	58 mph
		3—2	52 mph
		3—1	32 mph

Torque wrench settings (Automatic transmission)

	lb/ft	kg/m
Flexplate to crankshaft bolts	25	3.45
Torque converter to flexplate bolts	42	5.8
Converter housing to transmission bolts	25	3.45
Extension housing to transmission bolts	20	2.77
Transmission sump to case bolts	7	0.97

1 General description

1 The four-speed manual transmission used incorporates synchromesh on all forward gears, and is controlled by a remotely mounted floor-change lever. G.M. Automatic Transmission is available as an option on all models (see Section 16).

All forward gears are constant mesh and helically cut, and gear engagement is by hubs with sliding sleeves engaging teeth on the gears through intermediate synchromesh rings.

The gearbox 'cover' is at the bottom of the box and the forward gear selector forks are mounted on rails one at each side of the casing. The selector fork operating levers are mounted on a cross shaft across the casing. The reverse gear selector fork is mounted in the cover plate.

The laygear runs on needle roller bearings on the layshaft and end-float is governed by a thrust washer at each end.

An oil drain plug is located on the edge of the cover. The filler/level plug is located half way up the left side.

2 Gearbox — removal

1 Jack-up the car in the centre of the right hand body side frame mem-ber, and then support the car at the front and rear of this side member on proper stands (photo). If a pit is used this is not necessary, of course. If wheel ramps are used put them at the front and rear wheels on the same side of the car. In this way access to the gearbox and rear of the propeller shaft is equally satisfactory. Block the wheels resting on the ground. Drain the gearbox oil.

2 Remove the propeller shaft as described in Chapter 7.

3 To prevent loss of oil from the gearbox as it is being removed, cover the rear end with a polythene bag. Alternatively, drain the oil before the gearbox is removed.

4 Where applicable, remove the restraining cable fitted between the clutch and the rear crossmember.

5 Remove the self-tapping screws which retain the console insert; remove the insert.

6 Remove the self-tapping screws which retain the console; remove the console.

7 Remove the gearshift boot retainer.

8 The lever pivots in an inverted U-shaped carrier. The pivot pin is retained by an E-clip, which now has to be removed to allow the pin to be withdrawn, after raising the boot. (See Fig. 6.1).

9 Disconnect the speedometer cable by undoing the knurled retainer round the end of the outer cable on the side of the rear extension (photo). Where applicable, disconnect the reverse light leads.

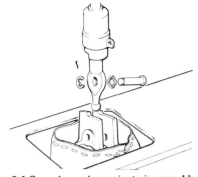

Fig. 6.1 Gear change lever pivot pin assembly

2.1 Stand supporting body side rail

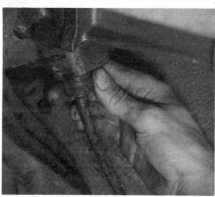

2.9 Undoing the speedo cable union

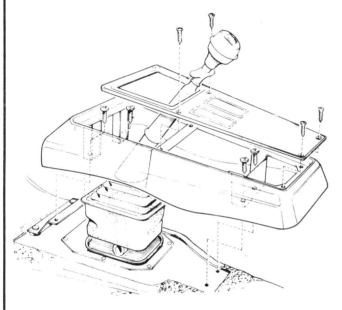

Fig. 6.2 Gear change lever console assembly (typical)

2.11 Removing the lower gearbox mounting bolts through the aperatures in the bellhousing

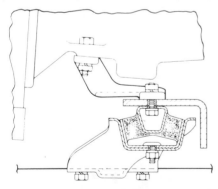

Fig. 6.3 Early type transmission mount - sectioned

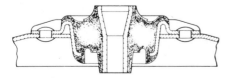

Fig. 6.4 Later type transmission mount - sectioned

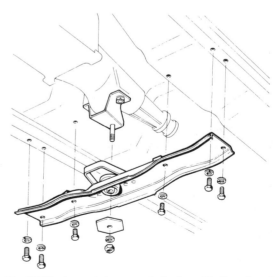

Fig. 6.5 The transmission mount attachment bolts and washers

10 Unhook the clutch operating lever return spring from the bracket bolted on the side of the casing. If the clutch is going to be dismantled and/or engine removed disconnect the clutch cable also.

11 Remove the two lower bolts which secure the gearbox to the clutch housing. These bolts fit from inside the housing into the gearbox and access to them is through the lower apertures in the housing. Use a cranked ring spanner to loosen and remove them (photo).

12 Support the edge of the clutch housing with a jack in preparation for removing the gearbox support crossmember.

13 Mark the crossmember so as to prevent confusion as to which way round it goes on replacement.

14 Undo the two bolts holding the crossmember at each end to the side rails and remove the nut securing it to the mounting stud in the centre. Take the crossmember off.

15 Carefully lower the jack under the bellhousing just enough to permit access to the two bolts which secure the top of the gearbox casing to the bellhousing. These bolt through the lugs on the gearbox into the bellhousing and are readily undone with a socket extension. Even though all four bolts are removed the gearbox will not fall.

16 Pull the gearbox to the rear, supporting it well so that it does not drop, and then take it out from under the car.

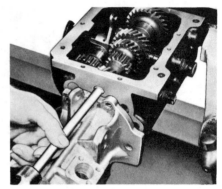

Fig. 6.6 Driving out the layshaft

3 Gearbox — dismantling

1 Place the complete unit on a firm bench or table and ensure that you have the following tools (in addition to the normal range of spanners etc) available:

a) Good quality circlip pliers, 2 pairs — 1 expanding and 1 contracting.

b) Copper headed mallet, at least 2 lb.

c) Drifts, steel 3/8 in.

d) Small containers for needle rollers.

e) Engineer's vice mounted on firm bench.

f) Method of heating, such as blow lamp or butagas stove.

Any attempt to dismantle the gearbox without the foregoing is not necessarily impossible, but will certainly be very difficult and inconvenient, resulting in possible injury or damage.

Read the whole of this section before starting work.

Take care not to let the synchro hub assemblies come apart before you want them to. It accelerates wear if the spines of hub and sleeve are changed in relation to each other. As a precaution it is advisable to make a line-up mark with a dab of paint.

Before finally going ahead with dismantling first ascertain the availability of spare parts — particularly shims and selective circlips which could be difficult to obtain.

2 Remove the gearchange mechanism by undoing the securing clips which locate the pins in both the selector shaft and control rod.

3 Undo the two bolts holding the gear lever carrier to the top of the rear cover.

4 Remove the flexible mounting from the rear cover (where applicable).

5 With the gearbox inverted remove the cover plate.

6 Undo the bolts securing the rear extension to the gear casing. Turn it so that the rear end of the layshaft is exposed.

7 Using a suitable diameter drift and working from the rear, drive the shaft out through the front of the casing. Note there is a locking ball bearing in a recess in the front end of this shaft to stop it rotating when fitted to the casing. Take care not to lose it.

8 When the layshaft has been removed carefully lift up the laygear, keeping it horizontal. Remove the needle rollers and spacers from each end. (Fig. 6.7).

9 Remove the thrust washers from each end of the casing round the layshaft openings.

10 The selector striking levers are held to the cross-shaft by tubular spring pins. These are driven downwards with a flat nosed punch just far enough to release the levers on the shaft.

Manoeuvre the shaft to the most advantageous position for driving out. If driven too far they might jam against the side of the casing.

Fig. 6.7 The laygear, showing the spacers and rollers

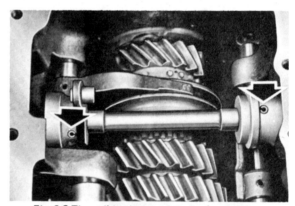

Fig. 6.8 The striking lever spring pins (arrowed)

Fig. 6.9 The later type reverse pinion

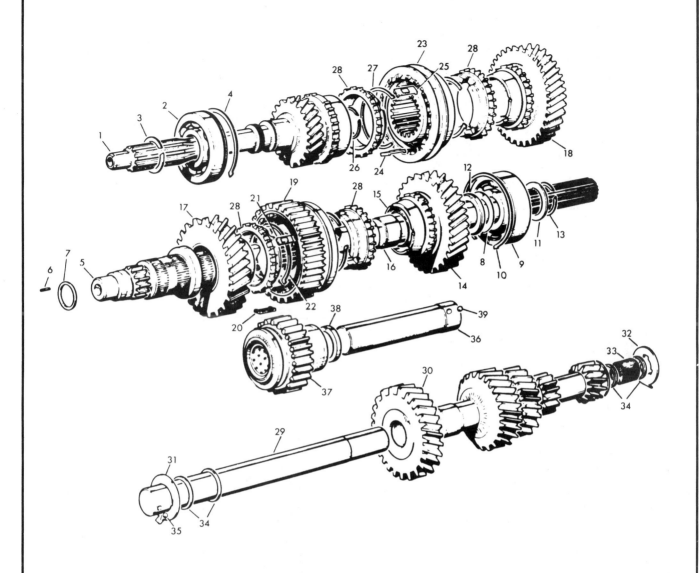

Fig. 6.10 Gearbox - internal shafts and gears

1 Input shaft	11 Thrust washer	20 Sliding key - slotted	31 Thrust washer front
2 Bearing - input shaft	12 Thrust washer	22 Spring	32 Thrust washer rear
3 Circlip	13 Circlip (selective)	23 3rd/4th synchro hub	33 Needle roller (see Fig. 6.7)
4 Circlip	14 First gear	24 Sliding key	34 Spacer rings (see Fig. 6.7)
5 Mainshaft	15 First gear bush	25 Sliding key	35 Shaft locking ball
6 Needle roller	16 First gear sleeve	26 Spring	36 Reverse pinion shaft
7 Spacer ring	17 Second gear	27 Circlip - selective	37 Reverse pinion
8 Mainshaft shim	18 Third gear	28 Synchro ring	38 Spacer
9 Mainshaft bearing	19 1st/2nd synchro hub	29 Layshaft	39 Shaft locking ball
10 Circlip (bearing/rear cover)	and reverse gear	30 Laygear	

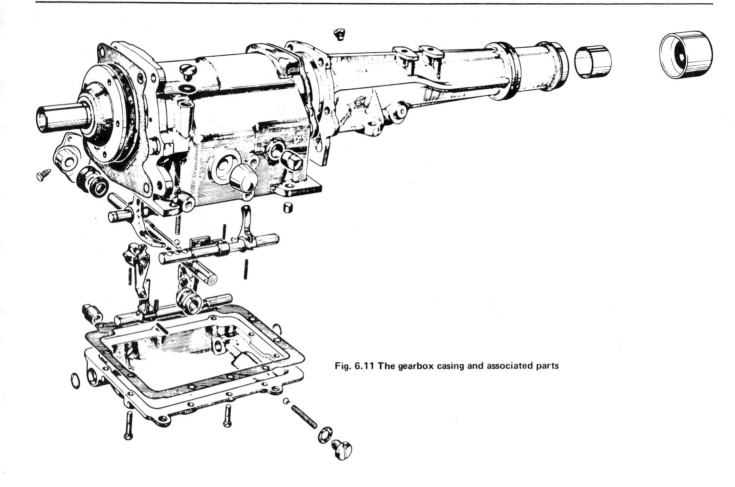

Fig. 6.11 The gearbox casing and associated parts

11 Draw out the cross-shaft and lift out the striking levers.

12 The selector forks are also held by spring pins to their respective rails. These should also be driven out, using a parallel pin punch, sufficiently to prevent jamming against the side of the casing.

13 The detent ball bearings and springs for the selector rails are contained in recesses in the casing side. Remove the screwed plug with a wide blade screwdriver to release the springs and ball bearings.

14 Once again, rotate the rear cover so as to expose the ends of the selector fork rails which are then drifted out from the rear to the front of the casing. Take care to watch that the forks do not jam while the rails are being drifted out through them.

15 Drift out the reverse pinion shaft next otherwise the mainshaft cannot be removed. On some early models there is a spacer collar between the rear face of the pinion and the casing. On later models the reverse pinion boss is lengthened. (Fig. 6.9).

16 Withdraw the mainshaft and rear cover assembly from the casing. Collect up the needle rollers from the counterbore of the input shaft — also the spacer ring.

17 Undo and remove the five bolts and spring washers that hold the input shaft bearing cover to the front of the casing. Withdraw the input shaft assembly.

18 Should it be necessary to remove the reverse gear selector fork and striking fork, first drift out the spring pins by working through the drain plug hole. Before driving out the shaft remove the detent spring and ball bearing by undoing the screwed plug in the housing.

19 The gearbox main casing is now stripped out. Thoroughly flush out the interior of the casing with paraffin and wipe clean with a lint-free cloth.

4 Mainshaft — dismantling

1 The mainshaft is held into the extension cover by a circlip behind the main bearing. The bearing is also a tight fit and to avoid damage the cover should be warmed over a suitable heat source first. Remove the rubber mounting block (where applicable) before holding the cover over a naked flame. Contract the circlip to release it from the bore of the casing, support the casing against the vice jaws and drive the shaft out from the rear with a soft faced mallet.

2 Remove the speedometer driven gear and spindle by undoing the two set screws, marking the position of the flat on the housing relative to the cover, and lifting it out.

3 With long nosed pliers remove the circlip inside the extension cover which retains the bearing.

4 Warm the extension cover over a heat source such as a butane gas camping stove and then clamp the flange in a vice.

5 Tap the tail end of the protruding mainshaft with a hammer and block of wood to drive the shaft and bearing out of the cover.

6 Without the services of a press it is essential to have an assistant when dismantling the shaft. The synchro hubs, gear sleeve and bearing are very tightly fitted and considerable force must be carefully applied to get them off.

7 Starting with the rear end of the shaft remove the circlips retaining the speedometer drive worm gear and drive off the gear with a suitable drift. It is keyed to the shaft with a small barrel key which should not be lost.

8 Remove the circlip on the shaft which retains the bearing by its inner race.

9 Support the front face of 1st gear over the jaws of the vice adjusting the jaw width to give maximum support to the gear without touching the gears below because the gear is next to the bearing.

10 With one person holding the assembly firmly, the rear end of the shaft needs firm striking with a heavy soft headed mallet. The shaft will be driven out through the gears.

11 Repeat this operation with the front face of the 2nd gear supported over the vice jaws in order to drive the shaft out through 2nd gear. 1st/2nd synchro hub and the centre sleeve on which 1st gear revolves.

12 Take note of the thrust washer and any shims fitted between the bearing and adjacent gear/hub.

13 The rear end of the shaft now being clear up tb the shoulder, remove the circlip from the opposite end which retains the 3rd/4th speed synchro hub in position.

14 Support the rear face of 3rd gear over the vice jaws and drive the nose of the shaft down through the gear and 3rd/4th synchro hub assembly. With the exception of the hub assemblies (dealt with in a later section), the mainshaft is now dismantled.

5 Input shaft — dismantling

1 The shaft and bearing are retained in the front cover by a circlip which also locks into a groove in the bearing outer race.

2 Grip the cover sleeve with the gear upwards and expand the circlip sufficiently to clear the groove in the bearing. At the same time tap the end of the shaft on the bench or a solid wood block to move it out of the casing.

3 To get the bearing off the shaft grip the shaft across the covered jaws of the vice at a place clear of the splines and drift the bearing down off it.

6 Synchro hubs — dismantling and inspection

1 Synchro hubs are only too easy to dismantle — just push the centre out and the whole thing flies apart. The point is to prevent this happening before you are ready. Do not dismantle the hubs without reason and do not mix up the parts of the two hubs.

2 The most important check to make is for any backlash in the splines between the outer sleeve and inner hub. If any is noticeable the whole assembly must be renewed.

3 Mark the hub and sleeve so that you may reassemble them on the same splines. With the hub and sleeve separated the teeth at the ends of the splines which engage with corresponding teeth of the gear wheels must be checked for damage or wear.

4 Do not confuse the keystone shape at the ends of the teeth with wear. This shape matches the gear teeth shape and it is a design characteristic to minimise jump-out tendencies. (Fig. 6.12).

5 If the synchronising cones are being renewed it is sensible also to renew the sliding keys and springs which hold them in position.

7 Synchro hubs — reassembly

1 The hub assemblies are not interchangeable so must be reassembled with their original or identical new parts.

2 The pips on the sliding keys are offset and must be assembled to both hubs so that the offset is towards the spigoted end of the hub.

3 One slotted key is assembled to each hub for locating the turned out end of the key spring.

4 It should be noted that the third and fourth clutch keys are shorter then the first and second clutch keys.

5 The turned out end of each spring must locate in the slotted key and be assembled to the hub in an anticlockwise direction as viewed from either side of the hub.

8 Gearbox components — inspection

1 It is assumed that the gearbox has been dismantled for reasons of excessive noise, lack of synchromesh on certain gears or for failure to stay in gear. If anything more drastic than this (total failure, seizure or gear case cracked) it would be better to leave well alone and look for a replacement, either secondhand or exchange unit.

2 Examine all gears for excessively worn, chipped or damaged teeth. Any such gears should be replaced. It is not practical to renew a first gear bush or reverse pinion bushes, and if they are worn, a complete assembly must be obtained.

3 Check all synchromesh rings for wear on the bearing surfaces, which normally have clear machined oil reservoir lines in them. If these are smooth or obviously uneven, replacement is essential. Also, when the rings are fitted to their gears — as they would be when in operation — there should be no rock. This would signify ovality, or lack of concentricity. One of the most satisfactory ways of checking is by comparing the fit of a new ring with an old one on the gearwheel cone. The teeth and cut outs in the synchro rings also wear, and for this reason also it is unwise not to fit new ones when the opportunity avails.

4 All ball race bearings should be checked for chatter and roughness after they have been flushed out. It is advisable to replace these anyway even though they may not appear too badly worn.

5 Circlips which are all important in locating bearings, gears and hubs should also be checked to ensure that they are undistorted and undam-

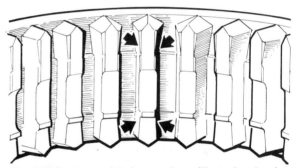

Fig. 6.12 Synchromesh hub outer sleeve. Illustration showing 'Keystone' shape of engagement dogs on all hubs

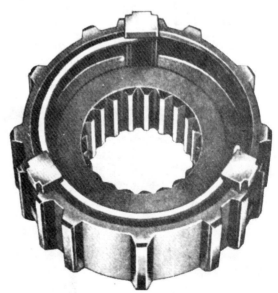

Fig. 6.13 The assembled synchro hub showing the spring ends

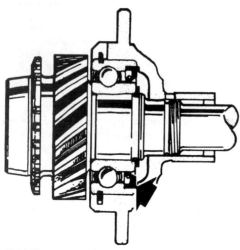

Fig. 6.14 The input shaft assembly with the bearing fitted

Arrow indicates the seal in the face of the bearing

aged. In any case a selection of new circlips of varying thicknesses should be obtained to compensate for variations in new components fitted, or wear in old ones. The specifications indicate what is available.

6   The thrust washers at the ends of the laygear should also be replaced, as they will almost certainly have worn if the gearbox is of any age.

7   Needle roller bearings between the input shaft and mainshaft and in the laygear are usually found in good order, but if in any doubt replace the needles as necessary.

8   For details of inspection of the synchro hub assemblies refer to Section 6.

9   Ensure that the gearbox rear cover bolt holes are clean and dry (for the application of Loctite during assembly).

9 Input shaft — reassembly

1   Fit a new oil seal into the housing in the bearing outer face. This should be installed with the seal towards the front of the gearbox. (Fig. 6.14).

2   The bearing can be driven onto the shaft with a piece of tube with an inside diameter of 1.125 in (28.575 mm) which will go over the shaft and butt against the inner race of the bearing. Do not drive the bearing on by the outer race. The circlip groove is off centre of the bearing and it should be nearest the gear on the shaft.

3   Make sure the bearing is driven fully up to the gear.

4   Put the circlip into the housing, expanding it with circlip pliers and then put the shaft and bearing in. Tap the shaft down so that the bearing first goes through the circlip and then make sure it is driven in far enough for the circlip to engage the groove.

10 Mainshaft — reassembly

1   Start with the tail end of the mainshaft and first place 2nd gear (the middle sized one of the three loose gears you have) onto the shaft with the gear teeth next to the shoulder of the shaft.

2   Place a synchro ring over the gearwheel cone.

3   Put the 1st/2nd gear synchro hub assembly (the one with the straight cut teeth on the outer sleeve) onto the shaft so that the teeth of the sleeve are nearest to the gear already fitted (photo).

4   The hub centre will need driving onto splines. A piece of 1.125 in (28.575 mm) internal diameter tube is ideal for this as it will be necessary to drive only the hub centre. It is also necessary to make sure that the cut outs in the synchro ring engage with the sliding keys in the hub when it is driven fully home. If you do not have a long enough piece of tube even then, use a drift or support the hub centre across the vice jaws and drive the shaft into it with a soft mallet (photo).

10.3 2nd gear, synchro ring and 1st/2nd gear synchro hub being put into the rear end of the mainshaft

10.4 Driving 1st/2nd gear synchro hub onto the shaft splines

10.5a Heating 1st gear hub sleeve

10.5b Showing the hubsleeve position on the shaft butted up to the synchro hub assembly

10.7 Fitting first gear. Note that the synchro ring is in position in the synchro hub

10.10 Placing the thrust washer and shim in position

10.11 Driving the bearing onto the shaft. Note the large circlip between the bearing and gear (arrowed)

10.12a Rear thrust collar being fitted

10.12b Circlip being fitted

10.13a Tapping the speedometer drive gear up to one circlip

10.13b Fitting the second circlip

10.14 Fitting 3rd gear to the front of the shaft

10.15a Placing the synchro ring and 3rd/4th hub onto the front of the mainshaft

10.15b Driving hub onto the splines. The outer sleeve has not yet been assembled to the hub

10.16 Fitting the circlip to retain 3rd/4th synchro hub

10.17 Pulling off the rear extension cover oil seal

10.18 Fitting a new rear extension oil seal

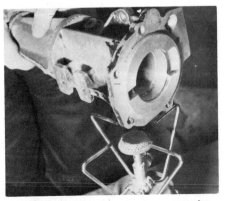

10.19 Warming the rear extension cover prior to fitting the mainshaft assembly into it

5   The hub sleeve for first gear is also a drive fit and goes on next. It helps, to heat it up. It is important to make sure that the edges of this sleeve are not nicked, burred or spread in the process of fitting. If two people are available it can be done with the vice jaw method. Make sure it butts tight up to the hub of the synchro assembly (photos).

6   Fit a synchro ring into the hub assembly, lining up the cut outs with the sliding keys.

7   Place 1st gear (the largest) onto the shaft with the cone section fitting into the synchro ring (photo).

8   Fit the large thrust washer.

9   At this stage it is theoretically necessary to check the measurement from the front face of the shoulder on which 3rd gear runs to the rear face of the thrust washer just fitted. This is because the longitudinal position of the mainshaft in the casing is controlled by the position of the rear bearing which goes on next. The measurement referred to should be between 5.781 – 5.783 in (147.837 – 147.888 mm). The design is such that shims need adding between the thrust washer and bearing to make up the correct distance.

10   Provided that only the bearing and synchro rings have been renewed one may replace the shims originally fitted without trepidation. If the synchro hub assembly and gears have been renewed then the shim thickness may need altering. For this, a large caliper gauge will need to be acquired to carry out the necessary measurement. Shim thickness can then be calculated. Available shims are listed in the specifications (photo).

11   With the thrust washer and shims in position the rear bearing is driven onto the shaft in the same way as the hubs. Replace the large circlip behind the bearing first — otherwise it will have to be spread excessively in order to get it in position afterwards. Be careful not to trap the shim in the circlip groove while the bearing is driven on (photo).

12   Having ensured that the bearing is driven fully up to the shims and thrust washer, fit the thrust collar and circlip in the shaft groove behind the bearing inner race. This is where a circlip of a different thickness may need selecting. Too thick a circlip will not go in, and too thin a circlip will allow the bearing to creep fractionally along the shaft until it butts up against the circlip. Select one which is a snug fit (photos).

13   The speedometer drive gear is next fitted to the main shaft. Line up the keyway first. Here again the correct thickness of the circlip on each side of the gear will prevent movement of the gear on the shaft (photos).

14   Turning to the front of the shaft fit third gear (the only loose gear left) onto the nose with the flat side up against the shoulder (photo).

15   Place a synchro ring over the gear cone and put the 3rd/4th hub assembly onto the shaft with the selector fork groove in the sleeve towards the front of the shaft. This hub will need driving on in the same way as the other end; once again the sliding keys must line up and fit into the synchro ring cut outs. Make sure that the hub assembly is driven on fully up to the third gear (photos).

16   Select a circlip which is a tight fit in the groove to retain the hub assembly on the shaft (photo).

17   Before fitting the mainshaft back into the rear extension cover fit a new rear oil seal. The old one can be taken out by clamping it in the vice and pulling the casing out (photo).

18   Carefully tap the new seal into position keeping it square and undistorted. Soak the felt ring with oil (NB, this job can be done with the gearbox installed and propeller shaft removed) (photo).

19   Warm the extension housing so that the main bearing on the shaft will enter easily (photo).

20   When the bearing is in position make sure that the retaining circlip fits the housing groove properly (photo).

21   Fit the gearbox mounting to the extension cover ensuring it is the correct way round.

11 Gearbox — reassembly

1   Make sure the mating faces of the casing and rear extension cover are clean, fit a new gasket in position and place the mainshaft assembly into the casing. Do not replace any bolts yet (photo).

2   Rotate the cover until the reverse pinion shaft hole is clear. Put the locking ball into the recess in the reverse pinion shaft and then guide the plain end into the casing.

3   Fit the reverse pinion with the spacer collar or lengthened boss towards the rear of the gearbox.

4   Rotate the shaft so that the locking ball lines up with the notch in the casing but before driving fully home, coat the end of the shaft with a non-setting gasket sealant.

5   Apply Loctite grade 270 to the rear cover bolt threads, fit them but do not fully tighten at this stage.

6   The 24 needle rollers should next be prepared for fitting to the input shaft onto the nose of the mainshaft. This can be done by either fitting them in the counterbore of the input shaft or around the nose of the mainshaft. (The latter method is less likely to cause dislodging of the needles on assembly. Use a little grease — not too much, to hold the needles in position (photo).

7   The spacer must be installed correctly. It is positioned at the mainshaft end of the needle rollers.

8   Check the input shaft mating surfaces on the cover and casing, and position a new gasket on the flange.

9   Fit a synchro ring (the remaining one) into the 3rd/4th synchro hub so that the cut outs engage the sliding keys.

10   Fit the input shaft into the casing so that the counterbore engages over the nose of the mainshaft without dislodging the needle rollers (photo).

11   Replace the front cover bolts, but do not tighten them fully at this stage.

12   The selector forks and rails are fitted next. It is best to have new cylindrical pins to secure the forks to the shaft. In subsequent paragraphs remember that you are working with the gearbox inverted so references to the left and right side are based on the box being the proper way up and looking from rear to front.

13   First/second selector fork has legs of unequal length and the rail is fitted from the front of the casing. The striking lug is fitted to the rail with the jaw for the lever towards the casing front.

14   Place the rail into the casing from the front on the left side. The three detent grooves are at the front end of the shaft and face the top of the casing when finally positioned.

15   Pass the rail through the striking lug.

16   Fit the selector fork into the 1st/2nd selector hub groove with the recessed face of the fork facing the front of the casing.

17   Pass the rail through the fork base and tap it home as far as it will go. The front end will come clear of the front of the casing (photo).

18   Pin the striking lug and selector fork to the rail using a flat nosed punch to fit the pins (photo).

19   The 3rd/4th selector fork rail is fitted on the other side of the casing. The selector fork should be fitted into the groove in the outer sleeve of the 3rd/4th gear hub with the recessed face facing the front of the casing like the other.

20   No separate striking lug is fitted on this rail. There is a cut out in the rail itself.

21   Pin the fork to the rail so that the cut out faces the interior of the casing (photo).

22   The cross shaft and striking levers are next assembled.

23   A conventional lip type seal is fitted into the casing for the right hand end of the shaft. This should be prised out and renewed while the opportunity presents itself. Lubricate the new seal lip with molybdenum paste or grease and drive it in open side first until it butts up against the shouldered recess in the casing (photos).

24   Insert the cross shaft, spigot end first into the casing from the right hand side.

25   Take up the striking lever which has two legs — one long — and put the shaft through it so that the long leg points to the bottom of the bore and the boss faces the side of the casing (photo).

26   Pass the shaft next through the other striking lever, the leg pointing to the top of the box and the boss facing the side of the casing (photo).

27   Manoeuvre both levers to line up with the holes in the shaft making sure that the set screw recess on the right hand end of the shaft faces the front of the casing. If this is not done correctly the operating lever

10.20 Fitting the mainshaft bearing circlip into the rear cover

11.1 Replacing the mainshaft into the gearbox casing

11.4 Reverse pinion shaft showing locking ball joint being driven fully home

11.6 Fitting needle rollers in input shaft counterbore

11.10 Replacing the input shaft into the casing. In this instance the synchro ring is fitted on the gear cover rather than in the synchro hub on the mainshaft

11.17 First/second gear selector rail with the fork and lug not yet pinned into position. The front of the casing is to the left of the photo

11.18 Pinning the 1st/2nd selector fork to the rail

11.21 Pinning the fork to the rail

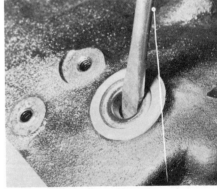
11.23a Prising out the old seal

11.23b Fitting a new seal for the cross shaft in the right hand side of the casing

11.25 Striking lever in correct position relative to 3rd/4th selector fork rail (before cross shaft has been put through it)

11.26 Striking lever in correct position relative to 1st/2nd selector fork rail (before shaft has been put through it)

11.28a Placing the pin in position on the striking lever

11.28b Pinning the striking lever to the cross shaft

11.31 Lay gear first thrust washer in position

11.32 Levering the lay gear into the casing

11.33 Fitting the layshaft

11.38 Fitting the selector fork rail blanking plugs to the front of the casing

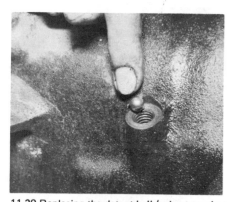

11.39 Replacing the detent ball (prior to spring and plug) in the casing

11.40 Refitting the cover plate and reverse selector rail. Note fork which will engage the pinion groove

11.41 Tightening gear casing cover bolts

11.43 Fitting speedometer driven gear and spindle with the housing

on the end of the shaft cannot be clamped on in the correct position.

28 Refit the spring pins to lock the striking levers to the shaft (photos).

29 The laygear is fitted next. The front end has 26 needle rollers with a spacer either side, and the rear end has two rows of 25 rollers with a space at each end and one in the middle. (Fig. 6.7). Put the needles and spacers in position using grease to prevent them dropping out.

30 Fit the thrust washers into the casing with the dimpled faces facing inwards. The washer with the flat edge goes at the rear with the edge in line with the casing edge.

31 The circular front washer is positioned so that the tab engaged in the groove (photo).

32 Carefully lower the laygear into the casing (large gear to the front) taking care not to disturb the thrust washers or needle rollers. Line up the holes of the casing and the gear (photo).

33 Put the locking bell in the recess of the layshaft and introduce the

plain end of the layshaft from the front of the casing end into the gear without upsetting the needle rollers (photo).

34 Tap it gently through the gear. The hole at the other end of the casing will be covered by the rear cover flange so as to ensure that the needle rollers are not disturbed, the bolts can be removed and the cover rotated to expose the hole. If the hole is left covered make sure that the cover bolts are not fully tightened. If they are, air may be trapped which could prevent the shaft being driven fully home.

35 Turn the shaft to line up the locking ball with the recess at the front of the casing and drive the shaft fully home.

36 At this stage rotate the mainshaft to ensure that everything revolves freely and smoothly.

37 Fully tighten the input shaft flange bolts and rear cover bolts and check once again that the shafts revolve freely.

38 Drive in the two cups that seal the selector fork rail holes in the front of the casing. They should be driven in open end first, just flush with the casing (photo).

39 Refit the detent balls, springs and screwed plugs into each side of the casing (photo).

40 The cover incorporates the reverse selector fork and rail. Having made sure that the mating surfaces are clean, fit a new gasket and replace the cover so that the fork engages the groove in the reverse gear pinion (photo).

41 Replace the cover bolts and tighten them. (photo)

42 Refit the detent ball and spring followed by the screwed plug into the cover if they have been taken out.

43 Fit the speedometer driven gear (not forgetting the thrust pad), a new seal (with circular spring on the small inner lip) and the housing (photo). The housing should be fitted as shown in Fig. 6.15.

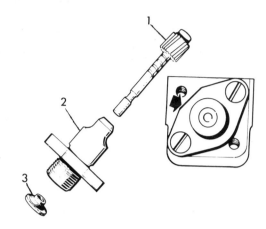

Fig. 6.15 Speedometer gear assembly and installed position

1 Driven gear
2 Housing
3 Seal

Inset Arrow shows the correct position of the flat on the housing

12 Gearbox — replacement

1 Replacement of the gearbox is a reversal of the removal procedure but certain matters have to be remembered.

2 The change mechanism should be assembled and fitted, and all gears engaged before reinstallation.

3 If you have overhauled the gearbox do not neglect the change mechanism as it is subject to wear and this results in a sloppy change action.

4 The clutch actuating lever is fitted by a spring clip to a ball ended stud in the bellhousing. Make sure this is fitted correctly as the gearbox input shaft has to be passed through the thrust bearing when the gearbox is replaced.

5 Do not forget to fit a new gasket between the gearbox face and the bellhousing. Hold it in position with some grease during assembly. Do not use sealing compound.

6 Make sure that the rear mounting and crossmember are fitted the correct way round. (See Figs. 6.3, 6.4 and 6.5).

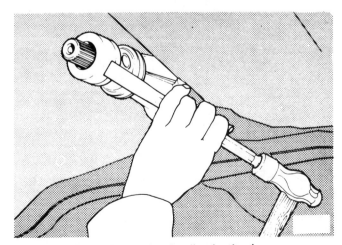

Fig. 6.16 Removing the oil seal and casing

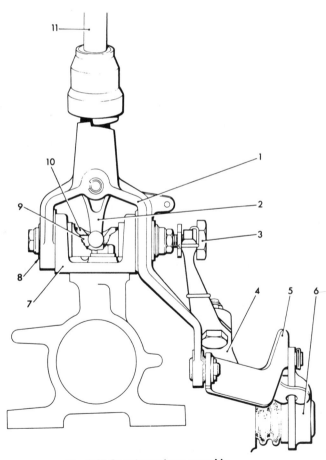

Fig. 6.17 Gearchange lever assembly

1 Intermediate lever
2 Finger
3 Adjuster
4 Selector bar
5 Control rod
6 Coupling
7 Carrier bracket
8 Bush
9 Pad
10 Pivot shaft
11 Upper lever

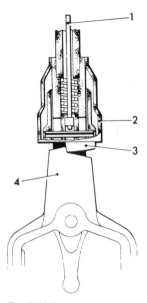

Fig. 6.18 Reverse abutment

1 Cable
2 Housing
3 Stepped abutment
4 Intermediate lever stop

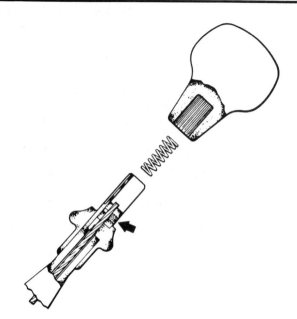

Fig. 6.19 Early gear shift lever

Grub screw arrowed

**Fig. 6.21 Component parts
of the later gear shift lever**

The stepped abutment is arrowed

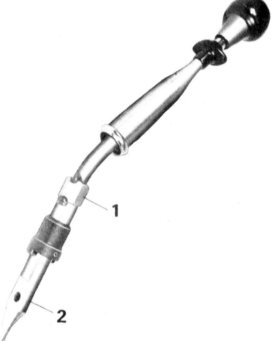

Fig. 6.20 Later gear shift lever

1 Tack welded nut
2 Gear shift finger

Fig. 6.22 Gear change lever cable adjustment

A = 0.02 - 0.04 inch (0.5 - 1.0 mm)
B = 0.012 - 0.020 inch (0.3 - 0.5 mm)

13 Extension housing oil seal — removal and refitting

1   Refer to Chapter 7 and remove the propeller shaft.
2   Using a chisel as shown in Fig. 6.16, knock off the old oil seal and casing.
3   The new seal and casing assembly may now be refitted using a suitable diameter drift.
4   Before refitting the propeller shaft smear the lip of the seal with a little general purpose grease to ensure the seal fine lip is not damaged. Check that the propeller shaft sleeve is free from burrs and scores.

14 Gearchange mechanism

1   Upon reference to Fig. 6.17 it will be seen that the gear shift upper lever (11) is pinned to a finger (2) which is able to pivot in an intermediate lever (1). The intermediate lever pivots on a bush (8) which is pressed into a carrier bracket (7), this being bolted to the transmission extension housing. The intermediate lever outer leg is extended downwards and is connected to the quadrant shaped striking lever shaft coupling (6) by a control rod (5). The spherical end of the finger engages in the intermediate lever pivot shaft (10) which runs in the carrier bracket bush and is loaded by a spring and pad (9) in the centre of the shaft. A selector bar (4) engages in a grooved adjuster (3) in the lever pivot shaft and connects the pivot shaft to the striking lever shaft coupling.
2   The forward or rearward movement of the upper lever is transmitted through the intermediate lever to the control rod. Sideways movement of the upper lever is transmitted through the finger and intermediate pivot shaft to the selector bar.
3   A safety device is incorporated in the gear change lever system whereby it is not possible to accidently engage reverse. This is made possible by a stepped abutment (3), Fig. 6.18, in the housing (2) at the lower end of the upper lever contacting a corresponding step (4) on the intermediate lever.
4   To engage reverse the abutment is lifted by a cable (1) which passes through the centre of the gear change lever and connected to a lift collar at the top of the lever. It is possible to fit a new cable once the gear change lever assembly has been removed from the car.
5   Disconnect the gearchange lever inside the car, as described in Section 2, paragraphs 5, 6, 7 and 8.
6   If it is necessary to gain access to the reverse gear abutment override cable on early models, pull off the lever knob, lift away the spring and then undo the grub screw located in the lever collar. Before withdrawing the cable from the lower end of the lever, drift out the spring pin that secures the gearshift finger and stepped abutment (Fig. 6.18). On later models, it is necessary to drive out the spring pin and remove the stepped abutment. After disconnecting the top end of the cable, the tack welds on the nut should be sawn through (where applicable) to allow the nut to be unscrewed and the lever separated. The cable can then be withdrawn.
7   On early models, reassembly is straightforward. On later models the nut must be finally tackwelded in place to prevent it from unscrewing.
8   When the gearchange lever has been refitted check that the selector bar is fully engaged in the groove of the adjuster before assembling the retainer. If necessary a bend can be introduced in the bar to provide full engagement.
9   When the gearchange upper lever is fitted to the intermediate lever, adjust the cable length so that there is a clearance 'A' (Fig. 6.22) between the underside of the abutment and the top of the intermediate lever of 0.02 — 0.04 in (0.5 — 1.0 mm). Engage 1st and 2nd gear and set the adjuster bolt in the lever pivot shaft so that clearance 'B' is 0.012 — 0.020 in (0.3 — 0.5 mm).

15 Fault diagnosis — manual gearbox

Note: It is sometimes difficult to decide whether it is worthwhile removing and dismantling the gearbox for a fault which may be nothing more than a minor irritant. Gearboxes which howl, or where the synchromesh can be 'beaten' by a quick gear change, may continue to perform for a long time in this state. A worn gearbox usually needs a complete rebuild to eliminate noise because the various gears, if re-aligned on new bearings will continue to howl when different wearing surfaces are presented to each other.

The decision to overhaul, therefore, must be considered with regard to time and money available, relative to the degree of noise or malfunction that the driver has to suffer.

Symptom	Reason/s	Remedy
Ineffective synchromesh	Worn baulk rings or synchro hubs	Dismantle and renew
Jumps out of one or more gears (on drive or over-run)	Weak detent springs or worn selector forks or worn gears	Dismantle and renew. (Detent balls and springs can be renewed without dismantling the gearbox).
Noisy, rough, whining and vibration	Worn bearings and/or laygear thrust washers (initially) resulting in extended wear generally due to play and backlash	Dismantle and renew
Noisy and difficult engagement of gears	Clutch fault	Examine clutch operation.

16 Automatic transmission — description

The automatic transmission replaces the conventional clutch and gearbox, and occupies the same space in the same way being bolted onto the rear of the engine. It comprises two basic parts — the torque converter and the three speed epicyclic gearbox.

The torque converter is a form of oil operated turbine which transmits the engine power from a multibladed rotor (the pump) directly connected to the crankshaft to another multibladed rotor (the turbine) directly connected to the input shaft of the transmission. At low engine revolutions, the oil driven by the pump has little force imparted to it, so the turbine does not move. When the pump speed increases, so the force of the oil is transferred to the turbine.

An intermediate multibladed rotor (the stator) regulates the flow of oil back to the pump after it has done its work through the turbine.

The gearbox consists of a ravignaux planetary gear set in constant mesh and the selection of the gears is by braking one or more of the components of this gear set.

This braking is effected by one of the three servo operated multi plate clutches and a band literally a brake band, which can be applied to the outer ring gear of the set. The automatic operation of three clutches and the low speed band is the complicated part, involving a servo hydraulic pump system controlled by road speed, inlet manifold

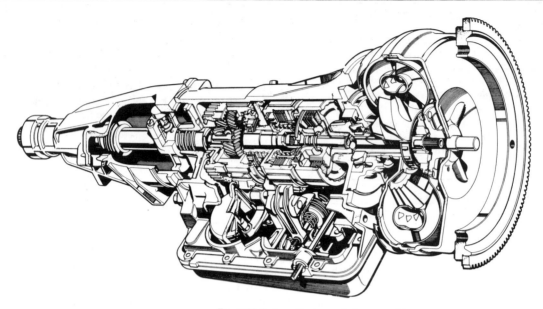

Fig. 6.23 Automatic transmission assembly

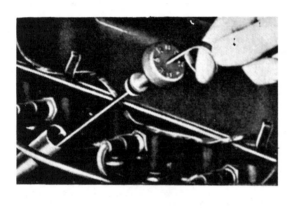

Fig. 6.24 Automatic transmission - fluid level dipstick

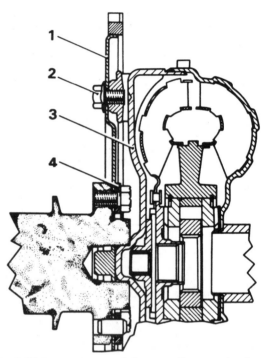

Fig. 6.25 Automatic transmission - coupling to engine flexplate

1 Flexplate	3 Torque converter
2 Flexplate to converter bolts	4 Distance plate

vacuum, and the position of the accelerator.

The capabilities of the automatic transmission are different from the manual system and in order that those unfamiliar with them may understand the difference, a full description of the function at starting, parking and stopping, in all of the five or six selector positions is given below.

'P' Park. In this position with the engine either stopped or running, no gears are 'engaged' and the gearbox output shaft is mechanically locked, which in effect means that the propeller shaft and rear axle are also locked. The car cannot be moved, therefore. The engine may be started in this position. In order to select the 'P' position, the selector lever button must be fully depressed. Do not select 'P' if the car is moving. Damage will result.

'N' Neutral. The conditions for neutral are the same as for 'P' except that the gearbox output shaft is not mechanically locked. The car will therefore, roll with the engine either running or stopped.

'R' Reverse. The button on the selector lever must be partially depressed to engage 'R'. In this position reverse gear is 'engaged'. If the engine is not running, it cannot be started unless the selector lever is moved to 'P' or 'N'. With the brakes applied the car will not move. With the

brakes off, increase in engine speed will move the car backwards. When the engine speed is decreased, the engine will act as a brake through the transmission. If the car is standing with the brakes off, it may roll at low engine speed in either direction. Reverse should not normally be selected whilst the car is moving.

'D' Drive. The selector position for normal driving requirements. In this position first gear is initially 'engaged' but, at low engine speed with the brakes off, the car may roll in either direction. The engine cannot be started in this position. With the engine speed increased, the car will move forward in low gear.

When the speed and load conditions are right, the transmission will automatically move to second gear 'engagement' and then subsequently to top gear. When speed decreases, the gears will automatically shift back down as far as first, again according to speed and load situation.

The engine does not act as a brake or overrun in any of the three speeds in the 'D' position.

'I' Intermediate. To select this position the lever button must be partially depressed. When selected, the automatic transmission will operate as in 'D' except that it will not move up out of 2nd. It should not be used in excess of 60 mph.

It is possible to change to 'I' when the vehicle is moving. It will immediately put the vehicle in 2nd gear until speed or throttle position may cause it to change down to first. The intermediate range is normally used in traffic or on uphill sections where one would tend to get a lot of changing going on between 2nd and top if in the 'D' position. Although there is no overrun braking in 1st gear, there is on 2nd gear in the 'I' position.

'L' Low. To select this position, the selector lever button is fully depressed. This position should not be selected above 35 mph. It would normally be used to provide engine braking on steep downhill sections of road, or to avoid unnecessary changing between 1st and 2nd in dense traffic or on continuous slow uphill climbs.

As implied the engine acts as a brake on overrun in this range.

Some points to bear in mind in the operation of automatic trans- mission are:

a) It is possible to obtain a quick change down to provide instant acceleration by depressing the accelerator fully. This change will not take place, however, if the vehicle is already in excess of the maxi- mum speed of the gear below.

b) Where continuous engine braking on overrun is wanted 'L' or 'I' ranges must be selected. It follows, therefore, that when shifting into these ranges when on the move, engine braking will take place if the car speed is high. On slippery surfaces the possibility of skids occur- ing must, therefore, be considered due to the sudden braking effect on the rear wheels.

c) It is not possible to push or tow-start the car.

d) If the car is to be towed for any reason, the speed must be kept below 30 mph (48 km/hr) and the selector be put in 'N'. Not more than 30 miles (48 km) should be covered. If there is a suspected fault in the transmission, the car should not be towed at all unless the propeller shaft is disconnected or the driving wheels raised to prevent the transmission being ruined.

e) Cars fitted with automatic transmission are also fitted with auto- matic chokes on the carburettor so that the engine speed is suitably governed until it is warmed up. There will be a tendency to a faster tickover and subsequent 'creep' when in any of the driving ranges, until the engine is fully warm. Engine tuning and smooth running is much more significant where automatic transmission is fitted.

f) Transmission fluid normally heats up in use. Severe or abusive use, or failure to keep cooling areas clean, can cause overheating and damage.

17 Automatic transmission — fluid level

1   The total capacity of the system is 9 Imperial pints (5.1 litres). A dipstick is provided in the filler pipe which is located on the right hand side and projects into the engine compartment at the rear of the engine. (Fig. 6.24).

2   To check the fluid level, the engine and transmission should be fully warmed up to normal working temperature. With the car stationary on level ground, engine ticking over at idling speed and the selector lever in 'P', remove the dipstick, clean it off, replace and remove again to note the level. The level must be kept between the 'Full' and 'Add' marks. From 'Add' to 'Full' calls for 1 Imperial pint (0.57 litre). Do not over-

fill or fuming and loss of fluid may occur. Use only the proper fluid for topping up the transmission and under no circumstances should addi- tives of any kind be mixed with it.

3   It is generally best to check the level after a normal run, otherwise, it is difficult to judge the correct working temperature. If starting from cold, then it will be necessary to select a drive range, apply brakes (driver in the driving seat for safety) and run the engine at a fast idle for no more than two minutes.

18 Automatic transmission — adjustments and attention

1   Automatic transmission systems are sophisticated and complicated and require specialist tools, experience and skill if they are to be pro- perly set up. As they tend to be the exception rather than the rule on anything other than large vehicles, it follows that the availability of the tools and frequency of experienced mechanics is rare. Non-professional experience is rarer still. Consequently the owner is not advised to tamper with his unit himself.

2   A cross section of the selector lever mechanism and starter inhibitor switch is given so that adjustment can be made to ensure that the oper- ation of the selector lever button and the safety start cut out are correct. It should not be possible to start the engine when the selector lever is in the 'D', 'I', 'L', or 'R' positions. Similarly it should only be possible to select 'L' or 'P' when the selector button is fully depressed, and 'I' and 'R' when it is partially depressed.

3   Details are given in the next Section on how to remove the trans- mission unit but, it must be emphasised that, full testing can only be carried out when it is known that the unit is beyond repair in its ins- talled position.

4   The test which the owner may carry out, if he suspects that there is either slip or otherwise, is the stall test. However, it will be necessary for a tachometer to be fitted to the engine. With the transmission fully warmed up, apply the brakes fully (chock the wheels too for safety), engage a drive range and press the accelerator to the floor. The engine speed should settle at 2100 — 2150 rpm. Do not maintain the test for more than 10 seconds or overheating will result. If the engine rpm are too high then the torque converter oil supply should be suspect, and then the low band servo in the transmission itself. If the rpm are too low then the engine is not delivering full power or the torque converter unit is faulty.

5   The lower part of the torque converter housing is fitted with a per- forated metal cover to permit cooling air into the housing. It is impor- tant to keep this clean as any restriction could result in overheating and loss efficiency and damage.

19 Automatic transmission — removal and replacement

1   Before making any attempt to remove the transmission, make sure your reasons are valid. In other words get expert diagnosis first if trans- mission malfunctioning is the reason.

2   If you are removing the engine from a car with automatic trans- mission, the two should be separated at the flexplate which connects the crankshaft to the torque converter. Do not try and separate the torque converter from the gearbox.

3   All the normal precautions for gearbox removal as described in Sec- tion 2, should be taken. It must be remembered that they are heavier than conventional gearboxes — approximately 110 lbs and therefore, adequate support must be provided.

4   Proceed to remove the crossmember support after having first slack- ened the transmission brace bolts at the sump bracket, and moving the starter as far forward as possible to clear the starter teeth on the flex- plate rim.

5   If an oil cooler is fitted it will be necessary to drain the oil out so that the cooler tubes may be disconnected from the transmission. Make sure the unions are perfectly clean first and seal the holes suitably to stop dirt entering. The combined filler/dipstick tube must be removed taking the same precautions.

6   The three bolts which hold the flexplate to the torque converter are accessible as soon as the semicircular sheet steel plate across the bottom half of the casing has been removed. These three bolts must be removed before the main housing bolts securing the transmission to the engine are undone, otherwise, a strain could be put on the flexplate which would distort.

7   Once the flexplate bolts are removed, the casing bolts can come out with the whole unit properly supported. The transmission is then drawn a little to the rear and lowered in the normal way.

8   If the flexplate is to be renewed, it may be unbolted from the crankshaft flange. Seal the bolts on replacement as for the flywheel.

9   When replacing the transmission, proceed in the reverse order of removal. Line up the painted balance marks on torque converter and flexplate. When tightening the transmission brace, tighten the bolts on the torque converter housing first and then those on the sump bracket.

Chapter 7 Propeller shaft

Contents

General description 1
Propeller shaft — removal, inspection and replacement ... 2
Universal joints — inspection 3

Specifications

Type	Tubular, 2-piece with centre bearing.	
Torque wrench settings	lb/ft	kg/m
Coupling flange bolts	18	2.5

1 General description

The drive from the gearbox to the rear axle is via the propeller shaft which is, in fact, a two-piece tube. Due to the variety of angles caused by the up and down motion of the rear axle in relation to the gearbox, universal joints are fitted to each end of the shaft to convey the drive through the constantly varying angles. In addition, universal joints are fitted at the centre bearing which is housed in a rubber-cushioned mounting. As the movement also increases and decreases the distance between the rear axle and the gearbox, the forward end of the propeller shaft is a splined sleeve which is a sliding fit over the rear of the gearbox splined mainshaft. The splined sleeve runs in an oil seal in the gearbox mainshaft rear cover, and is supported with the mainshaft on the gearbox rear bearing. The splines are lubricated by oil in the rear cover coming from the gearbox.

The universal joints each comprise a four way trunnion, or 'spider', each leg of which runs in a needle roller bearing race, pre-packed with grease and staked into the bearing journal yokes of the sliding sleeve and propeller shaft and flange.

2 Propeller shaft — removal, inspection and replacement

1 With the two-piece propeller shaft, it is necessary to replace the complete assembly if wear or malfunctioning is indicated. This means replacing the propeller shafts, universal joints, centre bearing and support as one complete entity.

2 Jack-up the rear of the car and support it on stands.

3 The rear of the shaft is connected to the rear axle pinion by a flange held by four nuts and bolts. Mark the position of both flanges relative to each other, and then undo the bolts.

4 Move the propeller shaft forward to disengage it from the pinion flange and then lower it to the ground.

5 After disconnecting the rear axle flange it is necessary to remove the two bolts and distance pieces securing the centre bearing support to the crossmember. The combined shafts and centre bearing assembly can then be withdrawn from the gearbox extension.

6 Place a receptacle under the gearbox rear cover opening to catch any oil which will certainly come out if the gearbox is tilted.

7 The crossmember which supports the centre bearing can be removed by releasing the two bolts that secure it to the underbody. These bolts are accessible beneath the floor carpet.

8 If the propeller shaft is removed for inspection, first examine the bore and counterbore of the two flanges which mate at the rear. If they are damaged in any way, or a slack fit, it could mean that the propeller shaft is running off centre at the flange and causing vibration in

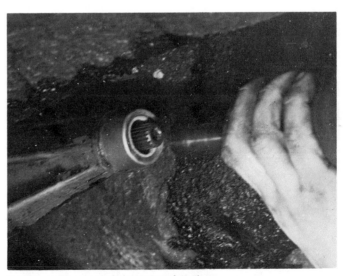

2.5 Removing propshaft from rear of gearbox

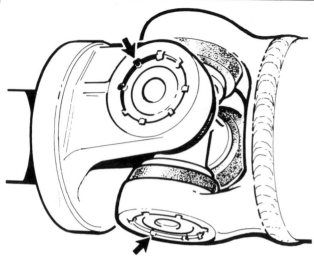

Fig. 7.1 Universal joints

Showing staking used instead of circlips for needle bearing retention

Fig. 7.2 Removing the centre bearing

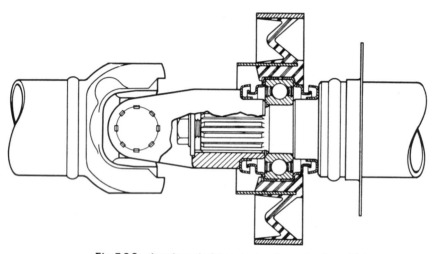

Fig. 7.3 Section through the centre bearing and universal joint
fitted on the propeller shaft

Fig. 7.4 Showing the distance pieces fitted between the centre
bearing support and the cross-member

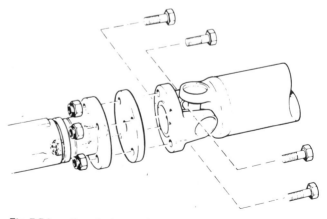

Fig. 7.5 Location of adaptor plate between the propeller shaft flange
and rear axle flange

the drive. If nothing obvious is wrong, and the universal joints are in good order, it is permissible to reconnect the flanges with one turned through 180° relative to the other. This may stop the vibration.

9 The replacement of the shaft is a reversal of the removal procedure. Ensure that the sliding sleeve is inserted into the gearbox end cover with care, and is perfectly clean, so as not to cause damage to, or failure of, the oil seal in the cover. Do not push the sliding sleeve fully onto the mainshaft or the sealing plug on the end of the sleeve may be damaged.

When reassembling ensure that a plain washer and lockwasher are assembled to the bolts which secure the crossmember to the underbody, and that two distance pieces are assembled between the centre bearing support and the crossmember (Fig. 7.4).

10 The flanges should be mated according to the position marks (unless a 180° turn is being done as mentioned in paragraph 8).

The four bolts should be fitted with the heads towards the universal joint. (Fig. 7.5).

3 Universal joints — inspection

1 Wear in the needle roller bearings is evident by vibration in the transmission, "clonks" on taking up the drive, and, in extreme cases, grating as the bearings break-up.

2 Preliminary inspection of the universal joints can be carried out with the propeller shaft on the car.

3 Grasp each side of the universal joint, and with a twisting action determine whether there is any play or slackness in the joint. Also try an up and down rocking motion for the same purpose. If there is any sign whatsoever of play, the joints need replacement. Unfortunately, this job cannot be done by the do-it-yourself enthusiast as the joint trunnions are staked into the yokes (Fig. 7.1). The only answer to this type of problem is to obtain a service replacement propeller shaft.

Chapter 8 Rear axle

Contents

General description 1
Halfshaft bearings and oil seals — removal and
replacement 4
Halfshaft — removal and replacement 3

Pinion, crownwheel and differential 6
Pinion, oil seal — removal and replacement 5
Rear axle — removal and replacement 2

Specifications

Type	Hypoid, semi-floating with underhung mounted pinion

Ratio

1800	3.73 : 1
2300	3.455 : 1

Oil capacity	2.5 pints (Imperial)/1.42 litres

Oil type	SAE 90EP

Torque wrench settings

	lb/ft	kg/m
Coupling shaft to propeller flange bolts	18	2.5
Coupling flange (pinion) nut	75	10.35

1 General description

The rear axle is of the semi-floating type with a hypoid final drive. The pinion is underhung and located within the final drive housing.

The rear axle casing assembly is located to the rear body members by means of four arms, two each side. Two of these are longitudinal and two diagonal, and their attachment points consist of steel bolts in rubber mounting bushes to hangers which are an integral part of the axle casing. All models incorporate a rear stabilizer bar connected between brackets each end of the rear axle and supported by links attached to the under-chassis.

The crownwheel and pinion assembly is supported in the axle housing by two taper roller bearings which are secured by end cap and bolts. Precise location is determined by positioning shims at the outer face of the bearing outer track.

The pinion runs in two pre-loaded taper roller bearings. The pinion is held in correct location to the crownwheel by shims located between the front face of the rear bearing outer track and the abutment face in the axle housing.

An oil seal is pressed into the end of the pinion housing to retain the lubricating oil.

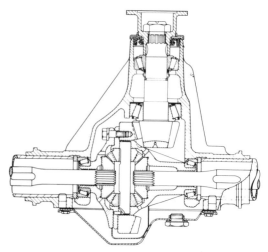

Fig. 8.1 Sectional view of the differential assembly

2 Rear axle — removal and replacement

1 Loosen the wheel nuts.

2 Raise and support the rear of the vehicle body, and remove the

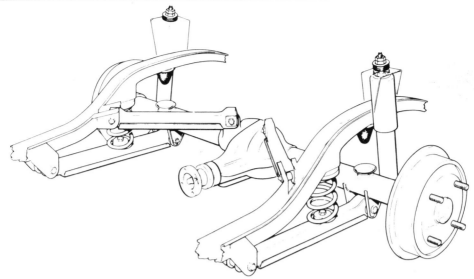

Fig. 8.2 Method of locating the rear axle to the suspension

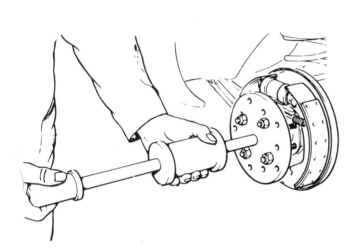

Fig. 8.3 Using a slide hammer to remove a halfshaft

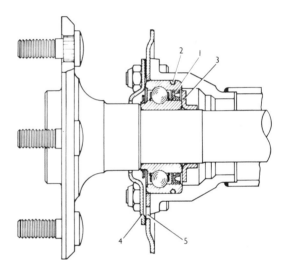

Fig. 8.4 Section through halfshaft bearing and housing

1   Oil seal
2   'O' ring in outer race
3   Bearing retaining ring
4   Retaining flange
5   Oil hole in brake flange plate

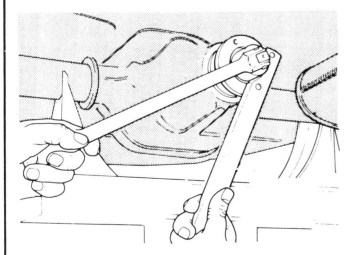

Fig. 8.5 Holding pinion flange and slackening nut

Fig. 8.6 Staking the pinion flange nut rim into the slot

wheels. The easiest way to do this is to jack the car under the centre of the differential unit.

3 When it is sufficiently high, stands should be placed under the longitudinal lower suspension arms.

4 The front wheels should be chocked to prevent any inadvertent movement. Under no circumstances should makeshift supports be used when doing work of this nature under the car.

5 Next, mark and disconnect the propeller shaft at the pinion flange as described in Chapter 7.

6 When the shaft is disconnected, allow the rear part to hang from the centre coupling.

7 Disconnect the handbrake cable clevis pin from the brake equalizer.

8 Disconnect the lower end of the flexible hydraulic fluid pipe where it is attached to a bracket on the rear axle.

9 Detach the lower end of each rear telescopic damper from the axle bracket by removing the two nuts and driving out the stud and bushes. For details see Chapter 11.

10 Remove the nuts and bolts from the longitudinal radius arm rear mountings on the axle, and then do the same with the diagonal arms where they locate to the brackets on the top of the differential casing. If a rear stabilizer bar is fitted, remove the nut and bolt that secures each end of the bar in its bracket and rubber insulator. Retain the insulators, and note that the slit in the rubber should be horizontal when reassembly takes place.

11 The whole axle assembly is now free and, by pushing the hydraulic dampers out of the way, it can be drawn out straight back from the car.

3 Halfshafts — removal and replacement

1 Loosen the wheel nuts.

2 Raise and support the side of the axle from which the halfshaft will be removed. Remove the wheel. **Note**: If both halfshafts are to be removed and the vehicle is raised level, oil may run out of the axle tubes. Precautions must be taken to prevent it running over the brake linings and the best way would be to remove the shoes, as described in Chapter 9.

3 Release the handbrake. Undo the bolt which holds the brake drum to the halfshaft flange and remove the drum.

4 Remove the nuts securing the halfshaft bearing retaining plate. This must be done through one of the holes in the halfshaft flange. As each bolt is undone and removed, the flange must be roated through 90° to the next bolt. Take care not to lose the four lockwashers.

5 The shaft can now be withdrawn and inspected. If the bearing is a very tight fit in the housing it will be necessary to borrow a slide hammer to fix to the flange to draw it out.

6 Carefully inspect the differential engagement splines for wear, and also the bearing and oil seal. If·the oil seal shows signs of failure it should be renewed. If the oil seal is to be renewed, the bearing will also have to be renewed because the oil seal is integral with the bearing.

7 Replacement of the halfshaft is a straightforward reversal of the removal procedure. See that the 0-ring on the outside of the bearing is seated in its groove. However, before replacement, ensure that the oil drain hole in the brake backplate is clear and coat the halfshaft with oil. Also coat with oil the bearing bore in the axle halfshaft tube; this will allow easy replacement. The bearing retainer plate nuts should be tightened to 18 lb ft (2.3 kg m) with clean dry threads.

4 Halfshaft bearings and oil seals — removal and replacement

If it is decided, after inspection, to replace the bearing and oil seal the procedure is as follows:

1 Slacken the bearing retainer ring by nicking it with a chisel. The retainer and bearing can be removed as one. As you will probably not have the correct Vauxhall pullers to remove the bearing, and the bearing is to be discarded, the following method of removal can be employed:

a) Clamp the bearing in a vice so that the halfshaft is parallel with the jaws.

b) Now using a hide hammer or mallet on the splined end of the halfshaft drive it back through the bearing and retainer. Note: A piece of wood MUST be interposed between the hammer and halfshaft.

2 Oil the new bearing journal and push the bearing down the halfshaft as far as it will go by hand. Ensure that the integral oil seal is facing toward the splines. Now drive the bearing right home against the shaft shoulder using a piece of steel tubing of a suitable length and diameter. Note that the tubing must only contact the bearing inner race, not the bearings, oil seal or outer race.

3 The bearing retainer can be driven home by the same method as the bearing, ensuring that the retainer ring collar faces the bearings.

4 Halfshaft replacement is described in Section 3.

5 Pinion oil seal — removal and replacement

If oil is leaking from the axle casing where the pinion emerges, it will mean that the oil seal needs renewal.

1 Raise the car, support it on stands and disconnect the propeller shaft as described in Chapter 7. The pinion flange nut will now be exposed.

2 In order to hold the flange, when undoing the nut, it will be necessary to make up a piece of flat bar with two holes at one end which can be bolted to the flange. This can then be held firm while the socket wrench turns the nut which is, initially, a very tight fit.

3 It will be seen that the pinion nut is staked into a groove on the pinion flange and when the nut is removed this staking will break away.

4 Before pulling the flange off the pinion splines, mark the positions of flange to pinion so that it may be replaced in the same position. Next, prise the dust shield from the flange.

5 The oil seal may then be dug out of the housing with a pointed punch and a hammer.

6 A new seal should be installed with the lip facing into the casing. Oil the seal lip and the pinion first and then carefully tap it home until it butts up to the bore face in the casing or is flush with the end of the housing, which ever occurs first. It may assist in fitting the seal square if a piece of pipe, which will fit over the pinion, is used to drive it home. Don't forget to refit the dust shield before replacing the flange.

7 Replace the pinion flange to the pinion ensuring the location marks made line up. Then fit the nut and tighten it to its specified torque.

8 Finally, stake the nut rim into the slot and reconnect the propeller shaft.

6 Pinion, crownwheel and differential

1 This Chapter has so far shown how to replace bearings and oil seals for the halfshafts and the pinion oil seal, as these are considered to be within the average owner-driver's competence and facilities. We do not recommend that owners go into the more complex problems of pinion to crownwheel settings, differential gear settings, differential side bearing replacement, or pinion bearing replacement.

Chapter 9 Braking system

Contents

Bleeding the hydraulic system 2
Brake load-conscious, pressure-reducing valve — description,
removal, installation and adjustment 14
Brake pedal — removal and replacement 15
Disc brakes — caliper removal, inspection and replacement ... 8
Disc brakes — disc run-out check 9
Disc brakes — inspection and replacement of pads 5
Drum and disc brakes — hydraulic pipes, rigid and flexible —
inspection, removal and replacement 6
Drum brakes — hydraulic wheel cylinders — removal, inspection
and replacement 7

Fault diagnosis — braking system 16
General description 1
Handbrake adjustment 4
Master cylinder — dismantling and reassembly 11
Master cylinder — removal and refitting 10
Rear drum brake shoes — inspection, removal and
refitting 3
Vacuum servo unit — checking, dismantling, servicing and
reassembly 13
Vacuum servo unit — general description 12

Specifications

Type ... ...   Hydraulically operated, front discs (Girling) and self-adjusting rear drums, (Lockhead) dual circuit with servo assistance. Cable operated handbrake to rear wheels.

Brake drums
Internal diameter ... ...   9.0 inch (229 mm)
Maximum run-out of braking surface ... ...   0.004 in (0.1 mm)

Disc brakes
Disc diameter ... ...   10.03 in (255 mm)
Disc thickness ... ...   0.375/0.38 in (9.5/9.65 mm)
Maximum run-out ... ...   0.004 in (0.1 mm)
Minimum thickness of friction pads ... ...   0.06 in (1.5 mm)

Torque Wrench Settings

	lb/ft	kg/m
Front brake flange plate to steering knuckle nuts	25	3.45
Rear brake flange plate to rear axle nuts	13	1.8
Disc caliper to steering knuckle bolts	33	4.55
Disc to hub bolts*	18	2.5
Girling tandem master cylinder tip valve nut	38	5.2
Pressure warning lamp actuator plug and adaptor	18	2.5
Parking brake equaliser pivot bolt nut	14	1.9

*Loctite grade C applied to threads except where tab washers are used

1 General description

1 The Magnum models are fitted with Girling disc brakes at the front and Lockheed self-adjusting drum brakes at the rear. They are operated by hydraulic pressure created in the master cylinder when the brake pedal is depressed. This pressure is transferred to the respective wheel cylinder or caliper cylinders by a system of metal and flexible pipes and hoses.

The tandem master cylinder is divided into two parts whereby the hydraulic system to the front wheels is not interconnected to that of the rear wheels. This means that if one brake line should fail there will still be braking effort on two wheels.

The drum brakes are of the internally expanding type with the shoes and linings moving outwards into contact with the rotating brake drum. The brake units are fitted with one wheel cylinder so enabling a one leading, one trailing shoe arrangement to be used. The term 'leading shoe' means that the leading edge of one shoe is moved into contact with the rotating drum by the wheel cylinder and a self servo or wrapping action of the brake shoe tends to pull it on further, thereby giving braking assistance.

The handbrake operates on the rear brakes only using a system of links and cables, with an equalizer assembly to ensure even braking on each rear wheel.

The front disc brakes fitted are of the conventional fixed caliper design. Each half of the caliper contains a piston which operates in a bore both being interconnected so that under hydraulic pressure these pistons move towards each other. By this action they clamp the rotational movement of the disc. Special seals are fitted between the piston and bore and these seals return to their natural shape and draw the pistons back slightly so giving a running clearance between the pads and disc. As the pads wear, the piston is able to slide through the seal so allowing wear to be taken up.

A brake servo unit is fitted as standard and this is fitted between the brake pedal and master cylinder and adds to the pressure on the master cylinder pushrod when the brake pedal is being depressed. (See Section 12).

A load conscious pressure reducing valve is incorporated in the system to ensure maximum braking retardation under all conditions without locking the rear wheels.

2   Bleeding the hydraulic system

1   The system should need bleeding only when some part of it has been dismantled which would allow air into the hydraulic circuit, or if the reservoir level has been allowed to drop so far that air has entered the master cylinder. If the vehicle has been left standing unused for any length of time it is possible also that air bubbles may have developed in the system due to the air absorbing nature of hydraulic fluid. Bleed nipples are found on each of the front wheels calipers and one only for the rear brakes to be found on the left hand backplate (photo). The hydraulic line goes through the right hand rear cylinder en route to the left rear cylinder.

2   Ensure that a supply of clean non aerated fluid of the correct specification is to hand in order to replenish the reservoir during the bleeding process. It is necessary to have someone available to help, as one person has to pump the brake pedal while the other attends to the bleed nipple. The reservoir level has also to be continually watched and replenished. Fluid bled out must not be reused. A clean clear glass jar and a 12 inch (305 mm) length of 0.125 inch (3.175 mm) internal diameter rubber tube that will fit tightly over the bleed nipples is also required.

3   With the engine switched off depress the brake pedal six times to make sure that there is no residual vacuum in the servo unit.

4   It is recommended that the rear brakes are bled first, then the left hand front and finally the right hand front.

5   Put a little hydraulic fluid in the bottom of the glass jar. Clean the bleed nipple and fit the tube onto the nipple and place the other end in the jar so that it is under the surface of the fluid. Keep it under the surface throughout the bleeding operation.

6   Unscrew the bleed screw half a turn and request the assistant to depress and release the brake pedal in short sharp bursts. Short sharp strokes are far better as they will force any air bubbles along the line with the fluid rather than pump the fluid past them. It is not essential to remove all the air first time. If the whole system has to be bled, attend to each wheel for three or four complete pedal strokes and then repeat the process. On the second time around operate the pedal sharply in the same way until no bubbles come out of the pipe into the jar. With the brake pedal in the fully depressed position tighten the bleed screw. Do not forget to keep the reservoir topped up throughout.

7   If the reason for bleeding has been a repair to a pipe or cylinder near a wheel then it should be normally necessary to bleed only the wheel of the line in question — PROVIDED that no fluid has been allowed to drain out of the disconnected line. If in any doubt bleed the whole system.

8   Depress the brake pedal which should offer a firm resistance with no trace of sponginess. The pedal should not continue to go down under sustained pressure. If it does there is a leak or the master cylinder seals have badly worn.

3   Rear drum brake shoes — inspection, removal and refitting

1   Chock the front wheels, apply the handbrake, jack-up the rear of the car and support on firmly based axle stands. Remove the wheel.

2   Release the handbrake then remove the single bolt retaining the brake drum. Withdraw the brake drum; if necessary it may be tapped outwards with a soft-faced hammer at the circumference.

3   Examine the friction surface on the interior of the drum. Normally this should be completely smooth and bright. Remove any dust with a dry cloth and examine the surface of any score marks or blemishes. Very light hairline scores running around the surface area are not serious but indicate that the shoes may be wearing or grit and dirt has found its way into the drum at some time. If there are signs of deep scoring the drum needs reconditioning or replacement. As reconditioning will probably cost as much as a new drum, and certainly more than a good secondhand one (obtained from car breakers), it is not recommended.

4   Inspect the drum stud holes for concentricity. If they are oval the drum must be discarded and a new one obtained.

5   Examine the brake shoes for signs of oil contamination, deep scoring,

2.1 A brake bleed nipple

3.6 Turning a slotted head washer with pliers

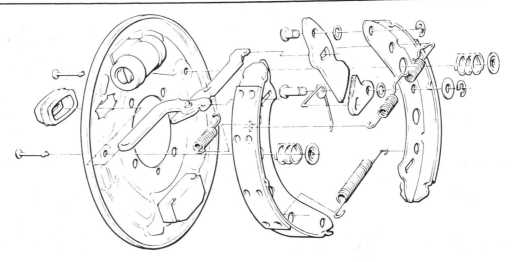

Fig. 9.1 The self adjusting rear brakes - exploded view

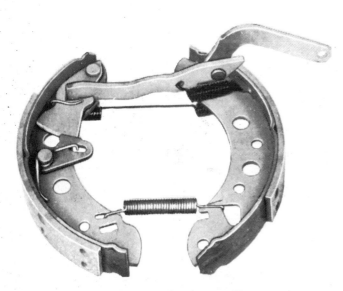

Fig. 9.2 The brake shoe assembly

Fig. 9.3 Withdrawing the brake shoes

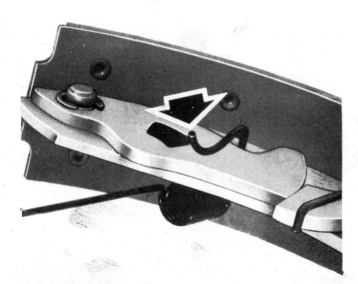

Fig. 9.4 The correct position (arrowed) for the ratchet plate and long return spring

or overall wear of the friction material. Deep scoring will be immediately apparent and will relate to any scoring in the drum. Oil contamination is evident where there are hard black shiny patches on the linings caused by the heat generated in braking which carbonises any oil that may have reached them. As a temporary measure, these areas can be rasped down but it is far better to replace the shoe. Normal wear can be judged by the depth of the rivet heads from the surface of the linings. If this is 0.025 inch (0.65 mm) or less, the linings should be renewed. With the bonded linings the minimum lining thickness is 0.0625 inch (1.6 mm).

6   With a pair of pliers turn the slotted washer on the pin so that it comes off the end of the pin. The spring, pin and washers can then be removed (photo).

7   Release the shoes from the lower pedestal then release the forward shoe from the wheel cylinder while holding the hooked end of the pull-off spring against the shoe web.

8   As soon as the shoes are removed make sure that the hydraulic cylinder pistons are prevented from coming out of the cylinders by tying wire or string around the cylinder.

9   The ratchet plate can be released from the brake shoe by removing the circlip, washer and clevis pin which retain it in position.

10 Replacement of the brake shoes is essentially the reverse of the removal procedure, but pay attention to the following points.

   a) When installing the brake shoes, lightly smear the ratchet plate pins, brake shoes operating lever pin and the mating surfaces of the

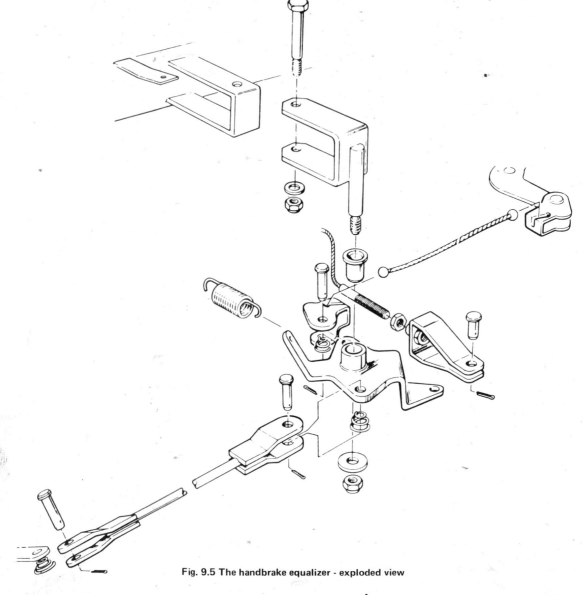

Fig. 9.5 The handbrake equalizer - exploded view

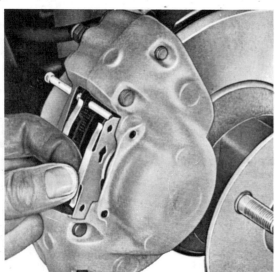

Fig. 9.6 Fitting the disc brake anti-squeal shims

A **B**

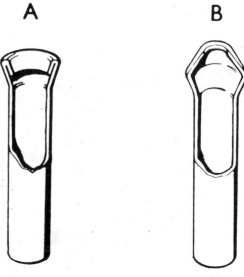

Fig. 9.7 Types of hydraulic pipe end flares

A Concave *B Convex*

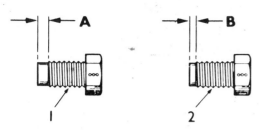

Fig. 9.8 Rear brakes hydraulic transfer pipe unions

1   RH A = 0.012 inch   2   LH B = 0.07 inch

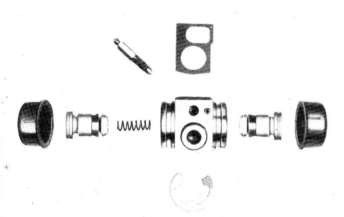

Fig. 9.9 The rear wheel cylinder - exploded view

flange plate with Castrol Girling Rubber Grease. Do not grease the ratchet teeth.
b) Ensure that the end of the parking brake operating lever is fully engaged in the slot in the rearward brake shoe (Fig. 9.2), and that the pull-off springs are correctly positioned.
c) Do not handle the brake linings, particularly if there is dirt or grease on your hands.
d) After fitting the drum and wheel, operate the handbrake several times to adjust the brakes.

4   Handbrake — adjustment

1   The handbrake front cable is connected to an equaliser attached to a mounting bracket on the rear axle. The equaliser is connected to the brake shoe levers by rods or cables.
2   The handbrake is automatically adjusted each time the rear brake shoes are adjusted to the drums. With time however, the operating cables may stretch and wear will develop in the brake rod clevis pins. When this happens it will be necessary to shorten the operating cable to take up the slack so that the handle does not have to be pulled too far in order to operate the brakes.
3   The handbrake is correctly adjusted when a force of 25 lb (11.35 kg) midway along the lever grip raises the lever four notches of the ratchet.
4   The adjustment is at the rear where the cable joins the lever attached to the equaliser assembly. If the locknut is loosened the threaded sleeve may be rotated and the cable tightened. The tightness should be gauged by ensuring that the clevis pins at the outer ends of the brake rods are not held so tightly that they cannot be revolved in position.
5   The equaliser assembly mounted on a bracket on the rear axle swing is designed to ensure that the handbrake is applied equally on both drums. After long service wear will develop in the clevis pins, clevises

and brackets to such an extent that rattles will develop, excessive backlash will be present and the strength of the assembly will be reduced. Such wear will be obvious and the pins, bushes and clevises should be renewed as required. Always keep the parts liberally greased.
6   When assembling a brake rod, ensure that a tapered coil spring is assembled between the lower side of the brake shoe lever or equaliser and the rod clevises, with the larger end of the spring against the clevis.
7   Rear cable clevises should be installed with the slotted side uppermost.

5   Disc brakes — inspection and replacement of pads

1   Thickness of the pads can be visually checked by jacking up the car and removing each front wheel, when the pads can be seen between the disc and caliper body. If the thickness of the friction material is less than 0.06 inch (1½ mm) they must be renewed. Sometimes the pads wear unevenly, but if one of a pair is under specification thickness, the pair should be renewed. As a general rule pads on both front wheels should be renewed even if only one needs it.
2   Remove the fluid reservoir cap and syphon out some fluid — say ¼ inch down. This will prevent the fluid overflowing when the level rises as the pistons are pushed back for fitting new pads.
3   To remove the pads, first pull the clips off the retaining pins and withdraw the pins.
4   Apply pressure to the faces of the old pads with the fingers, so pressing the pistons behind them back into the caliper. Then lift out the pads and shims from the caliper body (photos).
5   Refit new pads and new shims also if the old ones show signs of distortion or deterioration. Make sure that the shims are fitted with the arrow shaped hole in the top edge pointing in the direction of forward disc rotation (Fig. 9.6).
6   Replace the locating pins and clips.
7   Depress the brake pedal two or three times to position the pistons and pads once more, and top up the fluid reservoir to the specified level.

6   Drum and disc brakes — hydraulic pipes, rigid and flexible — inspection, removal and replacement

1   Periodically, normally at safety check services, all brake pipes, pipe connections and unions should be completely and carefully examined.
2   First examine for signs of leakage where the pipe unions occur. Then examine the flexible hoses for signs of chaffing and fraying and, of course, leakage. This is only a preliminary part of the flexible hose inspection, as exterior condition does not necessarily indicate the interior condition, which will be considered later.
3   The steel pipes must be examined equally carefully. They must be cleaned off and examined for any signs of dents, or other percussive damage, rust and corrosion. Rust and corrosion should be scraped off and, if the depth of pitting in the pipes is significant, they will need renewing. This is particularly likely in those areas underneath the car body and along the rear axle where the pipes are exposed to full force of road and weather conditions.
4   If any section of pipe is to be taken off, first of all remove the fluid reservoir cap and line it with a piece of polythene film to make it air tight, and replace it. This will minimise the amount of fluid dripping out of the system, when pipes are removed.
5   Rigid pipe removal is usually quite straightforward. The unions at each end are undone, the pipe and union pulled out, and the centre sections of the pipe removed from the body clips where necessary. Underneath the car, exposed unions can sometimes be very tight. As one can use only an open ended spanner and the unions are not large burring of the flats is not uncommon when attempting to undo them. For this reason a self-locking grip wrench (Mole) is often the only way to remove a stubborn union.
6   Flexible hoses are always mounted at both ends in a rigid bracket attached to the body or a sub-assembly. To remove them it is necessary first of all to unscrew the pipe unions of the rigid pipes which go into

them. Then with a spanner on the hexagonal end of the flexible pipe union, the locknut and washer on the other side of the mounting bracket need to be removed. Here again exposure to the elements often tends to seize the locknut and in this case the use of penetrating oil or 'Plus-gas' is necessary. The mounting brackets, particularly on the body-frame, are not very heavy gauge and care must be taken not to wrench them off. A self-grip wrench is often of use here as well. Use it on the pipe union in this instance, as one is able to get a ring spanner on the locknut.

7   With the flexible hose removed, examine the internal bore. If it is blown through first, it should be possible to see through it. Any specks of rubber which come out, or signs of restriction in the bore, mean that the inner lining is breaking up and pipe must be renewed.

8   Rigid pipes which need replacement can usually be purchased at any local garage where they have the pipe, unions and special tools to make them up. All they need to know is the total length of the pipe, and the type of flare used at each end with the union. This is very important as it is possible to have a convex flare at one end and a concave flare at the other.

   Note that on Lockheed brakes, the pipe linking the rear wheel cylinders has a different union at each end. This difference in in the length of the unthreaded portion.

9   Replacement of pipes is a straightforward reversal of the removal procedure. If the rigid pipes have been made up it is best to get all the sets (bends) in them before trying to install them. Also if there are any acute bends, ask your supplier to put these in for you on a tube bender. Otherwise you may kink the pipe and thereby restrict the bore area and fluid flow.

10   With the pipes replaced, remove the polythene film from the reservoir cap and bleed the system as described in Section 2. It is not necessary always to bleed at all four wheels. It depends which pipe has been removed. Obviously if the main one from the master cylinder is removed, air could have reached any line from the later distribution of pipes. If, however, a flexible hose at a front wheel is replaced, only that wheel needs to be bled.

7   Drum brakes — hydraulic wheel cylinders — removal, inspection and replacement

1   If it is suspected that one or more wheel cylinders is malfunctioning, jack up the suspect wheel and remove the brake drum.

2   Inspect for signs of fluid leakage around the wheel cylinder, and if there are any, proceed with instructions at paragraph 4.

3   Next get someone to very gently press the brake pedal a small distance. On rear brakes, watch the wheel cylinder to see that the pistons move out a little. On no account allow them to come right out or you will have to reassemble them and bleed the system. Then release the pedal and ensure that the shoe springs force the piston back.

4   A wheel cylinder where there is leaking fluid or which does not move at all (ie with a seized piston) will have to be fitted with new seals at least.

5   Remove the brake shoes as described in Section 3 and seal the fluid reservoir cap.

6   Remove the rubber dust cover and clip from the end of the cylinder,

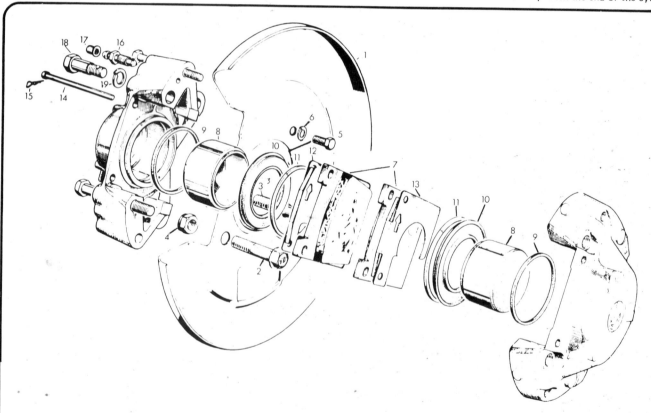

Fig. 9.10 Girling disc brake components

1 Disc shield	6 Lockwasher	11 Retaining ring	16 Bleed nipple
2 Bolt, steering arm to knuckle	7 Friction pad	12 Anti-squeal shim	17 Dust cap
3 Bolt, steering arm to knuckle	8 Caliper piston	13 Anti-squeal shim	18 Bolt, caliper to knuckle
4 Nut	9 Cylinder sealing ring	14 Retaining pin	19 Lockwasher
5 Bolt, shield to knuckle	10 Rubber boot	15 Clip	

and draw out the pistons on the inner end of which a seal will be fitted. Also remove the spring.

7 If the piston is seized in the cylinder it may be very difficult to remove, in which case it may be quicker in the long run to remove the cylinder from the wheel (see paragraphs 14 to 20).

8 Examine the bores of the wheel cylinders. Any sign of scoring or ridging in the walls where the piston seal travels means that the cylinder should be renewed.

9 If the cylinder is in good condition it will be necessary to renew only the seals on the piston. Pull the old ones off and carefully fit a new one over the long boss of each piston, engaging it over the raised rim. The lip of the seal must face away from the centre of the piston.

10 Clean out the interior of the cylinder with a dry cloth and ensure the piston is quite clean. Then use a little brake fluid and lubricate the piston seal before replacing the spring and pistons in the cylinder. Be careful not to damage or turn over the seal lip on replacement.

11 If the old seal shows signs of swelling and deterioration, rather than just wear on the lip, it indicates that the hydraulic fluid in the system may have been contaminated. In such cases all the fluid must be removed from the system and all seals renewed including those in the master cylinder. Flexible hoses should be checked too.

12 Replace the wheel cylinder dust cover.

13 Replace the brake shoes and drums, remove the fluid reservoir cap seal and bleed the hydraulic system (Section 2).

14 If the cylinders are to be replaced, unscrew the unions of the hydraulic pipes on the brake backplate.

15 Undo the pipe union behind the backplate (if applicable) and remove the bleed screw.

16 Prise out the E-clip which retains the wheel cylinder to the backplate using a small screwdriver.

17 Lift out the cylinder assembly.

18 Replacement is the reverse of the removal, but continue reassembly as described in paragraphs 9 to 13.

8 Disc brakes — caliper removal, inspection and replacement

1 If the caliper pistons are suspected of malfunctioning, jack up the car and remove the relevant wheel.

2 Examine for signs of fluid leaks and, if these are apparent, it will be necessary to remove the caliper and proceed as described from paragraph 4 onwards.

3 If there are no signs of leaking, get someone to depress the brake pedal and watch how the two disc pads come up to the disc. One may move very slowly or not at all, in which case it will be necessary to remove the caliper and proceed further.

4 Remove disc pads and shims as described in Section 5.

5 Seal the reservoir cap with a piece of plastic film.

6 Undo the hydraulic pipe union from the body of the caliper and draw back the pipe.

7 Undo the two bolts holding the caliper to the steering knuckle plate. **Do not** undo the bolts which clamp the two halves of the caliper together.

8 Lift the caliper off the disc.

9 Clean the exterior of the caliper assembly and then ease each rubber piston cover out of the grooves in the piston and the caliper body, and remove them.

10 It may be possible to pull the pistons out of their bores, but if not, it will be necessary to blow them out with pressure from an air pump hose attached to the hydraulic fluid inlet port. Support one piston while the other is blown out and then block the empty cylinder with a cloth while the other comes out. If one piston moves very slowly, remove this one before the other. If one piston does not move at all, it will have seized in the cylinder. Use a hydraulic cleaning fluid, or methylated spirits, to soak it for some time in an attempt to free it. If harsher measures are needed, try to confine any damage to the piston, and not the caliper body.

11 With the pistons removed, the fluid seal rings may be eased out of the piston grooves with a small screwdriver. Make sure that the piston

and groove are not damaged. Examine the bores and pistons for signs of scoring or scuffing. If severe, it is unlikely that a proper fluid seal will be possible and a new caliper assembly may be required. The part of the piston on the pad side of the seal groove may be cleaned up with steel wool if necessary. Take care to leave no traces of steel wool anywhere. Clean the cylinder bores using hydraulic cleaning fluid if possible, or methylated spirits otherwise.

12 Reassembly is an exact reversal of the dismantling process, taking care with the following in particular:

13 Ensure that the new fluid seal is seated properly in its groove.

14 The caliper mounting bolts have a nylon locking insert in the threads, and should be renewed. Tighten the bolts to the specified torque. Replace the pads as described in Section 5, remove the reservoir cap seal and bleed the system.

9 Disc brakes — disc run-out check

1 If the disc does not run true, then it will tend to push the disc pads aside and force the pistons further into the caliper. This will increase the brake pedal travel necessary to apply the brakes, apart from impairing brake efficiency and the life of the pads.

2 To check the disc run-out (trueness), jack-up the car and remove the wheel. Ensure the hub bearing has no free float in it.

3 Set a clock gauge micrometer on a firm stand up to a friction face of the disc, near the outside edge, so that a reading above 0.004 in (0.1 mm) is registered on the gauge.

4 Spin the hub and if the gauge registers more than $\pm$ 0.004 inch (0.1 mm), the disc is warped and needs renewing.

10 Master cylinder — removal and refitting

1 Wipe the top of the master cylinder reservoir and unscrew the filler cap. Place a piece of polythene sheeting over the filler neck and refit the cap. This will prevent syphoning of the hydraulic fluid during subsequent operations.

2 Wipe the arms around the union on the master cylinder body and then undo and detach the hydraulic pipes from their unions on the master cylinder body. Also detach the low brake pressure warning light cable.

3 Undo and remove the two nuts and spring washers that secure the tandem master cylinder to the servo unit and lift away the master cylinder.

4 Refitting the tandem master cylinder is the reverse sequence to removal. It will be necessary to bleed the brake hydraulic system as described in Section 2.

11 Master cylinder — dismantling and reassembly

1 The component parts are shown in Fig. 9.11.

2 Prior to dismantling wipe the exterior of the master cylinder clean of dirt. Undo and remove the two bolts that secure the plastic reservoir to the master cylinder body. Recover the two rubber seals.

3 Unscrew the low brake pressure warning switch and lift it away together with the 0-ring seal.

4 Unscrew and remove the pressure differential chamber plug and seal from the rear end of the master cylinder.

5 Plug the rear brake pipe connections and the control switch thread bore and remove the two pressure differential pistons and springs using an air jet on the front reservoir connection.

6 Remove the piston springs and seals.

7 Using a clean metal rod of suitable diameter depress the primary piston until it reaches the stop so that the pressure of the secondary piston is removed from the stop screw.

8 Unscrew the stop screw and remove the sealing washer. Release the pressure on the piston.

9 Lightly depress the primary piston again to relieve the pressure on

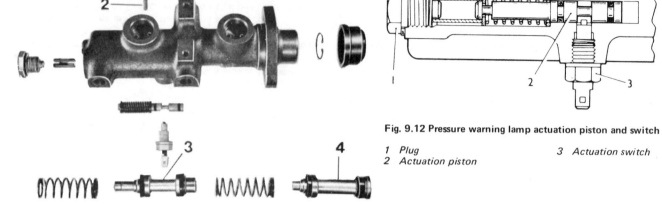

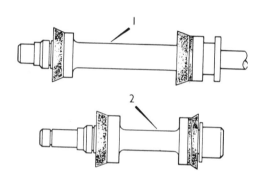

Fig. 9.12 Pressure warning lamp actuation piston and switch

1 Plug
2 Actuation piston

3 Actuation switch

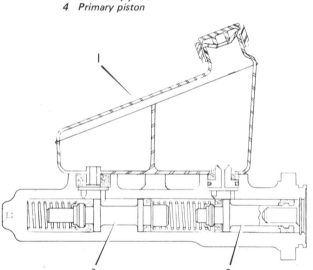

Fig. 9.11 Master cylinder - major components

1 Reservoir seal
2 Stop pin
3 Secondary piston
4 Primary piston

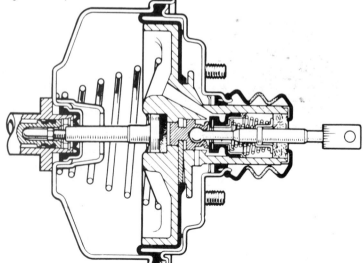

Fig. 9.14 Detail of seal assembly to pistons

1 Primary piston
2 Secondary piston

Fig. 9.13 Cross section through master cylinder

1 Reservoir
2 Primary piston
3 Secondary piston

Fig. 9.15 Brake servo unit - sectional view

the circlip located on the bore at the flanged end of the cylinder. With a pair of pointed pliers remove the circlip taking care not to scratch the finely finished bore.

10 Lift away the stop washer, and withdraw the primary piston assembly.

11 Withdraw the intermediate spring from the cylinder bore. Note which way round the primary piston seals are fitted and remove the seals from the piston.

12 The secondary piston assembly may now be removed by lightly tapping the master cylinder against a wooden base.

13 Withdraw the second spring from the cylinder bore. Note which way round the secondary piston seals are fitted and remove the seals from the piston.

14 Thoroughly wash all parts in either methylated spirits or clean approved hydraulic fluid and place in order ready for inspection.

15 Examine the bore of the master cylinder carefully for any signs of scoring, ridges or corrosion, and if it is found to be smooth all over, new seals can be fitted. If there is any doubt as to the condition of the bore, then a new cylinder must be fitted.

16 If examination of the seals shows them to be apparently oversize or very loose on their seats, suspect oil contamination in the system. Oil will swell these rubber seals, and if one is found to be swollen it is reasonable to assume that all seals in the braking system will require attention.

17 Before reassembly again wash all parts in methylated spirits or clean approved hydraulic fluid. Do not use any other type of oil or cleaning fluid or the seals will be damaged.

18 Commence reassembling by lubricating the bores with clean hydraulic fluid.

19 Smear the new secondary piston seals with hydraulic fluid and fit these to the secondary piston. Make sure that they are fitted the correct way round.

20 Smear the new primary piston seals with hydraulic fluid and fit these to the primary pistons. Make sure that they are fitted the correct way round.

21 Position the master cylinder between soft faces and clamp in a vice in such a manner that the main bore is inclined with the open end downwards.

22 Insert the spring and then the secondary piston assembly, second spring and the primary pistons assembly. To avoid any damage to the cup seals a flattened needle should be passed around the lip of each seal to assist entry into the cylinder bore.

23 Reposition the master cylinder so that it is now vertical with the open end upwards and place the top washer in position. Depress the primary piston slightly and fit the circlip.

24 Next fully depress the primary piston and fit the stop screw with a new sealing washer. Tighten the stop screw to a torque wrench setting of 4.3 − 7.0 lb ft (0.6 − 1.0 kg m).

25 Lubricate and fit new seals to the low brake pressure warning light differential pistons and fit the spring, two pistons, second spring and the differential pressure plug fitted with a new sealing washer. Tighten the plug to a torque wrench setting of 10.9 to 13.7 lb ft (1.5 − 1.9 kg m).

26 Fit new reservoir seals and then the plastic reservoir. Secure with two bolts. Reassembly is now complete.

12 Vacuum servo unit — general description

1 The vacuum servo unit is incorporated with a master cylinder and is operated directly from the brake pedal. It acts on all four wheels. When the pedal is depressed, suction from the induction manifold of the engine is applied to the piston inside the large cylinder bowl of the servo unit. The piston then moves a plunger, attached to its centre, applying additional pressure to the hydraulic master cylinder piston. If the servo unit should fail to operate, pressure from the foot pedal is still applied to the system but, of course, the pedal pressure required will be more than it would be if the servo was functioning.

The unit is mounted on brackets fitted to the pedal supports.

2 Servicing can be carried out but certain special tools are needed, although these can, of course, be made up by an enthusiast with reasonable facilities. The tools needed are for correct removal of the cover which has a bayonet type fixing into the shell, and a flange on which the master cylinder can be mounted to hold the whole unit firmly in a vice.

13 Vacuum servo unit — checking, dismantling, servicing and reassembly

1 The filter can be changed by drawing back the rubber boot from the end cover and withdrawing the retainer ring. The filter pad must be cut to remove it from the pushrod, as must the new one prior to fitting. Make sure the retainer is pressed back fully and the rubber boot properly engaged with five lugs in the end cover.

To remove the unit, disconnect the vacuum pipe and the hydraulic pipes from the master cylinder and undo the mounting stud units.

2 Before beginning dismantling, obtain a complete repair kit which will contain the necessary seals and diaphragm needed to recondition the unit. If in any doubt, it may be preferable to obtain an exchange unit.

3 Having removed the unit from the car together with the master cylinder, attach the cover removal tool to the four mounting studs and clamp one leg of the tool in the vice. Undo the nuts securing the master cylinder and take it off. It is possible at this stage to check the setting of the servo pushrod. It is critical and needs careful measurement with a suitable straight edge or gauge. The correct projection is 0.408 inch (0.36 mm) and must be accurate to within 0.005 inch (0.127 mm).

If incorrect, proceed with dismantling in order to adjust it. Remove the rubber mounting and then fit the slave flange on the studs in its place and tighten the nuts to 11 lb ft. (1.51 kg m).

4 Release the cover removal tool from the vice and clamp the whole assembly instead, by gripping the slave flange in the vice.

5 Mark the relative positions of the shell and end cover and turn the cover removal tool anticlockwise whilst maintaining pressure, until the cover can be released and the spring pressure relieved.

6 Remove the return spring stop from the shell. Leave the pushrod where it is.

7 Remove the slave flange from the master cylinder mounting stud and carefully push out the master cylinder seal and seal retainer. Take off the cover removal tool, and the pushrod retainer can be prised out of the valve body to release the rod. Pull off the rubber boot and take the filter retainer out of the valve body. Then separate the filter pad and valve from the end cover.

8 The valve bearing, seal and retainer may be prised out of the end cover.

9 Remove the diaphragm from the valve body and by holding it with the key downward, the valve rod and plunger assembly can be released when pressing the valve rod in. If this assembly is suspect it must be renewed.

10 Push out the reaction disc with a pencil from the valve body.

11 The pushrod adjuster can be turned if the stem is gripped in a vice near the head. One complete revolution represents approximately 0.035 inch (0.9 mm). If the adjuster requires less than 5 lb in (0.05 kg m) to turn it, it is too loose and a new one is required.

12 All parts should be cleaned with brake fluid and kept scrupulously clean and free from any bits of fluff that could come from certain types of cleaning cloth.

13 Where lubricant is necessary, use only Lockheed Disc Brake lubricant. Lubricate the valve rod and plunger, check that it is seating centrally and insert assembly into the valve body.

14 Refit the key, using light pressure on the valve rod to secure it in the body.

15 Fit the new diaphragm to the valve body making sure the centre sits properly in its groove.

16 Lubricate the reaction disc and put it back in the valve bore using the pushrod to seat it.

17 To fit the new end cover seal, bearing and retainer, it is best to use a

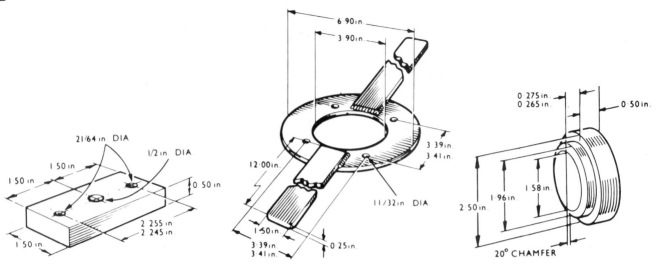

Figs. 9.16, 9.17, 9.18 Tool dimensions to assist service operations on the servo unit

Left: Slave flange   Centre: Cover removal tool   Right: Cover seal replacement mandrel

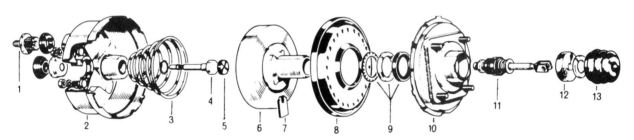

Fig. 9.19 Servo unit - exploded view

1 Suction pipe union and
   non-return valve
2 Body shell
3 Return spring
4 Piston rod
5 Seal
6 Piston
7 Piston rod locking plate
8 Diaphragm
9 Seal assembly
10 End cover
11 Pushrod
12 Filter
13 Pushrod and filter cover

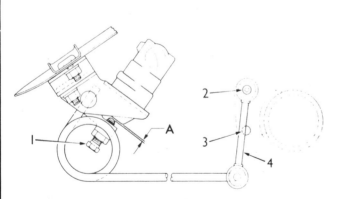

Fig. 9.20 Brake load - conscious pressure-reducing valve

1 Valve adjusting screw
2 Rear axle link connected to
   upper hole in axle bracket
3 Lower hole in axle bracket
4 Rear axle link to spring arm

A = dimension between valve and valve adjusting screw (0.020 inch)

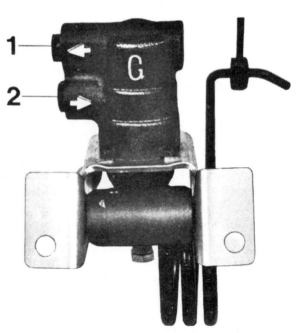

Fig. 9.21 Inlet and outlet ports to the load-conscious valve

1 Outlet port   2 Inlet port

mandrel of the type illustrated (Fig. 9.18). The lips of the seal should face away from the bearing ring and the flat side of the retainer goes in first.

18 Put the valve body into the end cover and put the filter over the forked end of the valve rod. Refit retainer and boot.

19 Fit the tool to the cover, once more, and the slave flange. Engage the spring stop in swollen end of the spring, and put it in the shell so that the recesses lock in position on the heads of the master cylinder mounting studs.

20 Lubricate the edge of the diaphragm where it will contact the lip of the shell and cover, and then line up the cover to the shell on the marks made previously. Dress the cover down carefully so as not to trap the diaphragm and turn it clockwise until it is up against the stops.

21 Remove the slave flange and insert the pushrod head into the valve body applying only enough pressure to seat it against the reaction disc.

22 Check the pushrod projection, as mentioned earlier, and if correct, press in the retainer using a piece of tube. Do not use excessive pressure. Then put the metal retainer in the shell over the pushrod, guarding against scratching the rod. Smear the rod with silicone grease and insert the rubber seal so that the pushrod adjuster and threads protrude. If this is not done properly, the shell could leak. It is most important also that the vent holes in the rubber seal are not blocked with any traces of dirt or lubricant, otherwise air might find its way into the master cylinder.

23 Before fitting the master cylinder in position, note the position of the vacuum hose connection which should be at 5 o'clock with the reservoir in the upright position. Press the master cylinder well home into its rubber seal before fitting the washers and nuts.

14 Brake load-conscious, pressure-reducing valve — description, removal, installation and adjustment

1 The load-conscious pressure-reducing valve ensures maximum retardation of the car under all conditions without the rear wheels locking before the front wheels. The valve mounting bracket is secured by bolts under the rear chassis, and the valve is in series with the rear brake hydraulic circuit. A plunger in the valve meters the hydraulic fluid and is operated by a spring arm connected to the valve and fitted to the rear axle by a link.

2 To remove the valve it is necessary to disconnect the two hydraulic pipes from the valve body, release the rear axle link from the spring arm and remove the two bolts securing the valve to the under chassis. Reassembly is the reverse of removal, but take care that the pipe from the master cylinder is connected to the lower port: this is marked with the inward pointing arrow. The pipe to the rear brakes is connected to the upper port, marked with an outward pointing arrow.

3 The metering plunger can be checked for operation, before removing the valve, by disconnecting the axle link and applying the brakes: the plunger should move away from the valve. When driving on a good road surface quite heavy braking of the car should be achieved without locking the rear wheels. The only accurate way of checking this is with a G-meter when at least 0.6 g should be observed before the wheels lock. Since most owners will not have access to one of these meters, if the operation of the valve is suspect i.e. the rear wheels locking during relatively moderate braking, it is recommended that the vehicle be checked at your local Vauxhall agent.

4 Should you decide that the rear wheels are locking at quite moderate braking forces, it is possible to adjust the valve. However, prior to adjustment you must ensure that the car is at kerb weight (i.e. unladen with fuel tank full), plus a driver or 154 lb on-board. When this condition is achieved, remove the connecting link from the upper hole in the rear axle bracket and temporarily mate it with the lower hole in the bracket. Check the clearance between the valve metering plunger and adjusting screw; this should be 0.020 in (0.508 mm). If the gap is outside this tolerance, loosen the locknut and rotate the adjusting screw to achieve this figure. Tighten the locknut.

15 Brake pedal — removal and replacement

1 If for any reason (such as worn out bushes), the brake pedal needs to be removed, follow the procedures as described for the clutch pedal in Chapter 5.

Fault diagnosis overleaf

16 Fault diagnosis — Braking system

Before diagnosing faults from the following chart, check that any braking irregularities are not caused by:
1   Uneven and incorrect tyre pressures.
2   Incorrect 'mix' of radial and crossply tyres.
3   Wear in the steering mechanism.
4   Defects in the suspension and dampers.
5   Misalignment of the body frame.

NOTE: For vehicles fitted with disc brakes at the front the references in the chart to front wheel shoe adjustments do not apply. The 'Reason/s' referring to hydraulic system faults or wear to the friction material of the linings still apply, however. Disc pads also come in different material and references to variations are also relevant.

Symptom	Reason/s	Remedy
Pedal travels a long way before the brakes operate	Automatic adjusters seized	Dismantle and repair as necessary
Stopping ability poor, even though pedal pressure is firm	Linings and/or drums and/or discs badly worn or scored	Dismantle, inspect and renew as required.
	Failure of one circuit in the dual hydraulic system	Check both circuits for hydraulic leaks and repair.
	One or more wheel hydraulic cylinders seized, resulting in some brake shoes not pressing against the drums (or pads against discs)	Dismantle and inspect wheel cylinders. Renew as necessary.
	Brake linings contaminated with oil	Renew linings and repair source of oil contamination.
	Wrong type of linings fitted (too hard)	Verify type of material which is correct for the car, and fit it.
	Brake shoes wrongly assembled	Check for correct assembly.
	Servo unit not functioning	Check and repair as necessary.
Car veers to one side when the brakes are applied	Brake pads or linings on one side are contaminated with oil	Renew pads or linings and stop oil leak.
	Hydraulic wheel cylinder(s) on one side partially or fully seized	Inspect wheel cylinders for correct operation and renew as necessary.
	A mixture of lining materials fitted between sides	Standardise on types of linings fitted.
	Unequal wear between sides caused by partially seized wheel cylinders	Check wheel cylinders and renew linings and drums as required.
Pedal feels spongy when the brakes are applied	Air is present in the hydraulic system	Bleed the hydraulic system and check for any signs of leakage.
Pedal feels springy when the brakes are applied	Brake linings not bedded into the drums (after fitting new ones)	Allow time for new linings to bed in
	Master cylinder or brake backplate mountings bolts loose	Retighten mounting bolts.
	Severe wear in brake drums causing distortion when brakes are applied	Renew drums and linings
Pedal travels right down with little or no resistance and brakes are virtually non-operative. (With dual braking systems this would be extraordinary as both systems would have to fail at the same time).	Leak in hydraulic systems resulting in lack of pressure for operating wheel cylinders	Examine the whole of the hydraulic system and locate and repair source of leaks. Test after repairing each and every leak source.
	If no signs of leakage are apparent all the master cylinder internal seals are failing to sustain pressure	Overhaul master cylinder. If indications are that seals have failed for reasons other than wear all the wheel cylinder seals should be checked also and the system completely replenished with the correct fluid.
Binding, juddering, overheating	One or a combination of causes given in the foregoing sections	Complete a systematic inspection of the whole braking system.

Chapter 10 Electrical system

Contents

AC Delco alternator systems - fault diagnosis 9
Alternators - dismantling and inspection 11
Alternators - general description 6
Alternators - removal, replacement and belt adjustment ... 10
Alternators - safety precautions 7
Battery - charging 5
Battery - electrolyte replenishment 4
Battery - maintenance and inspection 3
Battery - removal and replacement 2
Console illumination and switches 33
Electrical wiring - general 17
Flasher circuit - fault tracing and rectification 19
Fusible links, fuses and thermal circuit breaker 16
Headlamp beam - adjustment 22
Headlamps and bulbs - removal and replacement 21
Heater control illumination 34
Horns - fault tracing and rectification 20
Instrument voltage stabilizer unit 18
Lighting, windshield wiper and fog lamp switch connections 35
Lucas 15ACR or 17ACR alternator systems - fault diagnosis ... 8
Rear lights and flasher bulbs 24

Reverse lamp switch 38
Seven dial instrument panel - lamp, switch and voltage stabilizer renewal 31
Seven dial instrument panel - removal, servicing and replacement ... 32
Side and front turn signal lamps - removal and replacement ... 23
Starter inhibitor and reverse light switches 37
Starter motor (3M100/PE) - dismantling and reassembly 15
Starter motor (M35J/PE) - dismantling and reassembly 14
Starter motor - removal and replacement 13
Starter motor - testing in the car 12
Steering column stalk switches 36
Stoplamp switch 39
Twin dial instrument panel - lamp and switch renewal 29
Twin dial instrument panel - removal, servicing and replacement ... 30
Windscreen washers - fault finding 26
Windscreen wiper motor - dismantling, inspection and reassembly ... 28
Windscreen wiper motor - removal and replacement 27
Windscreen wipers - fault finding 25
General description 1

Specifications

Battery

Type	Lead acid, 12 volt
Rating:	
1800 cc	32 amp hours at 20 hour rate
2300 cc	38 amp hours at 20 hour rate
Earth	Negative

Alternators

	Lucas 15ACR	Lucas 17ACR	Delco-Remy DN460
Type	12	12	12
Voltage	28 amps	36 amps	28 and 35 amps
Output	4.3 ohms	4.16 ohms	—
Field resistance (± 5%)	0.20 in. (5 mm)	0.20 in. (5 mm)	—
Brushes - minimum length	7 - 10 oz	7 - 10 oz	—
Brush spring pressure	8 TRD	8 TRD	—
Regulator (incorporated)			

Starter motor (Lucas M35J/PE)

Brush length	0.38 in. minimum
Brush spring tension	See text
Commutator permissible thickness after skimming	0.080 in. minimum
Armature shaft endfloat	0.010 in. minimum
Solenoid switch test data:	
Series winding resistance	0.21 - 0.25 ohms
Shunt winding resistance	0.9 - 1.1 ohms
Starter test data:	
Free running current	65 amps at 8000 - 10,000 rpm
Lock torque	7 lb ft at 350 - 375 amps

Starter motor (Lucas 3M100/PE)

Brush length	0.38 in. minimum

Commutator permissible thickness after skimming	...	...	...					0.14 in. minimum
Armature shaft endfloat	...	...	...	...	...	...	...	0.010 in. maximum
Solenoid switch test data:								
Series winding resistance		...	...	...	...	...	...	0.25 - 0.27 ohms
Shunt winding resistance		...	...	...	...	...	...	0.76 - 0.80 ohms
Starter test data:								
Free running current	...	...	...	...	...	...	...	65 amps at 6000 rpm
Lock torque	...	...	...	...	...	...	...	16 lb ft at 545 amps

Windscreen wiper motor

Make	...	...	...	...	...	...	...	...	Delco-Remy
Total light running current consumption:								
High speed	...	...	...	...	...	...	...	5 amp
Low speed	...	...	...	...	...	...	...	2.5 amp
Wiper arm spring tension	...	...	...	...	...	...	...	24 oz

Fuses

A fuse block is mounted in the engine compartment on the bulkhead behind the dash panel and contains:
Three 35 amp fuses and one 50 amp fuse. There is provision for two spare fuses.

No. 4 fuse is fed via the thermal interruption and lighting switch. Two fusible links are fitted in the positive battery lead; one protects the lighting circuits and the other protects the remaining circuits, except the starter motor.

Fuse No. 1 protects	...	...	...	...	...	...	...	Horn, interior lamp, headlamp flasher (35 amp)
Fuse No. 2 protects	...	...	...	...	...	...	...	Stop lamp, turn signal lamp and warning lamps, oil and alternator warning lamps, fuel and temperature gauges, heater motor and reverse lights and heated rear window (50 amp)
Fuse No. 3 protects	...	...	...	...	...	...	...	Windscreen wipers, radio, cigarette lighter (35 amp)
Fuse No. 4 protects	...	...	...	...	...	...	...	Instrument lamps, rear lamps, number plate lamps, boot interior lamp and cigarette lighter bulb (35 amp)

Bulbs

Headlamps:								
Outer	...	...	...	...	...	...	...	12V, 50/37.5 watt, right-hand bias dip
Inner	...	...	...	...	...	...	...	12V, 50 watt, single filament
OR								
Outer	...	...	...	...	...	...	...	12V, 45/40 watt, Unified European, semi-sealed
Inner	...	...	...	...	...	...	...	12V, 45/40 watt Unified European, semi-sealed (45 watt filament used only)
Sidelights	...	...	...					12V, 4 watt mcc
Number plate, luggage boot light	...	...	...	...	...	...	12V, 5 watt mcc
Stop/tail lights	...	...	...	...	...	...	...	12V, 21/5 watt sbc (offset pins)
Turn signal lights	...	...	...	...	...	...	...	12V, 21 watt scc
Instrument panel, ignition warning		...	...	...	...	...	12V, 3 watt, wedge-base, capless
Other warning lights	...	...	...	...	...	...	12V, 1.5 watt, wedge-base, capless
Roof light	...	...	...	...	...	...	...	12V, 6 watt festoon
Floor console lights	...	...	...	...	...	...	12V, 2 watt, wedge-base capless
Automatic transmission selector light	...	...	...	...	12V, 1.2 watt, peanut
Heater control light	...	...	...	...	...	...	24V, 3 watt, wedge-base, capless

1 General description

1 The electrical system is of the 12-volt type and the major components comprise: A 12-volt battery with the negative terminal earthed, a starter motor which is fitted to the clutch bellhousing on the right-hand side of the engine, an alternator fitted to the front left-hand side of the engine, driven by the fanbelt from the crankshaft pulley, and a transistorised voltage control unit, integral with the alternator.

2 The 12-volt battery supplies a steady amount of current for the ignition, lighting, and other electrical circuits, and provides a reserve of electricity when the current consumed by the electrical equipment exceeds that being produced by the alternator. The output from the alternator is controlled by the voltage regulator, which ensures a high output if the battery is in a low state of charge or the demands from the electrical equipment high, and a low output if the battery is fully charged and there is little demand from the electrical equipment.

2 Battery - removal and replacement

1 Disconnect the negative (earth) lead from the battery terminal post and then the positive lead similarly. The leads are held by either a clamp which necessitates slackening the clamp bolt and nut, or by a screw driven through an all enclosing shroud.

2 Remove the battery clamp and carefully lift the battery out of its compartment. Hold the battery vertical to ensure that none of the electrolyte is spilled (photo).

3 Replacement is a direct reversal of this procedure. Note: Replace the positive lead before the earth (negative) lead and smear the terminals with petroleum jelly (vaseline) to prevent corrosion. Never use an ordinary grease as applied to other parts of the car.

3 Battery - maintenance and inspection

1 Normal weekly battery maintenance consists of checking the electrolyte level of each cell to ensure that the separators are covered by ¼ inch of electrolyte. If the level has fallen, top up the battery using distilled water only. Do not overfill. If a battery is overfilled or any electrolyte spilled, immediately wipe away the excess, as electrolyte attacks and corrodes any metal it comes into contact with very rapidly.

2 As well as keeping the terminals clean and covered with petroleum jelly, the top of the battery, and especially the top of the cells, should be kept clean and dry. This helps prevent corrosion and ensures that the battery does not become partially discharged by leakage through dampness and dirt.

3 Once every three months, remove the battery and inspect the battery securing bolts, the battery clamp plate, tray and battery leads for corrosion (white fluffy deposits on the metal which are brittle to touch). If any corrosion is found, clean off the deposits with ammonia or a solution of bicarbonate of soda and warm water, then treat the

area with a zinc based paint and/or underseal paint.

4 At the same time inspect the battery case for cracks. If a crack is found, clean and plug it with one of the proprietary compounds marketed by firms, such as Holts, for this purpose. If leakage through the crack has been excessive then it will be necessary to refill the appropriate cell with fresh electrolyte as detailed later. Cracks are frequently caused up the top of the battery cases by pouring in distilled water in the middle of winter *after* instead of *before* a run. This gives the water no chance to mix with the electrolyte and so the former freezes and splits the battery case.

5 If topping up the battery becomes excessive and the case has been inspected for cracks that could cause leakage, but none are found, the battery is being overcharged and the voltage regulator will have to be checked and reset.

6 With the battery on the bench at the three monthly interval check, measure its specific gravity with a hydrometer to determine the state of charge and condition of the electrolyte. There should be very little variation between the different cells and if a variation in excess of .025 is present it will be due to either:

    a) *Loss of electrolyte from the battery at some time caused by spillage or a leak, resulting in a drop in the specific gravity of the electrolyte when the deficiency was replaced with distilled water instead of fresh electrolyte.*

    b) *An internal short circuit caused by buckling of the plates or a similar malady pointing to the likelihood of total battery failure in the near future.*

7 The specific gravity of the electrolyte for fully charged conditions at the electrolyte temperature indicated, is listed in Table A. The specific gravity of a fully discharged battery at different temperatures of the electrolyte is given in Table B.

Table A
Specific Gravity - Battery fully charged

1.268 at 100°F or 38°C	electrolyte temperature
1.272 at 90°F or 32°C	" "
1.276 at 80°F or 27°C	" "
1.280 at 70°F or 21°C	" "
1.284 at 60°F or 16°C	" "
1.288 at 50°F or 10°C	" "
1.292 at 40°F or 4°C	" "
1.296 at 30°F or -1.5°C	" "

Table B
Specific Gravity - Battery fully discharged

1.098 at 100°F or 38°C	electrolyte temperature
1.102 at 90°F or 32°C	" "
1.106 at 80°F or 27°C	" "
1.110 at 70°F or 21°C	" "
1.114 at 60°F or 16°C	" "
1.118 at 50°F or 10°C	" "
1.122 at 40°F or 4°C	" "
1.126 at 30°F or -1.5°C	" "

4 Battery - electrolyte replenishment

1 If the battery is in a fully charged state and one of the cells maintains a specific gravity reading which is .025 or more lower than the others, and a check of each cell has been made with a voltage meter to check for short circuits (a four to seven second test should give a steady reading of between 1.2 to 1.8 volts), then it is likely that electrolyte has been lost from the cell with the low reading at some time.

2 Top up the cell with a solution of 1 part sulphuric acid to 2.5 parts of water. If the cell is already fully topped-up draw some electrolyte out of it with a pipette.

3 When mixing the sulphuric acid and water **never add water to sulphuric acid** - always pour the acid slowly onto the water in a glass container. **If water is added to sulphuric acid it will explode.**

4 Continue to top-up the cell with the freshly made electrolyte and then recharge the battery and check the hydrometer readings.

5 Battery - charging

1 In winter time when heavy demand is placed upon the battery, such as when starting from cold, and much electrical equipment is continually in use, it is a good idea occasionally to have the battery fully charged from an external source at the rate of 3.5 to 4 amps.

2 Continue to charge the battery at this rate until no further rise in specific gravity is noted over a four hour period.

3 Alternatively, a trickle charger, charging at the rate of 1.5 amps can be safely used overnight.

4 Specially rapid 'boost' charges which are claimed to restore the power of the battery in 1 to 2 hours are most dangerous as they can cause serious damage to the battery plates through overheating.

5 While charging the battery note that the temperature of the electrolyte should never exceed 100°F.

6 Alternators - general description

1 Basically the alternator, as its name implies, generates alternating current rather than direct current. This current is rectified (by diodes) into direct current so that it can be stored by the battery. The transistorised regulators are self-limiting in current output so they control only the voltage.

2 Apart from the renewal of the rotor slip ring brushes and rotor shaft bearings, there are no other parts which need periodic inspection. All other items are sealed assemblies and must be replaced if indications are that they are faulty.

7 Alternators - safety precautions

If there are indications that the charging system is malfunctioning in any way, care must be taken to diagnose faults properly, otherwise damage of a serious and expensive nature may occur to parts which are in fact quite serviceable.

The following basic requirements must be observed at all times, therefore, if damage is to be prevented:

1 ALL alternator systems use a *negative* earth. Even the simple mistake of connecting a battery the wrong way round could burn out the alternator diodes in a few seconds.

2 Before disconnecting any wires in the system the engine and ignition circuits should be switched off. This will minimise accidental short circuits.

3 The alternator must **never** be run with the output wire disconnected.

4 Always disconnect the battery from the car's electrical system if an outside charging source is being used.

5 Do not use test wire connections that could move accidentally and short circuit against nearby terminals. Short circuits will not blow fuses - they will blow diodes or transistors.

6 Always disconnect the battery cables and alternator output wires before any electric welding work is done on the car body.

8 Lucas 15 ACR or 17 ACR alternator systems - fault diagnosis

1 It is essential that when a fault occurs the correct procedure is followed to diagnose it. If it is not, the likelihood of damage is high. The safety precautions as described in Section 7 should always be observed.

2 No proper diagnosis is possible without an ammeter (0-100 amps range), a voltmeter (0-50 volts range) and a test lamp (12v 6 watt) being available. If you are unable to acquire these then leave the circuit checking to a competent electrician.

3 Check the obvious first, ie; battery, battery terminals, fanbelt tension and disconnected wires.

4 Follow the line of diagnosis as shown in the accompanying tables (Fig. 10.2).

9 AC Delco alternator systems - fault diagnosis

1 Fault diagnosis procedures in the manufacturer's service schedule are not readily interpreted into 'Do-it-yourself' terms. If a fault develops it is recommended that proper checks are made by a service

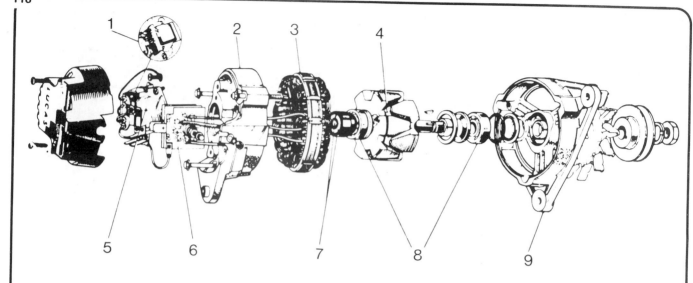

Fig. 10.1 Lucas 15ACR and 17ACR alternators

1 Regulator
2 Slip ring end cover
3 Stator
4 Rotor
5 Brush housing

6 Rectifier (diodes and heat sink)
7 Slip rings
8 Bearings
9 Drive end cover

10.3a The alternator connector sockets

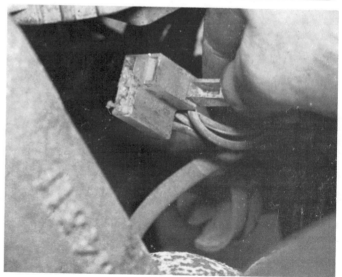

10.3b The alternator connector sockets

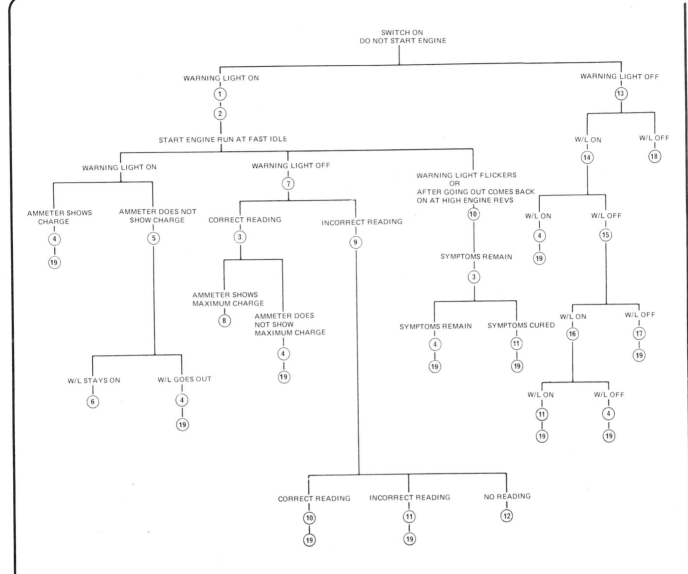

Fig. 10.2 Lucas 15/17ACR alternator system - fault diagnosis chart

1 Check fan belt(s) for tension and condition.
2 Disconnect main output connector and auxiliary connector. Install slave wire with a male Lucar terminal and a female Lucar terminal between alternator negative terminal and socket. Connect ammeter between alternator positive terminal and socket removed from this terminal. Reconnect auxiliary connector.
3 Remove rear cover from alternator. Re-install auxiliary connector, slave and ammeter wires. Bridge outer brush contact strip to ground. Adjust engine speed to give maximum output.
4 Install new or repair alternator.
5 Remove connector from field and sensing terminals (IND and B+). 'Switch ON' but do not start engine.
6 Check for short circuit in wire between alternator indicator terminal and warning light bulb.
7 Connect voltmeter between battery positive and negative terminals; increase speed to approximately 1500 rpm. Voltmeter should read 14.1 to 14.5 volts, ammeter reading 7.5 amp maximum. Higher amperage which would probably give lower voltage readings could indicate need to recharge battery before continuing with test.
8 If fan belt tension and condition are satisfactory, faulty battery or overloaded system is indicated. Comparison should be made between electrical loading and alternator output. 15ACR: 28 amp. 17ACR: 36 amp.
9 Remove voltmeter from battery and connect it between battery sensing terminal on alternator (B+) and ground (this should be made between electrical loading and alternator output. 15ACR: 28 amp. 17ACR: 36 amp.
10 Check battery terminals, ground strap connections, and wiring between battery and alternator for poor connection and resistive circuits.
11 Install new 8TR regulator.
12 Check wire from alternator B+ to starter solenoid for continuity.
13 Remove connector from alternator indicator socket and bridge double wires (brown/yellow 9/.012 in) connector to ground.
14 Remove rear cover from alternator, re-install socket connectors. Disconnect yellow wire from field diode heat sink.
15 Reconnect yellow wire to field diode heat sink. Connect slave wire between outer brush contact strip and ground.
16 Disconnect slave wire from outer brush contact strip and connect between inner brush contact strip and ground.
17 Check connecting wire between indicator and field terminals in socket connector for continuity.
18 Check warning lamp bulb. Check bulb-holder for loose connection. Check wire (brown/yellow) between alternator indicator terminal, warning lamp bulb and key-start switch for continuity. Note: warning lamp bulb must be 12 volt 2.2 watts.
19 Check that charging system operates satisfactorily by connecting voltmeter across battery terminals and ammeter in series with alternator output circuit. Impose approximate 28 amp (15ACR) or 36 amp (17ACR) load on battery, start engine and increase engine speed until ammeter reads maximum charge, 28 amp and 36 amp respectively. Remove load from battery. Ammeter should then drop slowly back to show trickle charge. Voltmeter should show 14.1 to 14.5 volts.

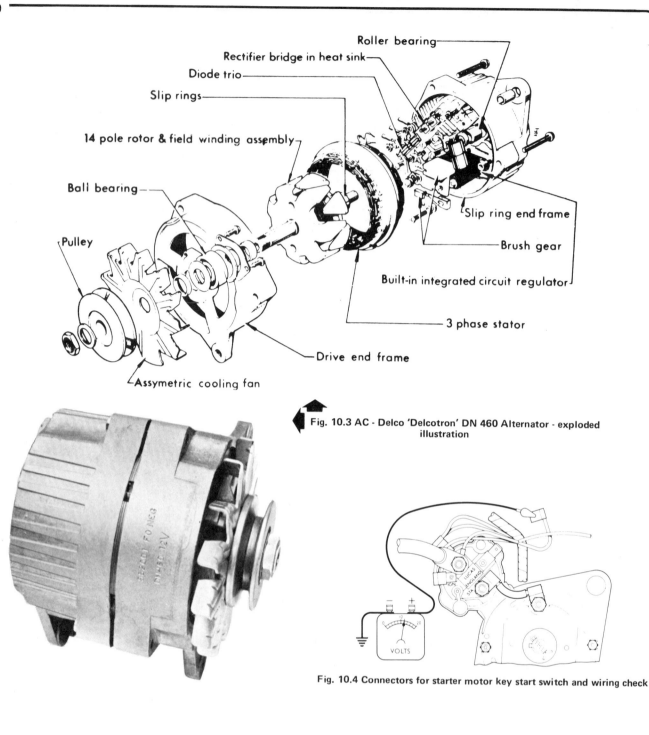

Roller bearing

Rectifier bridge in heat sink

Diode trio

Slip rings

14 pole rotor & field winding assembly

Ball bearing

Pulley

Slip ring end frame

Brush gear

Built-in integrated circuit regulator

3 phase stator

Drive end frame

Assymetric cooling fan

Fig. 10.3 AC - Delco 'Delcotron' DN 460 Alternator - exploded illustration

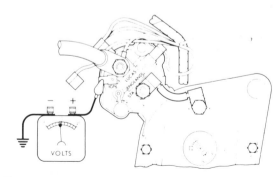

Fig. 10.4 Connectors for starter motor key start switch and wiring check

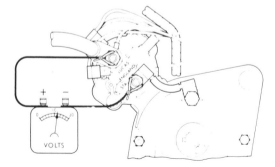

Fig. 10.5 Connections for starter motor solenoid check

Fig. 10.6 Connections for starter motor solenoid switch check

station which you know is equipped to deal with this make of alternator.

10 Alternators - removal, replacement and belt adjustment

1   Details of the alternator mountings and the procedures to be adopted when removing or adjusting them are given in Chapter 2, 'Fanbelt - adjustment',

2   Note that one of the mounting bolt holes in the alternator is fitted with a detachable split sliding bush. This enables the alternator to be put in position on the mounting brackets, without imposing any strain on the lugs when the bolts are tightened. It is essential that the lug *without* the bush (the front one) is tightened up first.

3   Electrical connections to the alternator are made through two multi-socket connectors (photos).

11 Alternators - dismantling and inspection

1   If tests indicate that the alternator is faulty it is possible that the slip ring brushes and slip rings may be the cause.

2   Alternators require the unsoldering of the stator connections to get at the brushes and slip ring and this is not recommended. If the diodes to which they are attached are overheated they could be damaged.

3   Therefore, we do not recommend dismantling as a general principle, as more damage could be caused to the system - not just the alternator, if a mistake is made.

4   When an alternator is diagnosed as unserviceable, it should only be as a result of a thorough check of the complete system. If this is not done a new unit could be completely ruined immediately following installation if something is also at fault elsewhere.

12 Starter motor - testing in the car

1   Disconnect the white/red wire from the solenoid and connect a voltmeter (or bulb) from the wire to earth. When the key start switch is operated the voltage should read 12v. Otherwise, the wiring or start switch is faulty (Fig. 10.4).

2   Reconnect the white/red wire and temporarily remove the LT wire from the ignition coil LT circuit to prevent the engine from starting. Connect the voltmeter across the two main terminals of the solenoid and a 12v reading should be given. When the key start is operated the voltage should drop to zero. If otherwise, the solenoid needs renewal (Fig. 10.5).

3   To check the cold start feed to the coil, disconnect the white wires from the 'IGN' terminal and connect the voltmeter from the terminal to earth. When the start switch is operated the reading should be at least 8 volts (Fig. 10.6). If there is no reading, renew the solenoid switch.

13 Starter motor - removal and replacement

1   Disconnect the battery earth lead.

2   Disconnect the heavy feed cable at the starter motor solenoid.

3   Disconnect the remaining leads at the starter motor solenoid (except the heavy lead to the starter motor), noting the cable colours to facilitate replacement.

4   Remove the two bolts and spring washers that secure the starter motor to the clutch housing and lift out the starter.

5   Refitting is the reverse sequence to removal.

14 Starter motor (M35J/PE) - dismantling and reassembly

1   If the starter motor fails to "turn over" the engine, although it is known that both the battery and starter motor solenoid are satisfactory, the starter motor should become suspect before allowing suspicion to fall on the engine. It may be just a simple renewal of brushes being required but, since it will be necessary to remove the starter motor to accomplish this, then it is worthwhile overhauling it at the same time.

2   The solenoid may be removed after detaching the short connecting cable from the other main terminal and removing the two securing nuts. If this is all that needs attention a new one can now be fitted over the existing plunger.

3   To dismantle the motor further, remove the short bolts (or through bolts) securing the commutator end bracket and brush gear to the yoke, then remove the split pin, washers and shims from the mainshaft. The end bracket may then be carefully removed. Do not lose the thrust washer located over the end of the shaft inside.

4   Next remove the bolts holding the drive end cover in position (if necessary) and the end cover complete with armature and shaft, may be drawn out of the yoke.

5   To separate the end cover from the armature it will be necessary to drive out the pin on which the engagement lever pivots. (See Fig. 10.8).

6   To take the drive pinion and clutch assembly off the armature shaft it will be necessary to drive the thrust collar down the shaft with a piece of suitable tube and then remove the circlip which is exposed (Fig. 10.9). If the driving gear assembly is worn the whole unit should be renewed. To check that the roller clutch is in good condition it should lock and take up the drive in one direction immediately it is turned. When turned in the opposite direction it should rotate smoothly and evenly. The whole clutch unit should also slide easily and without excessive play along the splines of the armature shaft.

7   Examine the brushes to ensure that they are not less than the permitted minimum length of 0.38 in. (9.6 mm). If they need renewal, obtain first the new ones. Two will be supplied complete with their terminal post and the other two separately for soldering the field coil end tags. On the starters which have an aluminium strip field winding, the old brushes should be cut off leaving a ¼ in. (7 mm) at least of the old copper wire to which the new brushes may be soldered. (You

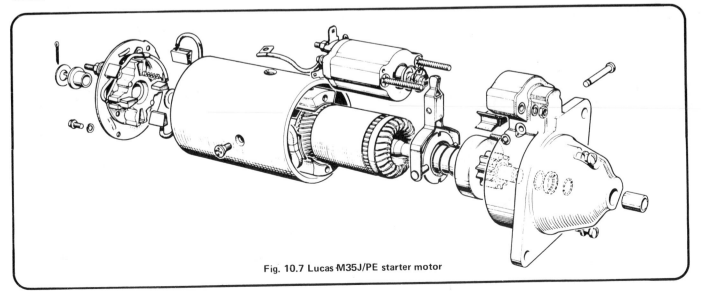

Fig. 10.7 Lucas M35J/PE starter motor

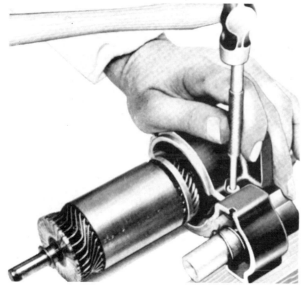

Fig. 10.8 M35J/PE starter pinion - driving out the pivot pin

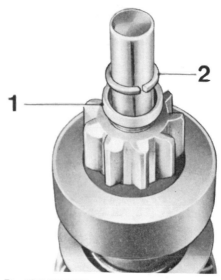

Fig. 10.9 M35J/PE starter pinion - pinion removal

1 Thrust collar

2 Jump ring

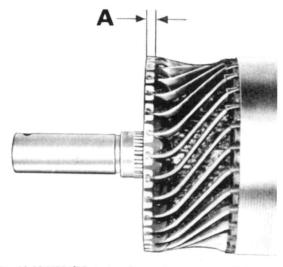

Fig. 10.10 M35J/PE starter - face end commutator thickness

A = 0.080 inch (2 mm) minimum

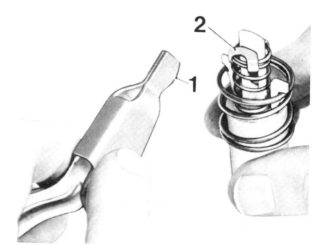

Fig. 10.11 M35J/PE starter pinion assembly - fitting lever to solenoid plunger

1 Radiused edge of lever

2 Retaining plate

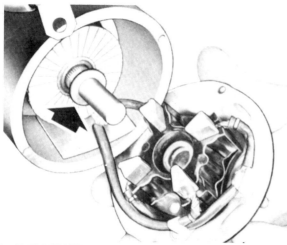

Fig. 10.12 M35J/PE starter motor - assembling commutator end cover. Note thrust washer (arrowed)

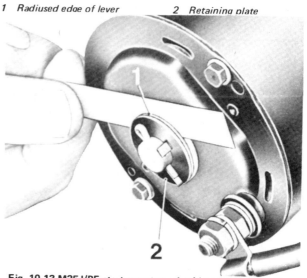

Fig. 10.13 M35J/PE starter motor - checking armature endfloat

1 Thrust plate

2 Shims

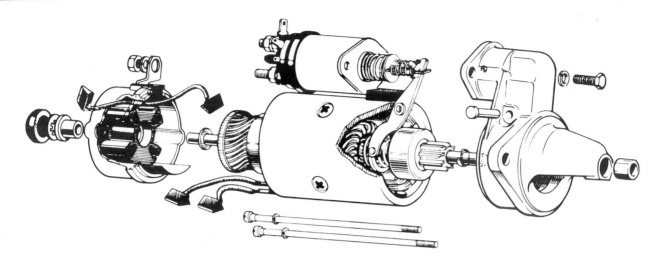

Fig. 10.14 Lucas 3M100/PE starter motor

cannot solder aluminium)! Make sure that the new brushes have sufficiently long leads and are in the proper position.

8 Clean up the face of the commutator with a petrol moistened rag. Light scoring may be cleaned up with fine glass paper. If there is deep scoring the commutator face may be skimmed in a lathe, provided it does not diminish in thickness below 0.080 in. (2 mm). Do not undercut the segment insulation (Fig. 10.10).

9 If it is ascertained that the field coil insulation has broken down it is recommended that the windings be removed, checked, and repaired by a specialist.

10 Check that the shaft is a good fit into each of the end plate bushes and renew the brushes if necessary.

11 Assembly is a procedure that must be carried out in sequence with attention to several points to ensure that it is correct.

12 First assemble the engagement lever to the solenoid plunger so that the chamfered corner faces the solenoid. Then make sure that the retaining plate is positioned correctly, relative to the lever (Fig. 10.10).

13 Next fit the drive pinion and clutch assembly on the armature shaft, fit the engagement lever fork to the clutch and assemble the whole lot together to the drive end cover. Then fit a new lever pivot pin and peen over the end to prevent it coming out.

14 Replace the yoke, and then lightly screw up the end cover bolts (if fitted).

15 Next place the thrust washer over the commutator end of the shaft, fit the brushes into their appropriate holders in the end cover and replace the end cover on to the shaft (Fig. 10.12). Both end covers have locating pips to ensure they are fitted correctly to the yoke.

16 Replace the through bolts or end cover bolts as appropriate and tighten them up at both ends.

17 Replace the thrust washer and shims to the end of the shaft, insert a split pin, and then measure the end float gap between the thrust washer and the end cover with a feeler gauge. It should be no more than 0.010 in. (0.25 mm) (Fig. 10.13). Additional shims should be added to reduce the end float as required.

18 Next replace the rubber pad between the drive end bracket (under the solenoid plunger housing) and the yoke, and refit the solenoid. Reconnect the short cable to the solenoid terminal.

19 Before replacing the starter in position after reassembly it is a good idea to check that it is functioning properly by connecting it temporarily to the battery.

15 Starter motor (3M100/PE) - dismantling and reassembly

1 This starter motor is similar to the M35J/PE motor described in the preceeding Section, apart from the following points.

2 The field coils are a series-parallel arrangement with the start and finish of the coils each connected to a brush. The electrical centre of the coils is earthed to the yoke. Armature end float is controlled by a retaining ring pressed on the armature shaft extension.

3 In order to remove the armature from the commutator end bracket

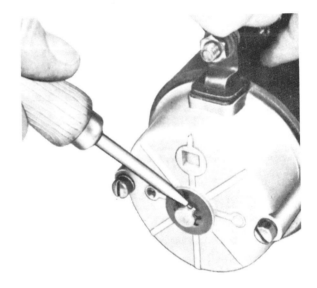

Fig. 10.15 3M100/PE starter motor - removing the end cap retaining ring

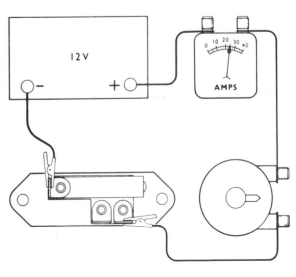

Fig. 10.16 Thermal circuit breaker test circuit

it is necessary to withdraw the end cap and remove the retaining ring by prising up the centre serrations, then remove the through bolts.

4   If it is required to renew the end bracket brushes it should be noted that they are obtained as spares complete with the terminal link and moulded rubber grommet.

5   Since the field coils are of copper strip the replacement brush leads can be soldered direct to the field coil ends. When cutting off the old brush leads note which brush is connected to which coil end; it will be seen that there is one long end and short end and this should be strictly adhered to when fitting the new brushes.

16 Fusible links, fuses and thermal circuit breaker

1   So that complete protection of the wiring circuit is assured the main feed cable from the battery has a section consisting of two fusible links which will burn out in the event of the fuse circuits failing or being bridged.

2   Four fuses are fitted in a separate fuse holder positioned on the engine side of the dash panel. The area adjacent to each fuse is marked from 1 to 4 for easy identification.

3   If any of the fuses blow, check the circuits on that fuse to trace the fault, before renewing the fuse. The circuits are listed in the Specifications.

4   Headlamp and sidelamp circuits are protected by a thermal circuit breaker. It can be tested by putting an ammeter and variable resistance in the circuit in series. The breaker should open at a current of 33 amps after 30 seconds to 3 minutes at 20°C (68°F).

5   The fuse block is mounted on the right-hand side of the front wheel arch. The connectors to the fuse terminals, however, are inside underneath. The thermal circuit breaker is alongside the terminals.

17 Electrical wiring - general

1   The modern developments in automobile wiring systems are perhaps more apparent in the Magnum range than in many other cars.

All individual circuits are gathered into neat harnesses secured to the body panels with clips. Multi-socket connectors join the three main harnesses together. The three being: engine harness, engine compartment harness, and a lighting and instrument harness.

2   The complete wiring protection offered by the fusible link, thermal link and fuses, means that any faults developing in any electrical component will not overload the circuit sufficiently to need repair. It can confidently be said, therefore, that unless the wiring harnesses are abused in any way, they are virtually fool-proof.

3   Checks can be made with the aid of a wiring diagram. Unless there is an obvious major burn up which would need renewal of the complete section of harness anyway, attempts should not be made to renew or bypass individual sections of any one particular circuit. A mistake could lead to major damage in view of the delicate nature of the charging circuit.

18 Instrument voltage stabiliser unit

In order that all gauges shall read accurately, a voltage stabiliser unit is used. This overcomes fluctuations in battery voltage which could cause inaccurate readings.

If suspect, it can be removed and tested with a 12 volt battery and voltmeter (see Sections 30 and 31).

Connect them as shown in Fig. 10.19. The voltmeter needle should pulsate evenly on each side of 10 volts.

If there is no reading, or the needle remains static, the unit is faulty and must be renewed.

19 Flasher circuit - fault tracing and rectification

1   The flasher unit is clipped to the top edge of the vertical parcel shelf panel adjacent to the steering column. On models fitted with a hazard warning system a second unit is mounted alongside (nearer the driver).

2   If, when operated to either side, the warning lamp on the dashboard stays on but does not flash and there is no audible warning, then one or both signal bulbs are not working.

3   If the warning bulb does not light and the frequency of flashing is slightly reduced, then the warning bulb is defective.

4   Before assuming that anything else is wrong (other than blown bulbs) make sure that the bulb caps and sockets are perfectly clean and corrosion free. Water, which may seep in due to a leaking seal or cracked lens, could cause this sort of trouble. Do not forget to check the fuse also.

5   Where there is total failure, the simplest check is to substitute a known good flasher unit. Finally check the switch if no other check reveals anything wrong.

6   The combined dip, horn, headlamp flasher and turn signal switch is mounted on the steering column with a clamp. Access to it can be gained after removing the column shroud. If the wires for the flasher circuit are detached and bridged, the fault can be isolated to either switch or wiring.

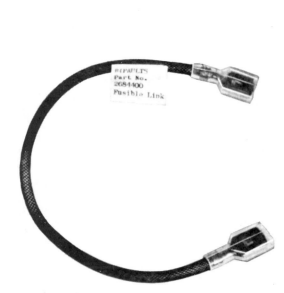

Fig. 10.17 A typical fusible link

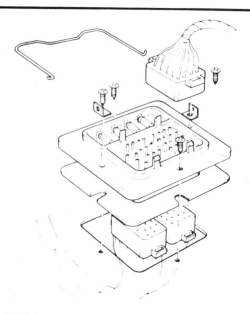

Fig. 10.18 Wiring system - bulkhead multiple connector socket and combined fuse box

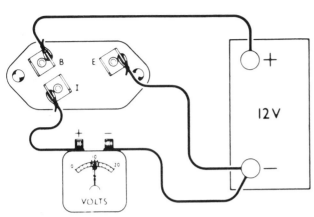

Fig. 10.19 Instrument voltage stabiliser unit. Connections for testing

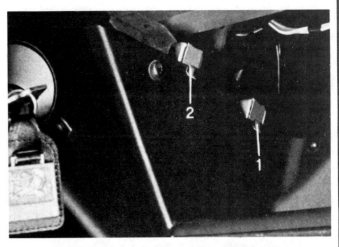

Fig. 10.20 Flasher circuit - position of flasher unit

1   Turn indicator unit   2   Hazard flasher unit

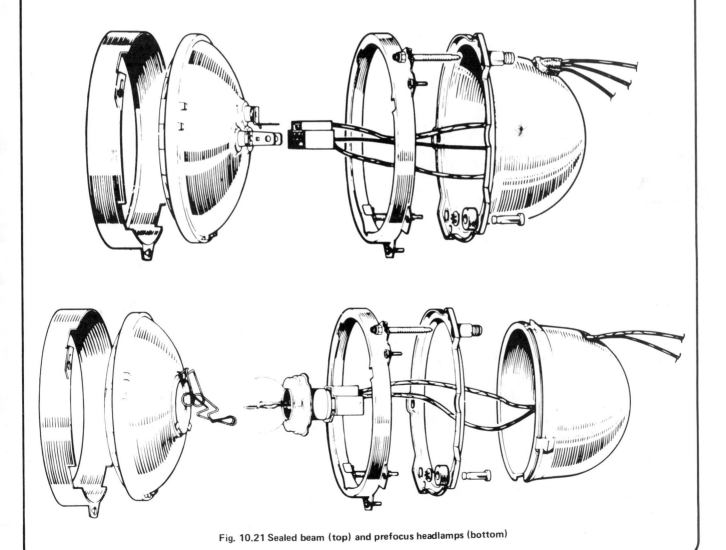

Fig. 10.21 Sealed beam (top) and prefocus headlamps (bottom)

Fig. 10.22 The light unit releasing screws (arrowed)

Fig. 10.23 Headlamp removal

20 Horns - fault tracing and rectification

1   If a horn works badly or fails completely, check the wiring leading to it for short circuits and loose connections. Check that the horn is firmly secured and that there is nothing lying on the horn body.
2   If the horn still does not work, or operates incorrectly, check the switch. This can be done by unscrewing the end cap on the combined switch. Bridge the two terminal blades and, if the horn works, check the contact piece inside the cap.
3   The horn adjusting screw is sealed on assembly to discourage tampering. If you do decide to tamper, it should be as a last resort only.
    Turn it anticlockwise to decrease the volume and clockwise to increase the volume.

21 Headlamps and bulbs - removal and replacement

1   The four lamp system comprises either sealed beam or Unified European pre-focus type light units, according to the regulations of the country in which the car is marketed.
2   All four lamps are in operation on main beam, but when dipped, only the outer lamp operates on a dip or supplementary main beam filament.
3   Access to the lamp bulb on pre-focus units is from the engine compartment. The spring dip which secures the bulb can be released after squeezing the sides of the plastic cover and the bulb can be withdrawn from the lamp mounting ring.
4   To withdraw a light unit, remove the appropriate radiator grille insert (see Chapter 12), then slacken the three crosshead retaining screws and turn the unit anticlockwise.
5   The headlamps are secured to the front end panel by four screws and speed nuts; these are accessible with the radiator grille inserts removed.

22 Headlamp beam - adjustment

1   Headlamp beam adjustment is best done with proper optical alignment equipment. However, if the lamps are seriously out, adjustment can be carried out on the two screws whose rear ends project into the engine compartment. Ideally, they are turned with a proper square section key.
2   The inner lamp should have a beam setting straight forward with $\frac{1}{2}^{\circ}$ downwards deflection. The outer lamps should be set when on dipped beams. They should then aim 2° down and 2° left (RHD) or 2° right (LHD).

Access to the rear lamp bulbs

Left — Saloon   Right — Estate

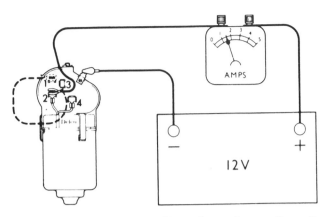

Fig. 10.25 Windscreen wiper motor (2 speed) - running test. Connection of battery and ammeter. Continuous line shows connection for low speed running. For high speed running move lead from terminal from 2 to 4. To check self-park move supply lead to terminal 3 and add another lead (dotted line) between terminals 1 and 2

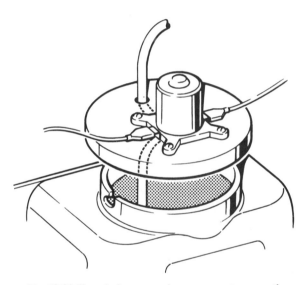

Fig. 10.26 The windscreen washer pump motor mounting

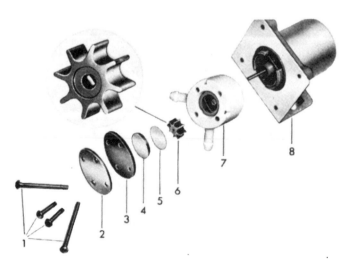

Fig. 10.27 The windscreen washer pump - exploded view

1	Bolts	5	Washer
2	End cover	6	Impeller
3	Seal	7	Housing
4	Distance piece	8	Motor body

23 Side and front turn signal lamps - removal and replacement

1   Access to the 2 bulbs can be gained after removal of the 2 lens securing screws. The bulbs should be pushed in and turned anticlockwise to remove them from their holders.
2   The lamp units are retained by 3 studs and nuts, accessible from behind the valance panel.

24 Rear lights and flasher bulbs - removal and replacement

1   Access to the rear lamp bulbs is from inside the luggage boot.
2   Remove the cover and then pull out the appropriate bulb holder held in by spring clips round the edge of the holder.
3   Replace the bulb in the holder and then refit the holder so that the tongues locate in the spaces in the holder.

25 Windscreen wipers - fault finding

1   If the wipers do not work when they are switched on first check the No. 3 fuse. If this is sound then there is either an open circuit in the wiring or switch, the wiper motor is faulty, or the pivot spindles or linkages may be binding.
2   If the wipers work intermittently then suspect a short circuit in the motor. Alternatively, the armature shaft end float adjustment may be too tight or the wiper linkage may be binding.
3   Should the wipers not stop when they are turned off there must be a short circuit in the switch or wiring.

26 Windscreen washers - fault finding

1   In the event of the electrically operated washers failing to deliver water to the jets, first check No. 3 fuse. If this is sound then there is either an open circuit in the wiring, switch or pump motor, or the pump motor may be seized.
2   The washer pump is mounted on the reservoir cap. There are 2 electrical connections, and one delivery tube to the washer jets.
3   Where necessary, the pump impeller can be renewed by removing the end cover, seal, distance piece and nylon washer which are retained by 4 bolts.
4   The washer jets are spherical and can be adjusted by inserting a pin in the jet orifice and moving it to the required angle.

27 Windscreen wiper motor - removal and replacement

1   The windscreen wiper motor has to be removed complete with the wiper operating links and arms, which are held in a rigid frame and comprise the complete windscreen wiper assembly.
2   Take off the windscreen wiper arm.
3   Remove from under the bonnet, the panel shrouding the ventilator. The wiper motor and crank assembly can be seen and it is held by two bolts through rubber bushes in the bracket. To get at the bolts, position the links by running the wiper and switching off the ignition when they are in the proper place. If the motor is no use, remove the link arms by detaching the clips.
4   When the bracket mounting bolts are removed, the whole assembly can be eased down and out and the electrical connections detached from the motor.
5   Having unclipped the links, the motor may be removed from the mounting bracket.
6   Replacement is the reverse of the removal procedure. The leads should be connected as follows:

1	–	Yellow	
2	–	Red	
3	–	Green	
4	–	Blue	
Ground terminal	–		Black

28 Windscreen wiper motor - dismantling, inspection and reassembly

1   Other than for normal wear, the bearings and gears in the motor

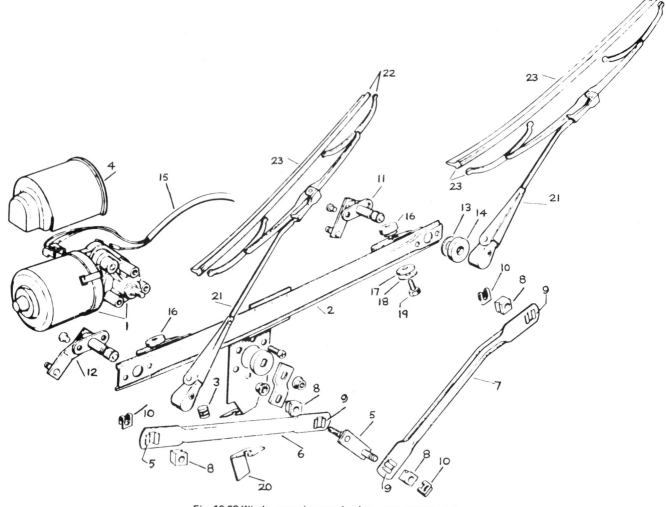

Fig. 10.28 Windscreen wiper mechanism - component parts

1 Motor assembly	7 Cross link	12 Wiper pivot housing	17 Washer
2 Wiper mounting bracket	8 Link fixing bush	(passenger side)	18 Washer
3 Retainer	9 Link fixing clip	13 Wiper spindle washer	19 Screw
4 Motor cover	10 Link fixing clip	14 Wiper spindle seal	20 Motor support bracket
5 Crank and pin assembly	11 Wiper pivot housing	15 Wiper wiring harness	21 Wiper arm
6 Drive link	(driver side)	16 Frame insulator	22 Wiper blade assembly
			23 Squeegee

should not deteriorate and if for any reason the motor should cease to function altogether, it is probably due to the wiper mechanism jamming or seizing which has overloaded the motor and burnt it out. In such instances the purchasing of either armature or field coils, and probably brushes as well, is hardly comparable to buying an exchange unit. If the motor ceases to function for no immediately obvious reason proceed as follows:

2   Remove the end frame by levering out the two retaining clips.

3   Remove the screw securing the terminal end cover to expose the drive gears.

4   The end frame and armature can be withdrawn together, care being taken to prevent loss of the nylon thrust bearing at the end of the worm shaft.

5   The brush plate and gear cover are a complete assembly and can be withdrawn together.

6   If any of the spindle brushes are worn, the cover complete (in which they are fitted) will need renewal, as they are not serviced (by Vauxhall) separately.

7   New carbon brushes may be fitted. It may be found preferable to solder their pigtail leads to the existing leads so leave sufficient length for soldering when cutting the old leads.

8   One of the most important features of reassembly is to make sure the endfloat in the armature and cross shafts is within Specification. Excessive endfloat is what causes jamming and stiffness leading to

overloading and a burnt out motor.

9   Make sure that the water shield and crank are assembled to the cross-shaft so that the relative positions of the self-park segment and crank are correct as indicated in the illustration (Fig. 10.31).

10 Before assembly begins lubricate the armature end frame bush with engine oil and put anti-scuffing paste on the thrust ball recess in the shaft.

11 Hold back the carbon brushes by hooking the leads over the tags on the brush holders. Then they can be released through the clip holes in the end cover, after the end cover has been replaced.

12 When the motor is reassembled, test it with an ammeter in circuit if possible. Even though it runs, if the current used is above 1 amp then trouble may be expected because something is stiff and causing extra loading which the windup cannot take. While the motor is running, tap the end frame to help settle the bearings. If necessary adjust the end thrust screw but watch the loading on the ammeter whilst doing so to see that it does not increase more than 1 amp.

13 Test that the self-park works by rearranging the wiring as shown in the connection illustration (Fig. 10.25).

14 If any of the nylon bushes in the pivots and link arms are worn, they can be removed and renewed by simply snapping them out of position. The pivot assembly can be renewed also. Drill out the rivets and re-rivet new units in position. Refit the motor.

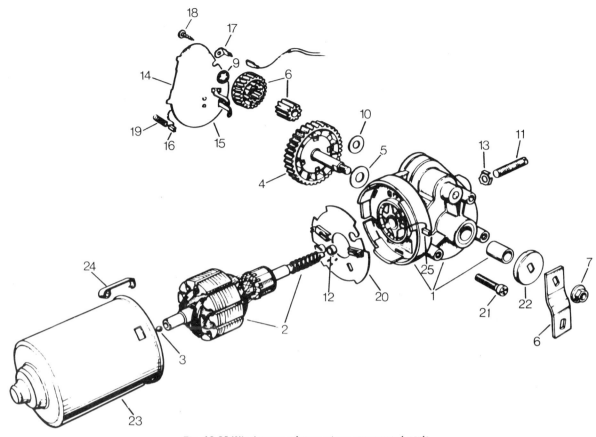

Fig. 10.29 Windscreen wiper motor - component parts

1 Housing and bearings assembly	7 Crank locknut	14 Gear cover	19 Brush spring
2 Armature	8 Worm wheel and pinion	15 Contact assembly	20 Brush gear assembly
3 Thrust ball	9 Worm wheel retainer	16 Brush and terminal assembly	21 Cover screw
4 Cross ahft and gear	10 Thrust washer	17 Terminal	22 Water shield
5 Thrust washer	11 Thrust screw	18 Terminal screw	23 Commutator end frame
6 Crank assembly	12 Thrust bearing		24 End frame clip
	13 Locknut		

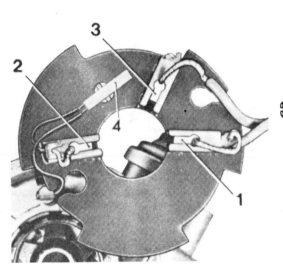

Fig. 10.30 Windscreen wiper motor illustration of brush plate

1 and 2 Slow speed brushes
2 and 3 High speed brushes
4 Safety cut-out bi-metal strip

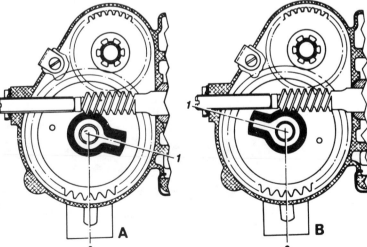

Fig. 10.31 Windscreen wiper motor - reassembly showing correct position of parking segment (1) relative to the crank (2)

A Left-hand drive   B Right-hand drive

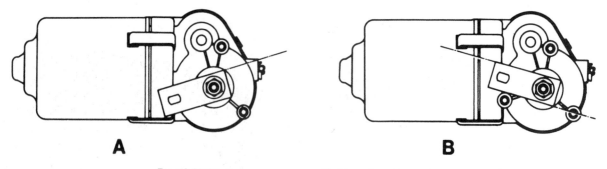

Fig. 10.32 Windscreen wiper motor. Position of crank at self-park

A Left-hand drive   B Right-hand drive

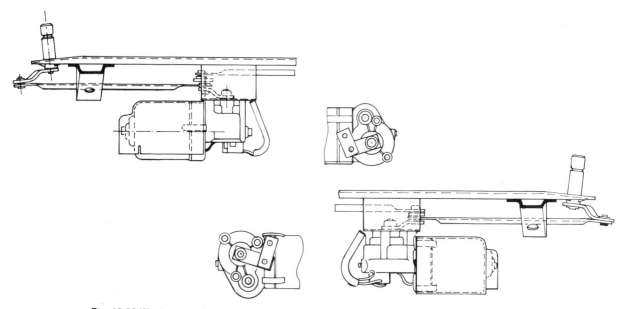

Fig. 10.33 Windscreen wiper mechanism assembly. Position of motor relative to mounting bracket

A Left-hand drive   B Right-hand drive

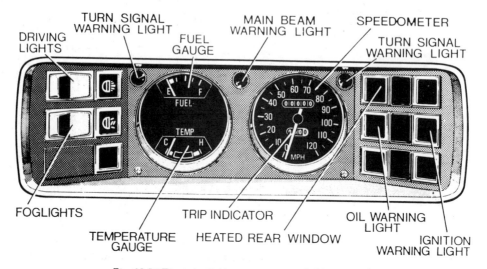

Fig. 10.34 The twin dial instrument panel (1800 models)

Fig. 10.35 Access to the instrument panel bulbs (twin dial)

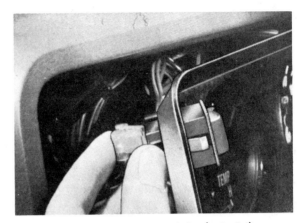

Fig. 10.36 Access to the switches (twin dial)

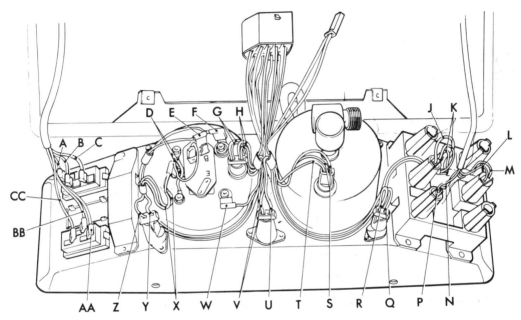

Fig. 10.37 The twin dial instrument assembly wiring

A   White/green (terminal 4)
B   Red/green (terminal 7)
C   Yellow/green (terminal 2)
D   Green/red
E   Green
F   Green/blue
G   Black

H   Red/white
J   White/brown
K   Green
L   Green
M   Brown/yellow
N   Black
P   Green/yellow

Q   Black
R   Green/white
S   Black
T   Red/white
U   Blue/white
V   Black
W   Green/black

X   Black
Y   Black
Z   Green/red
AA Brown (terminal 7)
BB Red/brown (terminal 4)
CC Blue (terminal 8)

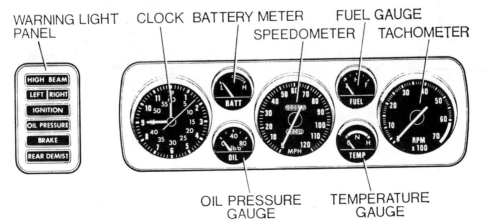

WARNING LIGHT PANEL

HIGH BEAM
LEFT   RIGHT
IGNITION
OIL PRESSURE
BRAKE
REAR DEMIST

CLOCK   BATTERY METER
SPEEDOMETER

FUEL GAUGE
TACHOMETER

OIL PRESSURE GAUGE

TEMPERATURE GAUGE

Fig. 10.38 The seven dial instrument panel (2300 models)

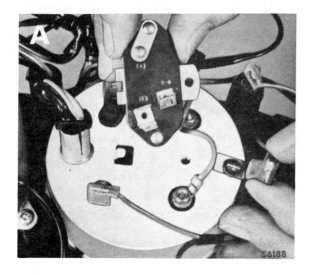

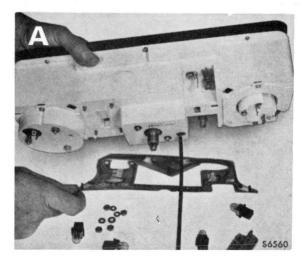

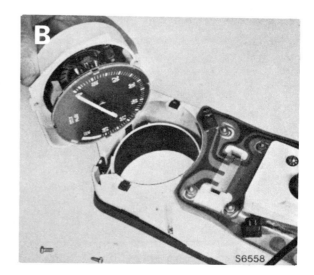

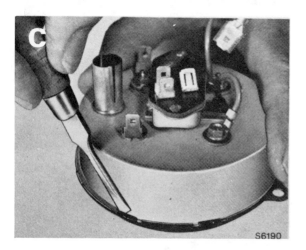

Fig. 10.39 Dismantling the twin dial instrument panel

A *Removing the voltment stabiliser*
B *Removing a main dial after removing the two
   retaining screws*
C *Removing the bezel and glass*

Fig. 10.40 Dismantling the sevel dial instrument panel

A *Removing the printed circuited*
B *Removing the tachometer dial*
C *Removing the fuel gauge dial*

29 Twin dial instrument panel - lamp and switch renewal

1 Access to the warning lamp bulbs at the side of the instrument panel, and the bulb in the speedometer, can be gained from above the driver's parcel shelf.
2 To gain access to the switches and remaining lamp bulbs, it is necessary to remove the 4 instrument assembly retaining screws, disconnect the speedometer cable and draw the assembly forwards.
3 The bulbs can be pulled out of their retainers.
4 Switches are retained by spring clips on the switch bodies which can be depressed to release. See Fig. 10.37 for the wiring connections.

30 Twin dial instrument panel - removal servicing and replacement

1 To permit the odometer (mileometer) trip control to be released, remove the instrument panel aperture filler which is retained by 4 screws.
2 Remove the instrument assembly as described in the previous Section, to permit the wiring to be disconnected.
3 The voltage stabilizer is secured to the rear of the instrument assembly by a single screw which also secures the ground terminal.
4 Testing of the stabilizer is described in Section 18.
5 The speedometer and instrument assembly are each secured by 2 screws. Removal is straightforward.
6 To gain access to the fuel or temperature gauges, ease back the tags and remove the bezel and glass from the instrument assembly.
7 The gauges can be withdrawn after removing the 2 securing nuts, but note the location of the insulating washers.

31 Seven dial instrument panel - lamp, switch and voltage stabilizer renewal

1 The bulb holders in the inner end of the instrument assembly and in the warning lamp panel can be removed after detaching the filler panel adjacent to the steering column. The voltage stabilizer can also be removed through this aperture. Testing of the stabilizer is described in Section 18.
2 The bulb holders at the outer end of the instrument assembly can be reached from above the driver's parcel shelf.

32 Seven dial instrument panel - removal, servicing and replacement

1 To remove the complete instrument assembly, release the two screws at each end and lift the assembly away together with the cover. If the printed circuit is removed, ensure that the instrument assembly is not held face down, or the gauges may drop through and damage the movement when the nuts are removed.
2 The clock and tachometer can be withdrawn from the rear of the instrument case after removing the two screws. The speedometer, battery condition meter, oil pressure, fuel and water temperature gauges, can be removed from the front of the case after removing the five screws securing the facia.
3 The warning lamp panel can be withdrawn, when the instrument assembly is removed, if the two retaining nuts and one screw are released.

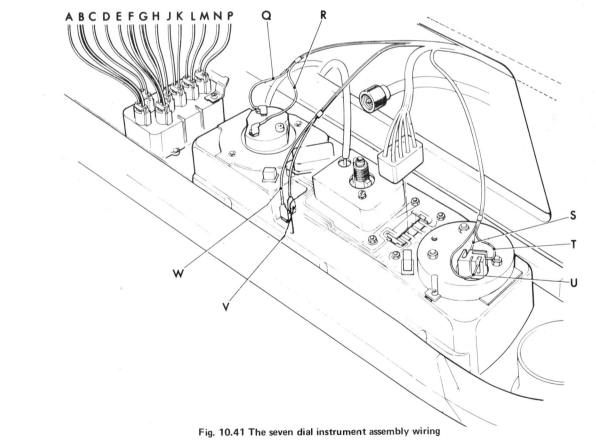

Fig. 10.41 The seven dial instrument assembly wiring

A Blue/white	G Green	M Green	S Green
B Black	H Brown/yellow	N Green/yellow	T White/black
C Black	J Green	P Black	U Black
D Green/red	K White/brown	Q Purple	V Black
E Green/white	L Green/brown	R Black	W Green
F Black			

33 Console illumination and switches

1   Access to the illumination lamps is either by removing four screws and detaching the insert or by removing the screws and detaching the whole assembly.
2   To gain access to the switches, remove the insert, then remove the appropriate switch(es) by removing two retaining screws. The switch connections are shown in Fig. 10.42.

34 Heater control illumination

1   Access to the heater control bulbs is gained by removing the control knobs, and the single escutcheon retaining screw and the escutcheon.

35 Lighting, windshield wiper and fog lamp switch connections

1   The switch terminals are numbered, and connections are made as follows:

Lighting
4 — Red/brown
7 — Blue/brown
8 — Blue

Wipers
2 — Yellow/green
4 — White/green
7 — Red/green
8 — Blue/green

Fog lamp
4 — Red/yellow
7 — Red
8 — Red/yellow

36 Steering column stalk switches

1   Early models are fitted with a single switch which operates the turn signals, headlamp dip, flasher and horn. Access to the horn contacts is gained by unscrewing the end cap.
2   Later models have twin stalk switches. One switch operates the turn signals, headlamp dip, flasher and horn push. The first 5° of the switch movement operates the turn signals without them 'locking on', so that lane-changing signals can be given. After the 5° of movement the switch is cancelled by the normal self-cancelling mechanism. Access to the horn button is gained by unscrewing the end cap. The other switch operates the wipers at full or half speed, and by moving it from the Off position towards the driver, provides a 'pulse-wipe' facility.
3   Switches can be removed by taking off the steering column canopy (see Chapter 11), and disconnecting the electrical connectors and removing the screw(s). **Note:** For twin stalk switches, the steering wheel must also be removed (see Chapter 11).

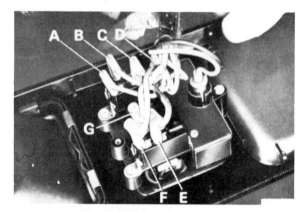

Fig. 10.42 The console switches

Windshield wiper switch
A Blue/light green (terminal 8)
B White/light green (terminal 4)
C Red/light green (terminal 7)
D Yellow/light green (terminal 2)

Lighting switch
E Brown/blue (terminal 7)
F Blue (terminal 8)
G Red/brown (terminal 4)

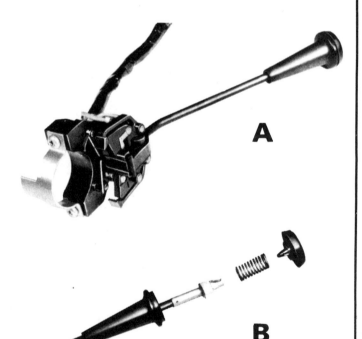

Fig. 10.43 A single steering column stalk switch (A) and the horn button (B)

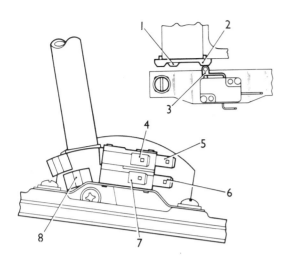

Fig. 10.44 Starter inhibitor and reverse light switches (early type)

1	Neutral cam	5	Yellow/white connection
2	Park cam	6	Green/brown connection
3	Roller	7	Green connection
4	Red/white connection	8	Reverse cam

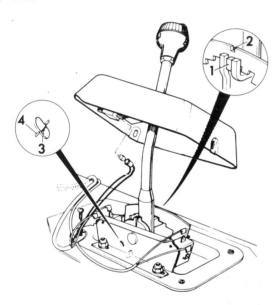

Fig. 10.45 Starter inhibitor and reverse light switches (later models)

1	Selector plunger	3	Line scribed on the cam
2	Cut-out in the selector plate	4	Line scribed on the switch bracket

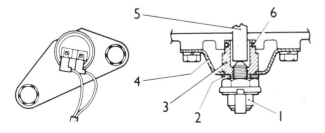

Fig. 10.46 Reverse lamp switch

1	Switch	4	Plate
2	Sealing washer	5	Striking lever shaft
3	Housing	6	'O' ring

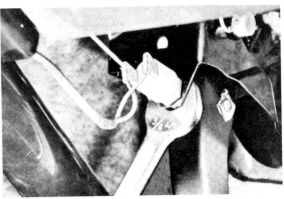

Fig. 10.47 Stop lamp switch adjustment

37 Starter inhibitor and reverse light switches

Early models

1   The switches are accessible after removing the console. They are attached to a bracket which is secured to the floor panel by two screws.
2   To adjust the switches, position them so that when the selector lever is at 'N' or 'P', the respective cam depresses the roller on the upper (inhibitor) switch. Now check that the starter will not operate when 'D', 'I', 'L', or 'R' is selected. Adjust the lower (reverse) switch so that the roller is depressed by the cam when 'R' is selected.

Later models

3   The switches are operated by a cam attached to a bracket, and secured by two nuts to the selector lever housing. The inhibitor switch is to the front of the car, while the cam is operated by a pin on the side of the selector lever.
4   Adjustment is possible after removing the selector lever console. First, set the selector lever in 'N' (neutral) and check that the selector plunger (1) is lined up with the cut-out (2) in the top of the selector plate. Next, slacken the two nuts securing the switch bracket and move the bracket until the line (3) on the cam is in alignment with the line (4) on the switch bracket. Tighten the switch bracket nuts and check that the starter will not operate when 'D', 'L', 'I' or 'R' is selected (Fig. 10.45).
5   Ensure that the roller on the reverse lamp switch is depressed by the cam when 'R' is selected. If the wiring has been disconnected ensure that they are replaced as follows: white/red and white/yellow to inhibitor switch, and green and green/brown to the reverse lamp switch.

38 Reverse lamp switch

Where a reverse lamp is operated by the gearchange lever, the switch is screwed into the rear end of the remote control housing on the gearbox. No adjustment is possible. When fitting a new switch ensure that the sealing washer is sound and that the O-ring is in position on the housing.

39 Stoplamp switch

1   The stoplamp switch is mounted on the brake pedal support bracket adjacent to the brake pedal. It is operated mechanically on depression of the brake pedal.
2   The switch should operate when the brake pedal is depressed. It can be adjusted by slackening the retaining nut, and moving it in relation to the brake pedal. This should be such that when the pedal is at rest, the plunger is pressed in only just enough to operate the switch. If set too near the pedal, it could restrict the return movement with serious consequences to braking.
3   If the switch is suspected of not working, first check that the circuit is working, by bridging the two terminals of the switch and noting whether the stop lights come on (with the ignition switch on). If they do, the switch is at fault. If not, check the stoplamp circuit wiring.

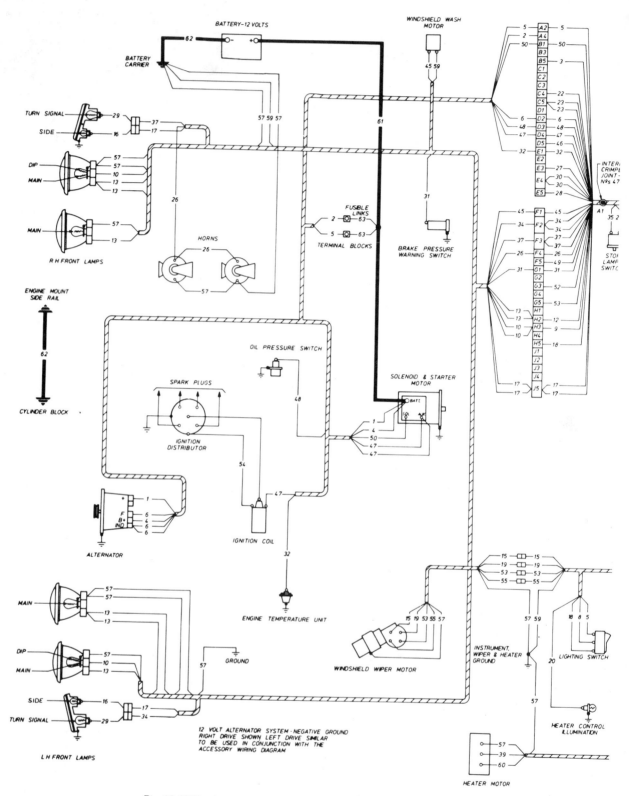

Fig. 10.48 Physical wiring diagram - Magnum 1800

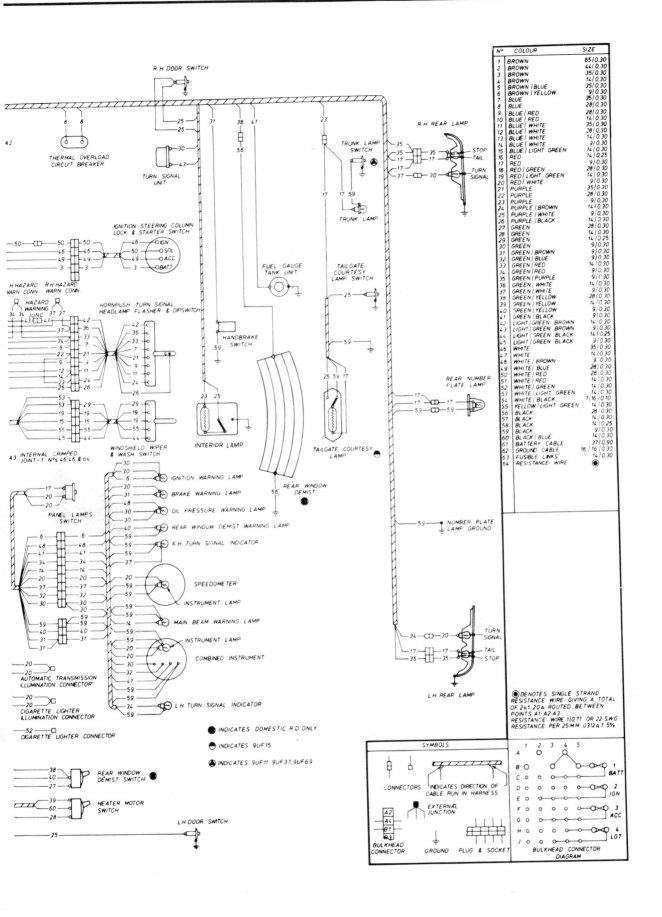

N°	COLOUR	SIZE
1	BROWN	65/0.30
2	BROWN	44/0.30
3	BROWN	35/0.30
4	BROWN	14/0.30
5	BROWN/BLUE	35/0.30
6	BROWN/YELLOW	9/0.30
7	BLUE	35/0.30
8	BLUE	28/0.30
9	BLUE/RED	28/0.30
10	BLUE/RED	14/0.30
11	BLUE/WHITE	35/0.30
12	BLUE/WHITE	28/0.30
13	BLUE/WHITE	14/0.30
14	BLUE/WHITE	3/0.30
15	BLUE/LIGHT GREEN	14/0.30
16	RED	14/0.25
17	RED	9/0.30
18	RED/GREEN	28/0.30
19	RED/LIGHT GREEN	14/0.30
20	RED/WHITE	9/0.30
21	PURPLE	35/0.30
22	PURPLE	28/0.30
23	PURPLE	9/0.30
24	PURPLE/BROWN	14/0.30
25	PURPLE/WHITE	9/0.30
26	PURPLE/BLACK	9/0.30
27	GREEN	28/0.30
28	GREEN	14/0.30
29	GREEN	14/0.25
30	GREEN	9/0.30
31	GREEN/BROWN	9/0.30
32	GREEN/BLUE	9/0.30
33	GREEN/RED	14/0.30
34	GREEN/RED	9/0.30
35	GREEN/PURPLE	9/0.30
36	GREEN/WHITE	14/0.30
37	GREEN/WHITE	9/0.30
38	GREEN/YELLOW	28/0.30
39	GREEN/YELLOW	9/0.30
40	GREEN/YELLOW	9/0.30
41	GREEN/BLACK	9/0.30
42	LIGHT/GREEN BROWN	14/0.30
43	LIGHT/GREEN BROWN	9/0.30
44	LIGHT/GREEN BLACK	14/0.25
45	LIGHT/GREEN BLACK	9/0.30
46	WHITE	35/0.30
47	WHITE	14/0.30
48	WHITE/BROWN	9/0.30
49	WHITE/BLUE	28/0.30
50	WHITE/RED	28/0.30
51	WHITE/RED	14/0.30
52	WHITE/GREEN	14/0.30
53	WHITE/LIGHT GREEN	14/0.30
54	WHITE/BLACK	7/16/0.10
55	YELLOW/LIGHT GREEN	14/0.30
56	BLACK	28/0.30
57	BLACK	14/0.30
58	BLACK	14/0.25
59	BLACK	9/0.30
60	BLACK/BLUE	14/0.30
61	BATTERY CABLE	37/0.90
62	GROUND CABLE	16/16/0.30
63	FUSIBLE LINKS	14/0.30
64	RESISTANCE WIRE	◉

RH DOOR SWITCH

THERMAL OVERLOAD CIRCUIT BREAKER

TURN SIGNAL UNIT

IGNITION STEERING COLUMN LOCK & STARTER SWITCH

IGN
SOL
ACC
BATT

LH HAZARD WARN CONN.   RH HAZARD WARN. CONN.

HAZARD WARNING

HORNPUSH, TURN SIGNAL, HEADLAMP FLASHER & DIPSWITCH

HANDBRAKE SWITCH

FUEL GAUGE TANK UNIT

TRUNK LAMP SWITCH

TRUNK LAMP

RH REAR LAMP
STOP
TAIL
TURN SIGNAL

TAILGATE COURTESY LAMP SWITCH

WINDSHIELD WIPER & WASH SWITCH

INTERIOR LAMP

INTERNAL CRIMPED JOINT-1 N°s 46,46 & 64

TAILGATE COURTESY LAMP

REAR WINDOW DEMIST

REAR NUMBER PLATE LAMP

IGNITION WARNING LAMP

BRAKE WARNING LAMP

OIL PRESSURE WARNING LAMP

REAR WINDOW DEMIST WARNING LAMP

RH TURN SIGNAL INDICATOR

PANEL LAMPS SWITCH

SPEEDOMETER

INSTRUMENT LAMP

MAIN BEAM WARNING LAMP

INSTRUMENT LAMP

COMBINED INSTRUMENT

AUTOMATIC TRANSMISSION ILLUMINATION CONNECTOR

CIGARETTE LIGHTER ILLUMINATION CONNECTOR

CIGARETTE LIGHTER CONNECTOR

LH TURN SIGNAL INDICATOR

NUMBER PLATE LAMP GROUND

TURN SIGNAL
TAIL
STOP

LH REAR LAMP

⬤ INDICATES DOMESTIC R.D ONLY

◗ INDICATES 9UF15

◓ INDICATES 9UF11, 9UF37, 9UF69

REAR WINDOW DEMIST SWITCH

HEATER MOTOR SWITCH

LH DOOR SWITCH

◉ DENOTES SINGLE STRAND RESISTANCE WIRE GIVING A TOTAL OF 2Ω 20a ROUTED BETWEEN POINTS A1·A2·A3 RESISTANCE WIRE 1/0.71 OR 22 SWG RESISTANCE PER 25 MM 0.312Ω ± 5%

SYMBOLS

CONNECTORS   INDICATES DIRECTION OF CABLE RUN IN HARNESS

EXTERNAL JUNCTION

A2
A4
B1
B3
BULKHEAD CONNECTOR

GROUND   PLUG & SOCKET

	1	2	3	4	5	
A						
B						1 BATT
C						
D						2 IGN
E						
F						3 ACC
G						
H						4 LGT
J						

BULKHEAD CONNECTOR DIAGRAM

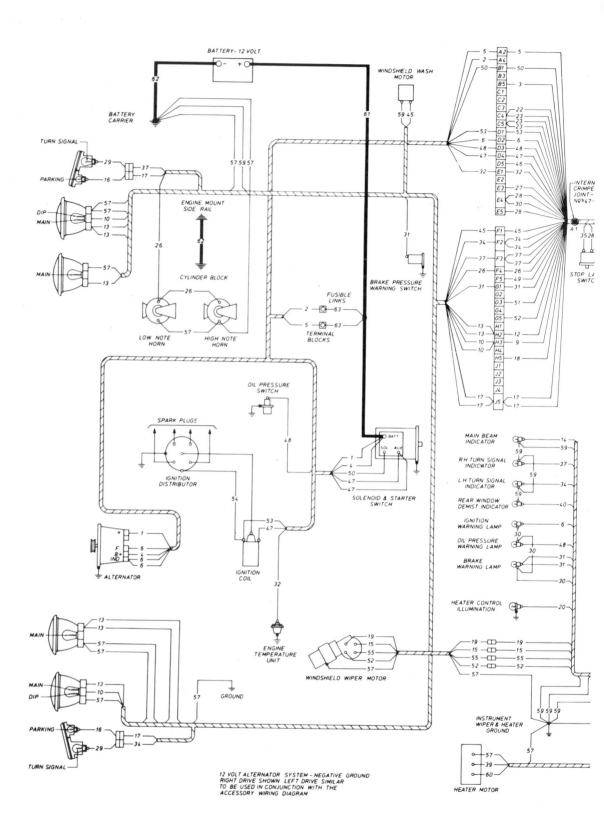

Fig. 10.49 Physical wiring diagram - Magnum 2300

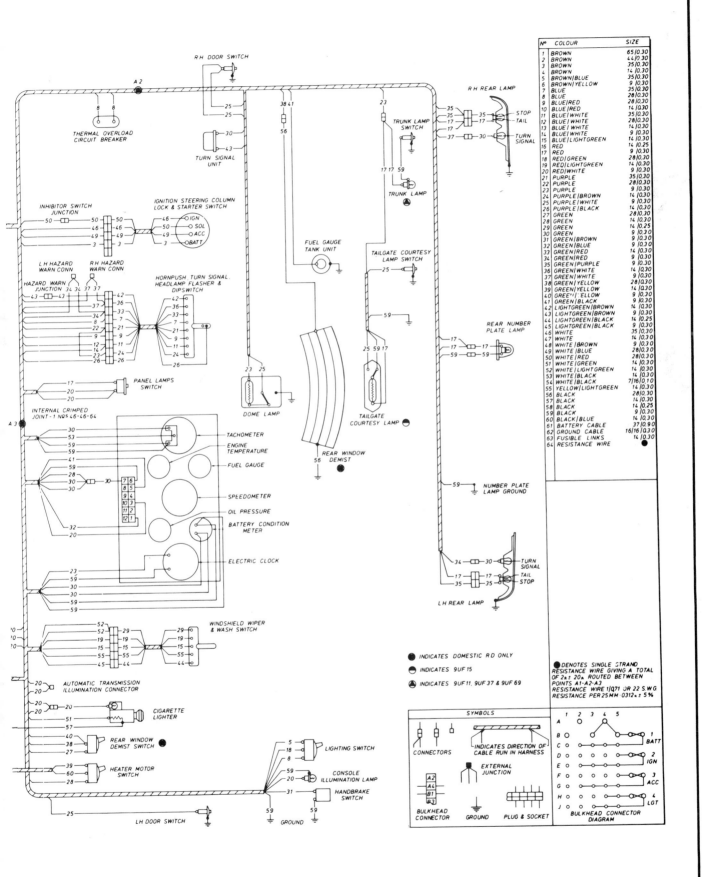

Nº	COLOUR	SIZE
1	BROWN	65/0.30
2	BROWN	44/0.30
3	BROWN	35/0.30
4	BROWN	14/0.30
5	BROWN/BLUE	35/0.30
6	BROWN/YELLOW	9/0.30
7	BLUE	35/0.30
8	BLUE	28/0.30
9	BLUE/RED	14/0.30
10	BLUE/RED	14/0.30
11	BLUE/WHITE	35/0.30
12	BLUE/WHITE	28/0.30
13	BLUE/WHITE	14/0.30
14	BLUE/WHITE	9/0.30
15	BLUE/LIGHTGREEN	14/0.30
16	RED	14/0.25
17	RED	9/0.30
18	RED/GREEN	28/0.30
19	RED/LIGHTGREEN	14/0.30
20	RED/WHITE	9/0.30
21	PURPLE	35/0.30
22	PURPLE	28/0.30
23	PURPLE	9/0.30
24	PURPLE/BROWN	14/0.30
25	PURPLE/WHITE	9/0.30
26	PURPLE/BLACK	14/0.30
27	GREEN	28/0.30
28	GREEN	14/0.30
29	GREEN	14/0.25
30	GREEN	9/0.30
31	GREEN/BROWN	9/0.30
32	GREEN/BLUE	14/0.30
33	GREEN/RED	9/0.30
34	GREEN/RED	9/0.30
35	GREEN/PURPLE	9/0.30
36	GREEN/WHITE	14/0.30
37	GREEN/WHITE	9/0.30
38	GREEN/YELLOW	28/0.30
39	GREEN/YELLOW	14/0.30
40	GREEN/YELLOW	9/0.30
41	GREEN/BLACK	9/0.30
42	LIGHTGREEN/BROWN	14/0.30
43	LIGHTGREEN/BROWN	9/0.30
44	LIGHTGREEN/BLACK	14/0.25
45	LIGHTGREEN/BLACK	9/0.30
46	WHITE	35/0.30
47	WHITE	14/0.30
48	WHITE/BROWN	9/0.30
49	WHITE/BLUE	28/0.30
50	WHITE/RED	28/0.30
51	WHITE/GREEN	14/0.30
52	WHITE/LIGHTGREEN	14/0.30
53	WHITE/BLACK	14/0.30
54	WHITE/BLACK	7/16/0.10
55	YELLOW/LIGHTGREEN	14/0.30
56	BLACK	28/0.30
57	BLACK	14/0.30
58	BLACK	14/0.25
59	BLACK	9/0.30
60	BLACK/BLUE	14/0.30
61	BATTERY CABLE	37/0.90
62	GROUND CABLE	16/16/0.30
63	FUSIBLE LINKS	14/0.30
64	RESISTANCE WIRE	●

RH DOOR SWITCH

A 2

THERMAL OVERLOAD CIRCUIT BREAKER

TURN SIGNAL UNIT

RH REAR LAMP

TRUNK LAMP SWITCH

STOP
TAIL
TURN SIGNAL

TRUNK LAMP

INHIBITOR SWITCH JUNCTION

IGNITION STEERING COLUMN LOCK & STARTER SWITCH

IGN
SOL
ACC
BATT

FUEL GAUGE TANK UNIT

TAILGATE COURTESY LAMP SWITCH

L H HAZARD WARN CONN

R H HAZARD WARN CONN

HAZARD WARN JUNCTION

HORNPUSH, TURN SIGNAL, HEADLAMP FLASHER & DIPSWITCH

REAR NUMBER PLATE LAMP

A 3

PANEL LAMPS SWITCH

INTERNAL CRIMPED JOINT - 1 Nº5 46-46-64

DOME LAMP

TAILGATE COURTESY LAMP

TACHOMETER

ENGINE TEMPERATURE

FUEL GAUGE

REAR WINDOW DEMIST

NUMBER PLATE LAMP GROUND

SPEEDOMETER

OIL PRESSURE

BATTERY CONDITION METER

ELECTRIC CLOCK

TURN SIGNAL
TAIL
STOP

LH REAR LAMP

WINDSHIELD WIPER & WASH SWITCH

AUTOMATIC TRANSMISSION ILLUMINATION CONNECTOR

CIGARETTE LIGHTER

REAR WINDOW DEMIST SWITCH

HEATER MOTOR SWITCH

LIGHTING SWITCH

CONSOLE ILLUMINATION LAMP

HANDBRAKE SWITCH

LH DOOR SWITCH

GROUND

● INDICATES DOMESTIC R D ONLY

◐ INDICATES 9UF 15

▲ INDICATES 9UF 11, 9UF 37 & 9UF 69

● DENOTES SINGLE STRAND RESISTANCE WIRE GIVING A TOTAL OF 2Ω ± 20Ω ROUTED BETWEEN POINTS A1-A2-A3 RESISTANCE WIRE 1/0.71 OR 22 S.W.G. RESISTANCE PER 25 MM ·0312 ± 5%

SYMBOLS

CONNECTORS

INDICATES DIRECTION OF CABLE RUN IN HARNESS

A2
A4
B1

BULKHEAD CONNECTOR

EXTERNAL JUNCTION

GROUND

PLUG & SOCKET

BULKHEAD CONNECTOR DIAGRAM

1 2 3 4 5

A
B — 1 BATT
C
D — 2 IGN
E
F — 3 ACC
G
H — 4 LGT
J

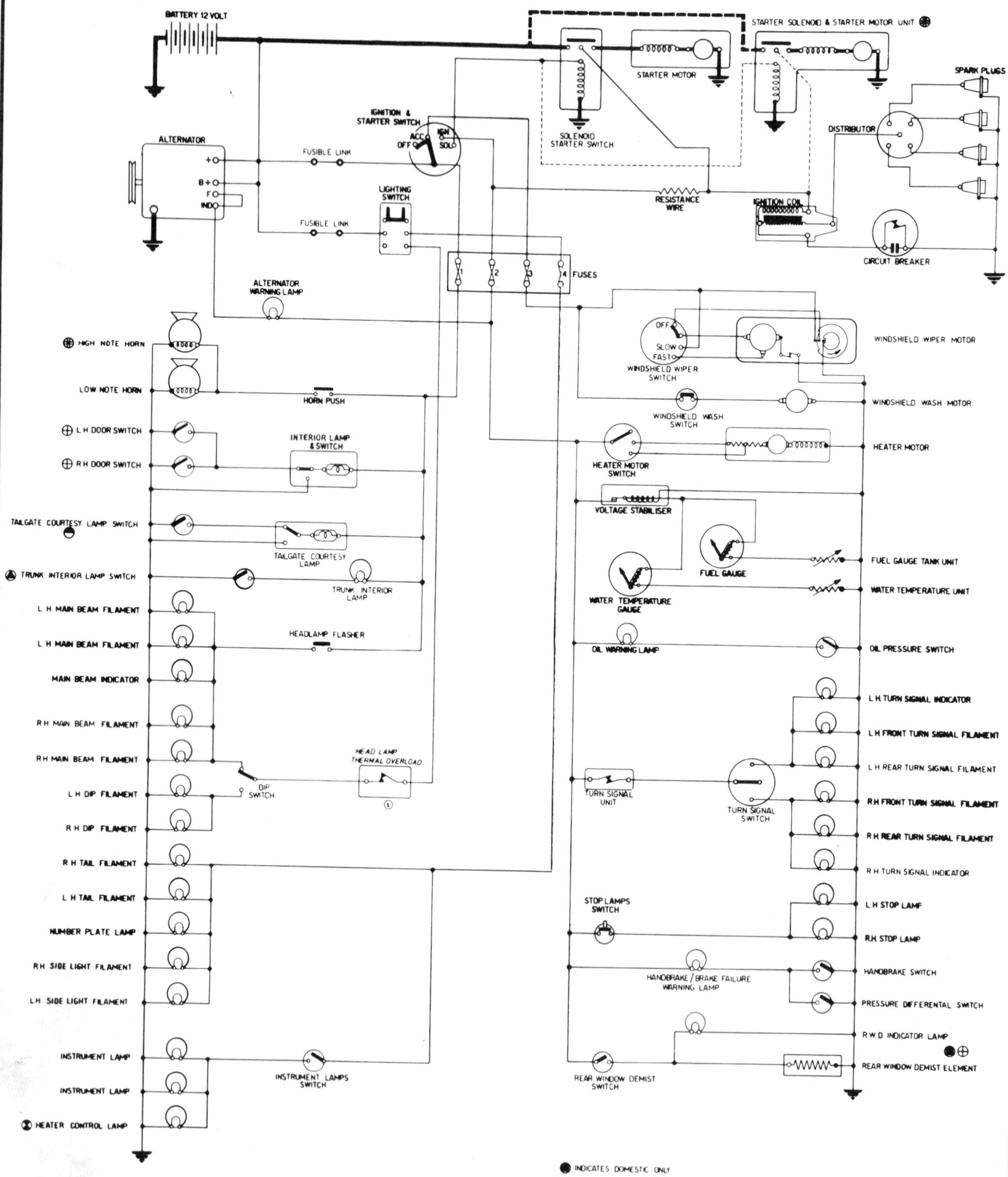

INDICATES DOMESTIC ONLY
INDICATES MODELS 9UD15, 9UE15 & 9UF15
INDICATES MODELS 9UE11, 9UE69, 9UF11, 9UF 37 & 9UF69
INDICATES MODELS 9UEA & 9UFA
INDICATES MODELS 9UDA 9UEA & 9UFA
INDICATES MODEL 9UFA ONLY

Fig. 10.50 Theoretical wiring diagram

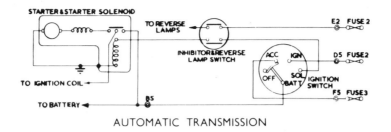

AUTOMATIC TRANSMISSION

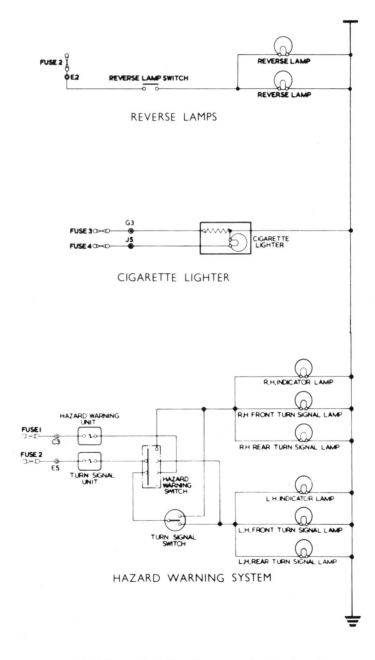

REVERSE LAMPS

CIGARETTE LIGHTER

HAZARD WARNING SYSTEM

Fig. 10.51 Theoretical wiring diagram - optional equipment

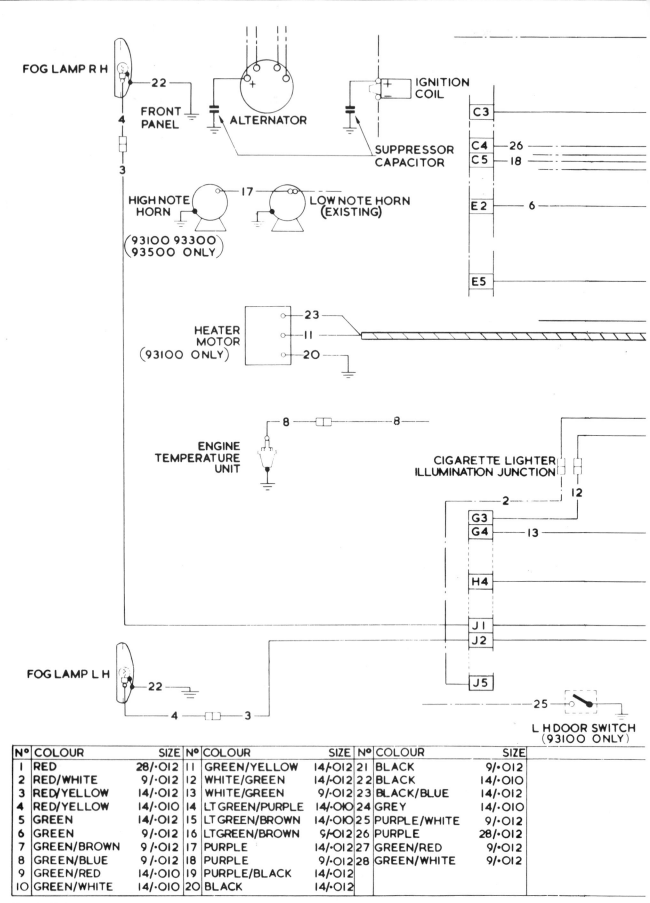

N°	COLOUR	SIZE	N°	COLOUR	SIZE	N°	COLOUR	SIZE
1	RED	28/·012	11	GREEN/YELLOW	14/·012	21	BLACK	9/·012
2	RED/WHITE	9/·012	12	WHITE/GREEN	14/·012	22	BLACK	14/·010
3	RED/YELLOW	14/·012	13	WHITE/GREEN	9/·012	23	BLACK/BLUE	14/·012
4	RED/YELLOW	14/·010	14	LT GREEN/PURPLE	14/·010	24	GREY	14/·010
5	GREEN	14/·012	15	LT GREEN/BROWN	14/·010	25	PURPLE/WHITE	9/·012
6	GREEN	9/·012	16	LT GREEN/BROWN	9/·012	26	PURPLE	28/·012
7	GREEN/BROWN	9/·012	17	PURPLE	14/·012	27	GREEN/RED	9/·012
8	GREEN/BLUE	9/·012	18	PURPLE	9/·012	28	GREEN/WHITE	9/·012
9	GREEN/RED	14/·010	19	PURPLE/BLACK	14/·012			
10	GREEN/WHITE	14/·010	20	BLACK	14/·012			

Fig. 10.52 Accessory wiring diagram   *Note: Some itmes are standard equipment on Magnum models*

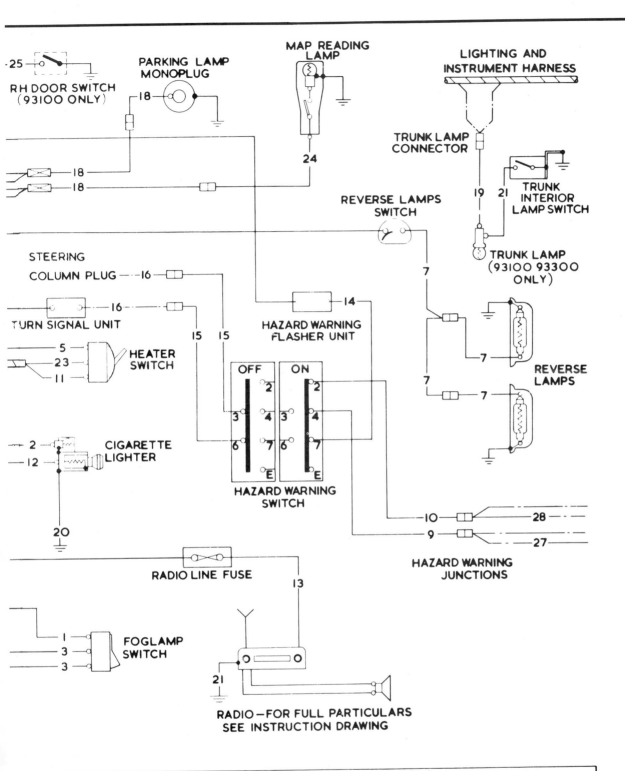

RH DOOR SWITCH
(93100 ONLY)

-25

PARKING LAMP
MONOPLUG

18

MAP READING
LAMP

24

LIGHTING AND
INSTRUMENT HARNESS

TRUNK LAMP
CONNECTOR

19   21

TRUNK
INTERIOR
LAMP SWITCH

TRUNK LAMP
(93100 93300
ONLY)

18
18

REVERSE LAMPS
SWITCH

7

7

7

REVERSE
LAMPS

STEERING
COLUMN PLUG — —16

16

TURN SIGNAL UNIT

5
23
11

HEATER
SWITCH

15   15

HAZARD WARNING
FLASHER UNIT

14

OFF   ON

2   2
3   4   3   4
6   7   6   7
    E   E

HAZARD WARNING
SWITCH

2
12

CIGARETTE
LIGHTER

20

7

7

10   28
9   27

HAZARD WARNING
JUNCTIONS

RADIO LINE FUSE

13

1
3
3

FOGLAMP
SWITCH

21

RADIO — FOR FULL PARTICULARS
SEE INSTRUCTION DRAWING

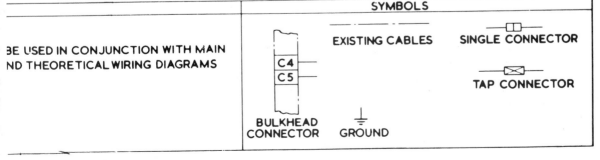

	SYMBOLS	
BE USED IN CONJUNCTION WITH MAIN	EXISTING CABLES	SINGLE CONNECTOR
ND THEORETICAL WIRING DIAGRAMS	C4 / C5	TAP CONNECTOR
	BULKHEAD CONNECTOR GROUND	

Chapter 11 Suspension and steering

Contents

Fault diagnosis - suspension and steering 25
Front crossmember - removal, checking and replacement 8
Front dampers - removal and replacement 3
Front and rear stabilizer bars - removal and replacement 12
Front springs - removal and replacement 4
Front suspension arm balljoints - removal and replacement ... 5
Front suspension arms - removal and replacement 6
Front suspension control rods - removal and replacement 7
Front wheel hub bearings - inspection and adjustment 13
Front wheel hub bearings - removal, inspection and replacement ... 14
General description 1
Rear dampers - removal and replacement 9
Rear springs - removal and replacement 10
Rear suspension arms - removal and replacement 11

Springs and dampers - inspection 2
Steering column lock 22
Steering column, steering shaft and bearings - removal, inspection and replacement 23
Steering gear - examination, adjustment, removal and replacement 16
Steering geometry - checking and adjustment 19
Steering knuckle and steering arm 18
Steering mechanism - inspection 15
Steering shaft coupling - removal and replacement 21
Steering trackrod outer balljoints - removal and replacement ... 17
Steering wheel - removal and replacement 20
Wheels and tyres 24

Specifications

Front suspension

Type	Independent, coil springs, with single lower arms, wishbone upper arms and stabilizer bar

Rear suspension

Type	Coil spring, four arm location with stabilizer bar (except Estate)

Steering

Type	Rack and pinion
Make	Burman or Cam gears
Oil capacity	¼ pint (Imperial)/(0.14 litre)

Steering geometry

Toe-in measured on rims at height of wheel centre	0.45 in toe-in to 0.45 in toe-out
Camber angle	2° negative to 0°
Steering pivot (king pin) inclination	7° 55' to 10° 25'
Castor angle	2° 30' to 4°
Toe-out on turns	Outer wheel 18° 30' from straight with inner wheel at 20°

Dampers (shock absorbers)

Type	Telescopic double acting front and rear

Wheels and tyres

Wheel type	Styled, 5J x 13, pressed steel

Tyre sizes and types:
  1800 models ... ...   155SR x 13, radial ply
  2300 models ... ...   175/70HR x 13, radial ply
Tyre pressures (normal running)*
  155SR x 13 ... ...   24 lb/in^2 (1.69 kg/cm^2)
  175/70HR x 13 ... ...   24 lb/in^2 (1.69 kg/cm^2)
Tyre pressure (high speed running)*
  155SR x 13 ... ...   28 lb/in^2 (1.97 kg/cm^2)
  175/70HR x 13 ... ...   28 lb/in^2 (1.97 kg/cm^2)
Tyre pressures (maximum gross vehicle weight)*
  155SR x 13 ... ...   30 lb/in^2 (2.11 kg/cm^2)
  175/70HR x 13 ... ...   28 lb/in^2 (1.97 kg/cm^2)

Note: Tyre pressures must be checked when the tyres are cold since they increase considerably when warm

Torque wrench settings

	lb f ft	kg f m
Front crossmember upper mounting to body nuts	19	2.6
Front crossmember rear mounting to body bolts	32	4.4
Spring upper mounting to crossmember bolts	32	4.4
Upper wishbone pivot bolt	55	7.6
Lower arm pivot bolt	42	5.8
Upper balljoint securing bolts (replacement)	22	3.0
Steering knuckle to balljoint nuts	33	4.6
Steering arm to steering knuckle	25	3.45
Trackrod end to steering arm nut	24	3.3
Damper top mounting bolt	32	4.4
Damper lower mounting bolt	57	7.9
Control rod to lower arm bolts	32	4.4
Rear suspension arms to hangers and axle mounting bolts	38	6.5
Rear spring to suspension arm mounting nut	19	2.6
Steering wheel nut	45	6.2
Steering gear to crossmember bolts	19	2.6
Steering column upper support bracket bolts	17	2.35

1 General description

The Magnum suspension system is based on four coil springs - one at each wheel. At the front, the wheels are suspended independently on an upper wishbone and lower arm, with the spring fixed to the lower arm and passing through the wishbone to an upper anchorage on the ends of the axle beam pillars.

The live rear axle is located by four arms, two being longitudinal pivoted at the forward end on plates welded to the frame side rails, and at the rear fixed to flanges on the outer ends of the axle tubes.

The other two arms also pivot at their front ends on brackets welded to the frame side rails (behind the longitudinal arms) and run at an angle of approximately 45° to mounting lugs integral with the differential casing.

The rear coil springs are located between the rear ends of the longitudinal arms and the side frame rails which curve up at that point. All pivoting is done on steel bushed rubber mountings which require no maintenance.

Double acting telescopic hydraulic dampers are used front and rear, those at the front being positioned inside the coil spring and mounted at the same points as the spring. Those at the rear are attached to the flange on the outer end of the axle tube at the bottom, and the upper end to a special support bracket fixed to the side rail.

Stabilizer bars are fitted at the front and rear (front only on Estate cars) to improve handling characteristics. These are mounted in rubber bushes and are connected to the suspension lower arms and front axle crossmember braces at the front and to the outer ends of the rear axle and underbody at the rear.

The steering is rack and pinion of conventional design, and the products of either of two manufactures is fitted, namely Burman or Cam Gears. These can be identified by the manufacturer's name cast on to the bottom of the gear housing. The assembly, comprising a housing, rack and pinion, is supported in rubber mountings on the front of the axle crossmember. The rack is mounted in one end of the housing by a bush, and at the other by a spring loaded adjustable yoke which also maintains engagement with the pinion. The pinion is mounted between ball thrust bearings, the pre-loading of which is also adjustable. The inner ends of the steering tie rods are attached to the rack by adjustable balljoints. The outer ends are fixed to the steering knuckle by sealed balljoints.

The steering column is the safety type with a collapsible 'lattice work' section in the column which will crumple on impact. The shaft itself is able to telescope and it is retained in its normal position by injections of plastic material which will shear on impact.

A steering column lock is fitted as standard.

2 Springs and dampers - inspection

1 With the tyre pressures correct, fuel tank full and the car standing on level smooth ground, bounce it up and down a few times and let it settle. Then measure the distance from the lower arm fulcrum bolt centre to the ground, and from the rear longitudinal arm front bolt centre to the ground.

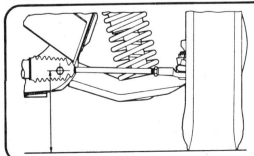
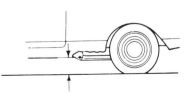

Fig. 11.1. Measurement points for front and rear body height

If there is a difference of more than 0.125 in (6 mm) side for side at front and rear, then further investigation for either a broken spring or faulty damper is necessary. If no consistent measurements can be obtained after several 'bouncings' it usually indicates that a damper is binding and should be renewed (Fig. 11.1).

2   Dampers may be checked by bouncing the car at each corner. Generally speaking the body will return to its normal position and stop after being depressed. If it rises and returns on a rebound, the damper should be suspect. Examine also the damper mounting bushes for any sign of looseness and the cylinders themsleves for traces of hydraulic fluid leaks. If there is any sign of the latter, the unit must be renewed. Static tests of dampers are not entirely conclusive and further indications of damper failure are noticeable pitching (bonnet going up and down when the car is braked and stopped sharply), excessive rolling on fast bends, and a definite feeling of insecurity on corners, particularly if the road surface is uneven. If you are in doubt it is a good idea to drive over a roughish road and have someone follow you to watch how the wheels behave. Excessive up and down 'patter' of any wheel is usually quite obvious, and denotes a defective damper.

3   In some instances, it is possible to bleed a damper but this first entails removal (Section 3 or 9). Bleeding is carried out by holding the unit upright, extending to ¾ of the full travel, inverting then fully compressing. This should be repeated twice and if there is still free-play, the unit is unserviceable and must be replaced. This bleeding procedure should always be carried out when installing a replacement unit.

3   Front dampers - removal and replacement

All figures in text refer to Fig. 11.8.

1   Removal of the dampers is made easier with the special Vauxhall tool to compress the spring, but is not essential.

2   Jack-up the car so that the front wheel is clear of the ground by a few inches.

3   Undo the three nuts (39, 57) which hold the lower damper mounting plates to the lower suspension arm and also the nut (54) on the lower damper mounting bolt (51) (Fig. 11.2).

4   Place a block under the front wheel and then lower the car so that the brackets and lower damper mounting come clear of the arm. Remove the lower mounting pin and detach the brackets.

5   Remove the upper mounting bolt and nut (49, 50) and the damper may be withdrawn from below. Before installing a replacement damper it should be bled as described in paragraph 3 of the previous Section.

6   The lower damper mounting bushes may be renewed separately if required but the top bush is part of the damper and is not supplied separately.

7   Reassembly is a reversal of the removal procedure but, for convenience, refit the lower mounting bushes and brackets loosely before reconnecting the top. Tighten all nuts to the specified torques.

4   Front springs - removal and replacement

All figures in text refer to Fig. 11.8.

1   Proceed as for front damper removal as described in Section 3, as far as paragraph 4 inclusive. Slacken also the nut (36) on the lower arm fulcrum pin (35). The coil spring is now held in compression by the lower steering joint (24) to the steering arm. Obviously the joint cannot be separated from the arm without taking measures to control the expansion of the spring when the lower arm is released. With a spring compressor this is no problem. A spring compressor can be made using short lengths of iron rod with the ends bent over to form hooks. Three of these will hold the coils of the spring sufficiently to enable the lower arm to be disengaged.

2   Alternatively, one may proceed as follows: Jack-up the lower suspension arm and then support the car under the front crossmember in the centre.

3   Place a block of wood between the spring upper mounting and the upper wishbone to hold the wishbone up in position.

4   Disconnect the lower suspension arm balljoint as described in Section 5.

5   Lower the jack under the lower suspension arm until the spring is relaxed. The spring may then be detached.

6   Replacement is a reversal of this procedure. Make sure that the spring locates correctly in the lower arm seat and that the tapers of

the balljoint pin and steering knuckle are perfectly clean and dry before reconnection.

7   When the weight of the car is finally resting on the suspension, retighten the lower arm fulcrum bolt to the specified torque.

5   Front suspension arm balljoints - removal and replacement

1   The front suspension balljonts will need renewal if they are worn beyond the acceptable limits. This wear is one of the items checked when MOT tests become necessary. The lower joint can be checked by jacking the cap up so that the wheel hangs free and then placing another jack under the lower suspension arm and raising the arm so that movement in the joint can be detected. If there is any movement the joint must be renewed.

2   To remove the joint, first take off the self-locking nut (32) (Fig. 11.8) from the pin located in the steering knuckle.

3   Separate the joint from the knuckle. This can only be done with surety by using a claw clamp. However, it is possible to drive through but only if the knuckle is firmly supported. The joint will almost certainly be damaged in the process. Another method is to strike the side of the knuckle where the pin goes through whilst holding the head of another hammer on the opposite side. This has a squeezing out effect on the tapered pin. The lower suspension arm will only move a limited way as it is held by the front damper.

4   The car should then be jacked-up under the front crossmember, a block placed under the wheel, and the car lowered again until the lower balljoint is clear of the knuckle and can be got at for removal from the arm.

5   To remove the joint from the arm, first remove the circlip and washer.

6   Using a piece of tube, drive the joint out of the arm. It may be necessary to put a block of wood under the arm to provide a firm support for this (Fig. 11.4).

7   Drive in a new joint so that the splines engage in the arm. Then fit the special washer with the float lined up and the concave side upwards and replace the circlip (Fig. 11.5).

8   Reconnect the pin to the steering knuckle ensuring that the mating surfaces of the taper are clean. Replace the nut.

9   The upper arm balljoint can be checked by jacking the car up and rocking the wheel whilst holding the joint to detect any play. If there is any play the joint must be renewed. This necessitates removal of the upper wishbone (see Section 6).

10 With the upper wishbone removed, the four rivets holding the joint must be drilled out without damaging the holes in the arm.

11 The holes in the arm must then be drilled out to 5/16 inch (8 mm). The new joint will be supplied with the necessary mounting bolts. Install these with the heads uppermost and tighten the nuts to the specified torque.

12 Replace the arm as described in Section 6.

6   Front suspension arms - removal and replacement

Figures in the text refer to Fig. 11.8.

1   The suspension arms will need to be removed if the bushes are worn. Also the upper suspension arm needs to be removed in order to renew the balljoint.

2   To remove the upper arm, jack-up the suspension under the lower arm and then remove the upper balljoint from the steering knuckle. This entails removal of the unit. The joint can then be removed as described in Section 5.

3   Next, remove the long fulcrum bolt (21) and nut (23) which hold the wishbone to the crossmember. If necessary, it is permissible to bend back the lashing eye (used for securing the car when carried on a transporter) which may get in the way when withdrawing the bolt. The arm can then be taken off.

4   To renew the bushes (13) calls for care as the arms of the wishbone must not be distorted during the course of removing and replacing the bushes. It is best to get the old ones out by cutting through them.

5   New bushes should be lubricated with soapy water and drawn in. Use a long nut and bolt together with a tubular spacer (on the inside of the arm) and large washers to ensure the bushes are drawn in square. Under no circumstances should attempts be made to drive the bushes in with a hammer.

6   Replace the arm in the reverse order of removal but do not tighten

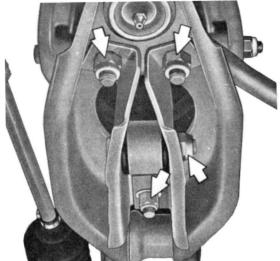

Fig. 11.2. Front suspension lower arm. Nuts (arrowed) to be removed when removing damper lower mounting

Fig. 11.4. Front suspension lower balljoint - driving out a joint with a piece of tube

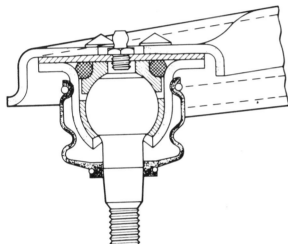

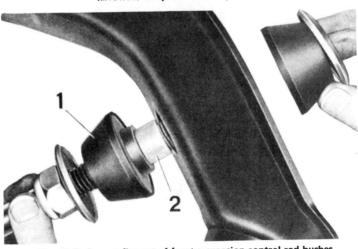

Fig. 11.5. Front suspension lower balljoint - correct position of flat (arrowed) on special assembly washer

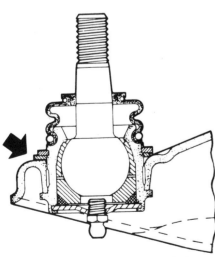

Fig. 11.3. Front suspension upper and lower balljoints — Cross section. Note special washer and retaining circlip (arrowed) for lower joint retention in the arm

Fig. 11.6. Correct fitment of front suspension control rod bushes

1   Rubber bush with collar   2   Spacer

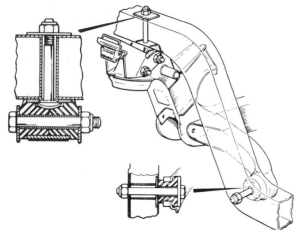

Fig. 11.7. Front suspension crossmember. Detail of body frame mountings

the nut on the fulcrum bolt to the full torque until the weight of the car is resting on the suspension.

7   To remove the lower suspension arm, proceed as for removal of the front spring as described in Section 4. Then remove the fulcrum bolt, and the arm can be drawn away from the mounting brackets.

8   The single large bush needs careful treatment when removed, otherwise the arm may be distorted. Do not try and drive it out. Use a bolt, spacer and washers and draw it out. Note that there is a steel sleeve on the outside of the bush which must not be left behind.

9   The new bush should be oiled on the steel sleeve to assist fitting. Make sure it is drawn in from the side that will not let it foul the lip inside the arm. When installed, the centre sleeve should project equally on each side.

10 Replacement of the arm is in the reverse order of removal. Do not tighten the fulcrum bolt nut until the weight of the car is resting on the suspension.

7   Front suspension control rods - removal and replacement

All numbers refer to Fig. 11.8.

1   The front suspension lower arms are stabilised fore and aft by a rod (37) which is bolted to their outer ends, and located in rubber bushes (40) at the other end into the front crossmember support stays. The length of the rod is adjustable to achieve the correct degree of castor angle on the front wheels.

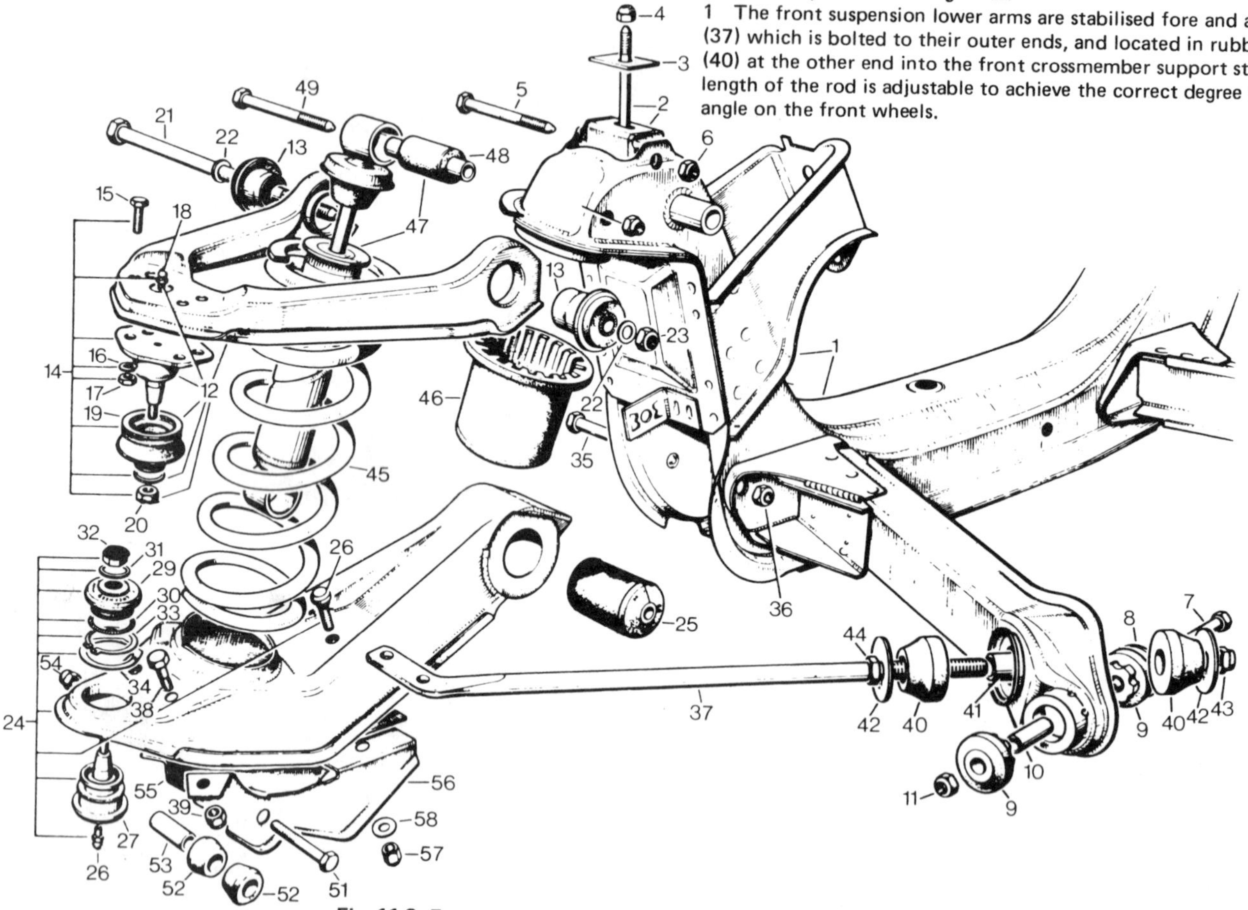

Fig. 11.8. Front suspension and crossmember - exploded illustration

1 Main crossmember	16 Washer	31 Boot ring	46 Spring insulator *
2 Crossmember mounting	17 Nut	32 Nut	47 Damper assembly
3 Plate	18 Grease nipple	33 Circlip	48 Damper bush
4 Nut	19 Boot	34 Washer	49 Damper mounting bolt
5 Mounting bolt	20 Nut	35 Lower arm bolt	50 Nut
6 Nut	21 Upper arm bolt	36 Nut	51 Damper mounting bolt
7 Brace mounting bolt	22 Washer	37 Control rod	52 Bush
8 Washer	23 Nut - self-locking	38 Control rod securing bolt	53 Spacer
9 Insulator	24 Lower arm assembly	39 Nut	54 Nut
10 Spacer	25 Lower arm bush	40 Insulator	55 Anchor bracket
11 Nut	26 Bolt	41 Spacer	56 Anchor bracket
12 Upper arm assembly	27 Lower arm balljoint	42 Washer	57 Nut
13 Upper arm bushes	28 Grease nipple	43 Nut	58 Washer
14 Upper arm balljoint	29 Boot	44 Nut	
15 Bolt	30 Spring garter	45 Spring	

* The spring insulator fits between the spring and damper at the top end.

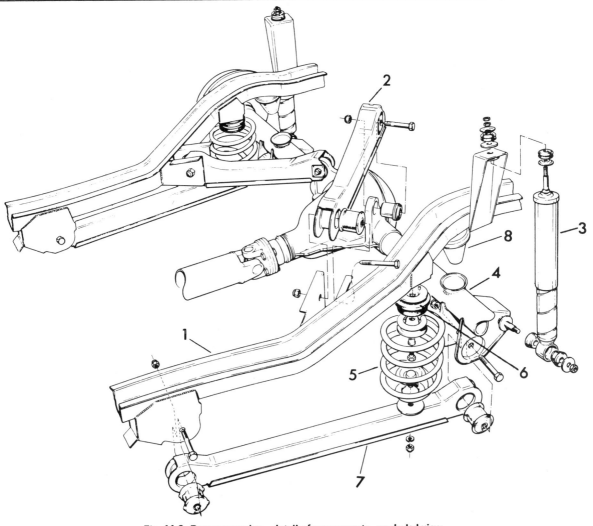

Fig. 11.9. Rear suspension - detail of components - exploded view

| 1 | Body frame side rail | 3 | Telescopic damper | 5 | Spring | 7 | Lower longitudinal arm |
| 2 | Upper radius arm | 4 | Rear axle tube | 6 | Upper spring seat | | |

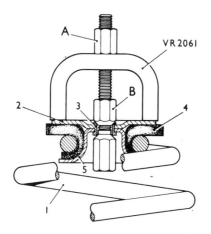

Fig. 11.10. Rear suspension - spring upper seat detail cross section showing special tool being used to peen the centre bush

A,B	Peening tool	3	Bush
1	Spring	4	Insulator
2	Upper seat	5	Retainer

2 If the control rod bushes need renewal it will be necessary to remove the rod first.

3 Jack up the suspension under the lower arm and remove the two nuts and bolts (38 and 39) securing the forward end to the suspension arm.

4 Slacken the two nuts (43 and 44) noting the position of the inner one first in relation to the thread. Then remove the end one (43) followed by the washer (42) and half bush. The rod may then be drawn out.

5 Return the inner nut to its original position before fitting new bushes and then replace the arm in the reverse order of removal. Fit the bushes correctly (Fig. 11.6).

6 Tighten the rear nut to the specified torque.

7 It is advisable to have the steering geometry checked at a garage, with suitable testing equipment, after removal and replacement of these control rods.

8 Front crossmember - removal, checking and replacement

1 Under certain circumstances it may be advantageous to remove the front suspension, as a complete assembly, from the car. It is attached to the underbody side members at two points on each side, one at the top and the other at the rear of the bracing arm at each side as shown in Fig. 11.7.

2 With the car jacked up and supported on stands under the body, disconnect the steering column from the steering gear (see Section 16) and disconnect the hydraulic brake line unions.

3 Support the axle beam in the centre and then undo the nuts from

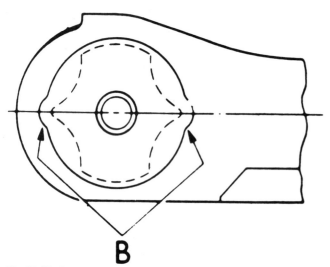

Fig. 11.11. Rear suspension arm bushes

1 Plain bush
2 Steel jacketed bush
   (heavy duty)

A Lip in arm fabrication
   requiring bush to be pressed
   in, in direction of arrow

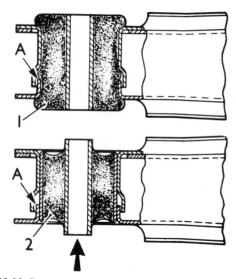

Fig. 11.12. Rear suspension - longitudinal arm front bush showing
Special locating lugs (B) to fit in arm preventing rotating of bush

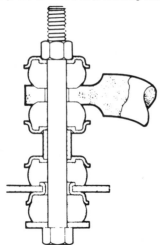

Fig. 11.13. Front stabiliser bar assembly
Showing the assembly order of the bushes, cups and washers

the upper and lower mounting bolts - four in all. Then remove the
lower bolts, and the axle assembly can be lowered from the car.
4   Renew the axle mountings, if necessary, before replacing the axle
assembly.

9 Rear dampers - removal and replacement

1   The rear dampers will need removal if their mounting bushes are
worn or if indications are that the unit is no longer performing
properly.
2   It is not necessary to raise the car to remove the dampers but, if it is
raised, the axle should be supported as well.
3   To detach the top mounting, remove the rubber plug from the
wheel arch inside the boot when the two upper nuts will be accessible.
The slotted spindle will need holding firmly whilst the nuts are
removed.
4   The lower mounting eye may be disconnected by removing the nut
on the mounting pin and pulling it out.
5   Replacement is a reversal of the removal procedure but ensure that
the damper is first bled as described in paragraph 3, of Section 3. All
bushes are renewable; care should be taken to arrange the bushes and
washers correctly as shown in Fig. 11.9.
6   Tighten the top securing nuts down to the bottom of the stud
threads.

10 Rear springs - removal and replacement

1   Jack-up the car and support the body under the rear frame
members on stands. Then support the axle on a jack.
2   Undo the lower spring mounting stud nut which is underneath the
longitudinal suspension arm.
3   Lower the jack under the axle until the suspension arm is clear of
the spring.
4   Using a socket wrench, remove the upper bolt which is in the
centre of the upper spring seat and fits into a captive nut in the side
member.
5   Lift out the spring complete with the upper mounting seat.
6   New springs, spring seats, rubber insulators and retainers are
supplied individually. They are all assembled and held together by
the centre bush which is peened over on to the upper seat. Fig.11.10
shows a cross section of the assembly with a special Vauxhall tool
used to draw the new bush into position and peen over the top. If
other improvised tools are used to carry out this job, the main thing
to remember is that the upper seat spring retainer must be held
tightly together when the bush is being peened over.
7   Note that the upper seat has a dowel peg which locates in a
corresponding hole in the sidemember. This must be correctly
positioned when refitting the spring assembly which is otherwise a
straightforward reversal of the removal procedure.

11 Rear suspension arms - removal and replacement

1   If the rubber mounting bushes at each end of any of the arms are
worn, it will be necessary to remove the arms to replace them.
2   The upper (radius) arms are bushed at the front end and bolted
between brackets on the rear body frame member. The rear end
locates over a lug on the rear axle, which is rubber bushed and is
secured by a bolt and nut.
3   Simply by removing the nuts and bolts at each end, the arm can be
removed.
4   The front bush should be removed and replaced in exactly the
same manner as described for the front suspension lower arm in Section
6.
5   The rear bush will need drawing out of the lug on the axle using a
long nut and bolt with a tubular spacer and large flat washers. The new
bush should be drawn in, in the same manner after it has been well
lubricated with soapy water.
6   Replace the arm and bolts but before tightening the nuts to the
specified torque let the weight of the car settle on the springs.
7   The lower (longitudinal) arms can be removed after first raising
and supporting the car on stands under the body side frame members
and placing a jack under the axle.
8   Remove the nut securing the lower spring mounting plate to the

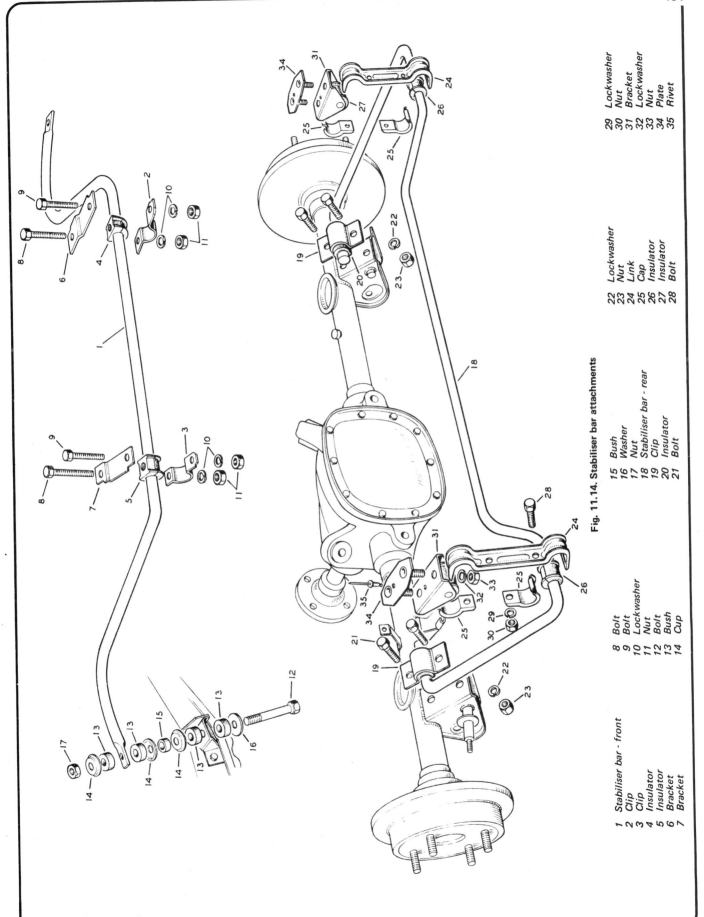

Fig. 11.14. Stabiliser bar attachments

1	Stabiliser bar - front
2	Clip
3	Clip
4	Insulator
5	Insulator
6	Bracket
7	Bracket

8	Bolt
9	Bolt
10	Lockwasher
11	Nut
12	Bolt
13	Bush
14	Cup

15	Bush
16	Washer
17	Nut
18	Stabiliser bar - rear
19	Clip
20	Insulator
21	Bolt

22	Lockwasher
23	Nut
24	Link
25	Cap
26	Insulator
27	Insulator
28	Bolt

29	Lockwasher
30	Nut
31	Bracket
32	Lockwasher
33	Nut
34	Plate
35	Rivet

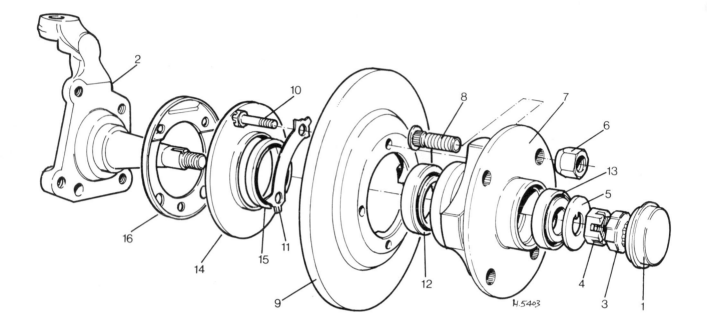

Fig. 11.15. Front hub assembly - exploded view

1	Dust cap	5	Washer	9	Brake disc	13	Bearing, outer
2	Steering knuckle	6	Wheel nut	10	Bolt	14	Shield, outer
3	Retainer	7	Hub	11	Tab washer	15	Oil seal
4	Nut	8	Wheel stud	12	Bearing, inner	16	Shield, inner

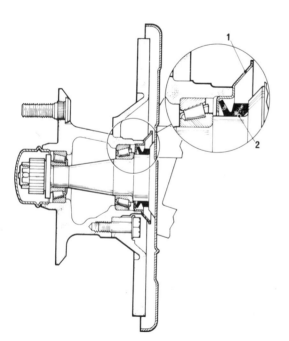

Fig. 11.16. Sectional view of the later type hub assembly

1 Sealing collar   2 Seal

arm and then lower the jack until the arm is clear of the spring.

9   Remove the mounting bolts and nuts at each end and the arm can then be detached.

10 The same precautions for removal and replacement of the bushes apply as for the upper amrs. In addition, the front bush has two locating ridges which must bet set correctly into the arm as shown in Fig. 11.12.

11 When refitting the arm, replace the mounting bolts but do not tighten the nuts to the specified torque until the weight of the car is resting on the springs.

12 Front and rear stabilizer bars - removal and replacement

1   The front stabilizer bar is attached to the front axle crossmember braces through rubber-mounted brackets. Flanges on the ends of the bar are connected by rubber bushes, link bolts and nuts to the suspension lower arms. Removal is straightforward and involves no special techniques.

2   The rear stabilizer bar is connected between brackets at each end of the rear axle and is supported by links attached to the underbody. Again, removal is straightforward.

3   When either the front or rear bar is removed, inspect it for distortion or corrosion; fit a new bar if necessary. Inspect the rubber bushes for evidence of deterioation and renew if necessary.

4   When reassembling, install the front stabilizer bar, bushes, cups and spacers in the order shown in Fig. 11.13. Assemble a flat washer against the bolt head and tighten the nut to the end of the thread.

5   When reassembling the rear stabilizer bar the only critical point is that the rubber insulators should be installed with the slit horizontal.

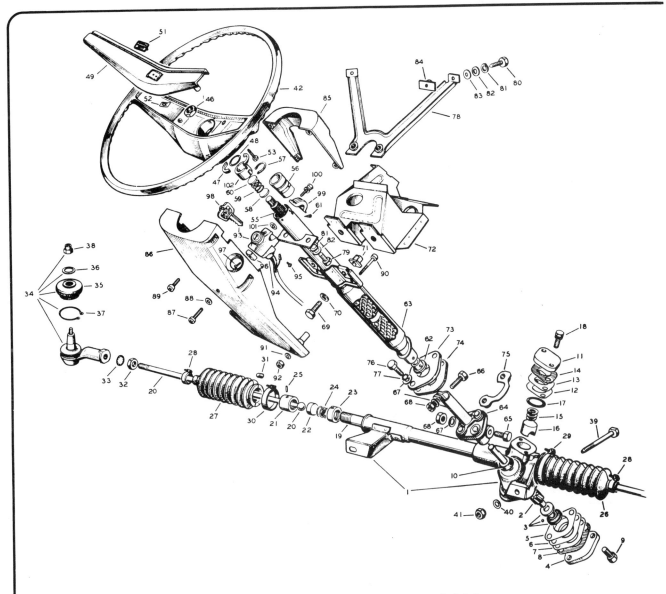

Fig. 11.17. Steering column and steering gear - exploded view

1	Housing and bush assembly	26	Boot	56	Housing	81 Lock washer
2	Pinion, rhd	27	Boot	57	Circlip	82 Washer
3	Bearing	28	Clip	58	Washer	83 Washer
4	Cover	29	Clip	59	Spring	84 Plate assembly
5	Shim, .005 in.	30	Clip	60	Washer	85 Canopy (upper)
6	Shim, .0075 in.	31	Cap	61	Screw	86 Canopy (lower)
7	Shim, .0925 in.	32	Locknut	62	Bearing assembly (lower)	87 Screw
8	Gasket	33	Washer	63	Cover	88 Washer
9	Bolt	34	Joint assembly	64	Coupling assembly	89 Screw
10	Seal	35	Boot	65	Bolt	90 Screw
11	Cover	36	Retainer	66	Bolt	91 Washer
12	Shim, .005 in.	37	Circlip	67	Washer	92 Nut
13	Shim, .0075 in.	38	Nut	68	Nut	93 Steering column lock
14	Gasket	39	Bolt	69	Bolt	94 Ignition and starter
15	Spring	40	Washer	70	Lockwasher	switch
16	Yoke	41	Nut	71	Nut	95 Screw
17	'O' ring	42	Steering wheel	72	Support assembly	96 Key release button
18	Bolt and washer	46	Nut	73	Bracket steering column	97 Screw
19	Rack, rhd	47	Collar		support (lower)	98 Key
20	Tie rod	48	Band	74	Insulator, steering column	99 Clamp
21	Housing	49	Pad assembly		lower support	100 Bolt
22	Seat	51	Medallion	75	Plate	101 Washer
23	Locknut	52	Clip	76	Bolt	102 Direction indicator
24	Spring	53	Screw	77	Lockwasher	cancelling sleeve
25	Pin	55	Steering shaft	78	Brace assembly	
				79	Bolt	
				80	Bolt	

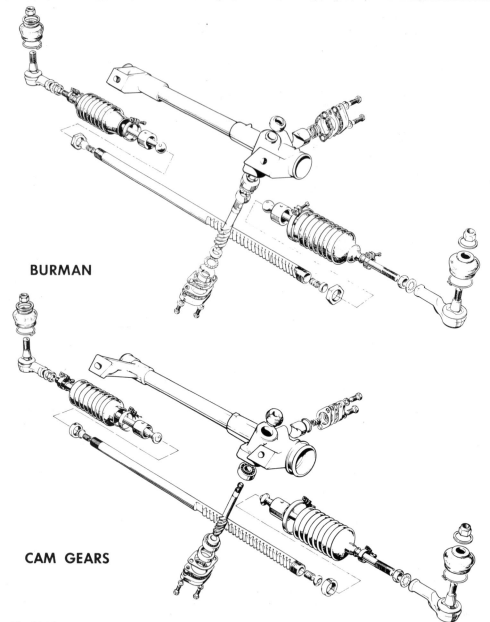

BURMAN

CAM GEARS

Fig. 11.18. Steering gear exploded illustrations showing differences between Burman and Cam gears types

Fig. 11.19. Steering shaft coupling showing peg (arrowed) on shaft which engages in slot in coupling

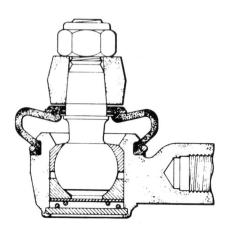

Fig. 11.20. Steering track rod outer end balljoint cross section

13 Front wheel hub bearings - inspection and adjustment

1   The steering qualities of the car will deteriorate if the front wheel bearings are maladjusted or worn.
2   To check the bearings, first jack-up the car so that the wheel is clear of the ground. Check that the wheel spins freely with the brakes off.
3   Then grip the edge of the tyre at the top and bottom and try and rock it in a vertical plane. If movement can be felt it is normally due to looseness in the bearing but at the same time it should be noted whether there is any sign of lateral movement in either the upper or lower suspension arm balljoints. (If there is, they must be renewed as described in Section 5).
4   There should be no detectable movement in the wheel bearings and if there is, they should be adjusted. Fig. 11.15 gives an exploded view of a front hub.
5   Remove the wheel and then tap the dust cover out of the centre of the hub.
6   Remove the split pin and retainer, using a tubular spanner, tighten the nut whilst continuing to revolve the wheel. Then slacken the nut off and retighten it until there is 0.002 in (0.051 mm) gap between the face of the nut and the knuckle spindle washer.
7   Back the nut off a little further, if necessary, so that the retainer and (new) split pin can be fitted then check that the wheel rotates freely without binding. The total endplay must now be between 0.002 and 0.005 in (0.051 to 0.127 mm). If any roughness is felt on spinning the wheel the bearings should be removed for further examination.
8   Provided that the adjustment is satisfactory, bend over the ends of the split pin and replace the dust cap. Finally fit the wheel and lower the car to the ground.

14 Front wheel hubs and bearings - removal, inspection and replacement

1   Jack-up the car and remove the roadwheel.
2   Remove the brake caliper, as described in Chapter 9.
3   Remove the hub grease cap, split pin and nut retainer.
4   Remove the hub nut and the washer behind it which is keyed to the shaft.
5   Withdraw the hub together with the brake disc.
6   The bearing races will have come off with the hub, and the inner race of the outer bearing will be loose so that it can be taken out.
7   The inner bearing will need to be driven out with a drift from the inside of the hub. Locate the drift against the outside race. The oil seal will come out with the bearing. **Note:** If a sealing collar is fitted between the oil seal and the inner bearing, pick out the oil seal first of all then remove the sealing collar (Fig. 11.16). The outside race of the outer bearing should come out easily, but may need tapping from the inside with a drift.
8   Thoroughly clean the bearings and examine the rollers and races for signs of wear. If in doubt, renew them. Wear can be detected by running perfectly clean, lightly oiled bearings in their races and feeling for traces of roughness. Blue discolouration indicates overheating, but brown discolouration will only be lubricant stain and is not to be taken as an adverse indication.
9   Reassembly of outer bearing races into the hub is a reversal of the removal procedure. Make sure that the open ends of the tapers of the outer races face outwards from the centre of the hub. Pack the inner bearing inner race and rollers with a general purpose grease, and place it in position in the hub.
10 With the inner bearing fit a new seal, which recesses into the hub behind the bearing. The lip of the seal should face to the centre of the hub. **Note:** If a sealing collar is fitted, this will need to be installed before the oil seal (Fig. 11.16), which itself is different from the previously used type. The sealing collar and revised seal can be used to replace the earlier seal provided that the ground surface of the seal land on the steering knuckle and the entire mating surface of the seal are coated with Loctite Grade AVX.
11 Pack the outer bearing inner race and rollers with the recommended grease, place it in position and refit the complete hub assembly to the spindle. Replace the washer and nut, then adjust the hub bearing, as described in Section 13.
12 Replace the dust cap, which should be half full of the recommended grease.

13 Replace the disc brake caliper (refer to Chapter 9, if necessary).
14 Replace the roadwheel and lower the car to the ground.

15 Steering mechanism - inspection

1   The steering mechanism on the Magnum is uncomplicated and easy to check. The owner can save himself a lot of trouble by regular examination, apart from, of course, keeping a check for his own safety.
2   Assuming that the suspension joints and bushes and front wheel bearings have been checked and found in order, the steering check involves tracing the amount of lost motion between the rim of the steering wheel and roadwheels. If the rim of the steering wheel can be moved more than ½ inch (13 mm) as its periphery with no sign of movement at either, or both, of the front wheels it may be assumed that there is wear at some point. If there are signs of lost motion, jack up the car at the front and support it under the front crossmember so that both wheels hang free.
3   Grip each wheel in turn and rock it in the direction it would move when steering. It will be possible to feel any play. Check first for any sign of lateral play in the balljoints which connect the tie rods from the steering gear to the steering arms on the wheel knuckles. This is the more common area for wear to occur and, if any is apparent, the balljoint/s must be renewed.
4   Having checked the balljoints, next grip the tie rod and get someone to move the steering wheel. Do this with the bonnet open and if there is any play still apparent, look first to see whether the coupling in the steering column shaft is causing the trouble. If it is, it should be renewed.
5   Finally, if play still exists, it must be in the steering gear itself. This is more serious (and expensive). If either of the rubber boots at each end of the gear housing is damaged, resulting in loss of oil from the unit, then various bearings and teeth on the rack and pinion may have been severely worn. In such cases renewal of the complete steering gear assembly may be necessary. Certainly adjustments will be required.

16 Steering gear - examination, adjustment, removal and replacement

1   Assuming that all balljoints and front wheel bearings are in order, it may be necessary to remove and replace, or renovate, the steering gear if there is excessive play between the steering shaft and the steering tie rods. This can be checked by gripping the inner end of both the rods in turn near the rubber boot, and getting someone to rock the steering wheel. If the wheel moves more than about ½ inch (13 mm) without moving the steering tie rod, then the wear is sufficient to justify overhaul. If the rubber boots have leaked oil they will also need renewal and, in order to do this and effectively refill the unit with the proper oil, it is easiest in the long run to remove the assembly from the car.
2   To remove the steering gear from the car, first slacken the upper half of the coupling from the steering column by undoing the pinch bolt. Then disconnect both tie rod outer ball joints from the steering arms as described in Section 6. The three mounting bolts holding the assembly to the front crossmember may then be removed and the unit taken off. If the coupling tends to stick on the splines of the steering column do not strike it, but ease it off by moving the steering wheel from side to side.
3   If it is necessary to replace only the rubber boots and refill the assembly with lubricant, remove both outer balljoints from the tie rods together with the locknuts, having noted their original position carefully. Slacken off the boot retaining clips noting their position in relation to the assembly housing. If the steering arms are dirty, clean them thoroughly and slide off the old boots.
4   Refit the clips to new boots and slide them onto the rods. Tighten the clips in position on one boot only. Stand the unit on end, refill the housing with ¼ pint (no more) of SAE 90 EP lubricant, and then refit the other boot and tighten the clips.
5   It is possible to alleviate some of the play in the gear (between rack and pinion) by checking that the yoke pre-load is correct.
6   Remove the yoke cover plate and remove the shims and spring followed by the yoke.
7   Replace the yoke and cover without the spring or any shims and lightly tighten the bolts.
8   Measure the gap between the cover and the housing with a feeler gauge. The thickness of the shims should be the gap measurement

plus 0.0005 to 0.003 in (0.013 to 0.076 mm) on Burman units, or
plus 0.0005 to 0.006 in (0.013 to 0.152 mm) on Cam Gear units.
Make up the shim packs accordingly and reassemble. Adjust the shims
required to give a maximum turning torque on the pinion of 12 lb in.
9   Similarly, any sign of endfloat and slackness in the pinion shaft
may be taken up by removing the cover opposite the pinion extension
and reducing the thickness of the shims behind the cover accordingly.
In this case the shims should be 0.001 to 0.005 in (0.025 to 0.127 mm)
less than the measured clearance between the cover and housing.
10 It must be emphasised that the adjustments mentioned in this
paragraph are not sufficient to compensate for extreme wear. Before
making them, therefore, it must be decided whether the wear apparent
is beyond adjustment, or sufficient to warrant adjustment anyway.
11 Any play in the tie rod *inner* balljoints may be adjusted but involves
drilling and re-pinning the joints and this calls for precision work.
12 Replacement of the assembly is a reversal of the procedure as
described in paragraph 2. Make sure that the steering rack is in its
central position and, if the coupling has been detached from the pinion,
line up the bolt hole in the lower part of the coupling with the flat on
the pinion. Replace but leave the bolt slack. When fitting the upper
coupling to the column line up the peg with the coupling slot. When
everything is assembled tighten first the steering gear mounting bolts,
then lower the lower coupling pinch bolt followed by the upper pinch
bolt. Before tightening the cotter pin nut securing the coupling flange
to the pinion shaft make sure that the hub of the steering wheel is not
rubbing on the column shroud below it. This may be caused by the
steering column dropping down a little when the steering gear unit was
disconnected. Lift the steering wheel before tightening the cotter
clamp nut. Tighten all nuts and bolts to the correct torques as specified.
13 The front wheel toe-in should then be checked at a garage with the
proper equipment.

17 Steering trackrod outer balljoints - removal and replacement

1   The removal of the balljoints is necessary if they are to be renewed,
or if the rubber boots on the steering gear are being renewed.
2   It is not necessary to jack the cap up but the increase in height
above ground level may make it more convenient to do so.
3   Slacken the self-locking nut, completely remove it to clear the
threads, and replace it after oiling the threads until the head of the nut
is level with the end of the stud. This will protect the threads in
subsequent operations if the same joint is being replaced.
4   If a claw clamp is being used to 'break' the taper of the joint pin

from the steering arm, the joint may be disconnected without further
ado.
5   If no claw clamp is available and it is necessary to strike the pin out,
it is essential to provide a really firm support under the steering arm
first. A firm tap with a normal weight hammer is all that is then
necessary to move the pin out of the steering arm. Another method
is to strike one side of the arm whilst holding the head of another
hammer against the opposite side. This tends to 'squeeze' the taper
pin out.
6   If the nut now turns the pin when trying to remove it, (despite
the precaution taken in paragraph 3) jam the pin back into the arm
with the jack to hold it whilst the nut is removed. If difficulty is
experienced with a joint being renewed then cut it off.
7   Once the balljoint is clear of the arm, slacken the locknut but leave
it at its original position. The joint may then be removed and a new
one fitted by screwing it up as far as the locknut. The pin should
point upwards and then be fitted into the steering arm.
8   As the nut is self-locking it will be necessary to prevent the pin
turning whilst tightening it. This can be done by putting a jack under
the joint so that the weight of the wheel rests on the taper.
9   Tighten the locknut on the tie rod.
10 It is advisable to have the front wheel alignment checked as soon
as possible.

18 Steering knuckle and steering arm

1   Neither the steering knuckle (or stub axle as it is sometimes called)
nor steering arm, normally need any attention. It is possible, however,
in the case of severe shock or damage to the front suspension and
steering, that either or both of them could be bent or distorted. If it is
necessary to remove them for checking or renewal proceed as follows:
2   Remove the front hub as described in Section 14.
3   Detach the upper and lower wishbone balljoints, as described in
Section 5.
4   Detach the steering arm outer balljoint, as described in Section 17.
5   Separate the steering knuckle from the steering arm by undoing
the bolts and nuts which hold them together.
6   Reassembly and replacement is a reversal of the procedure. Bleed
the brake system when reassembly is complete (see Chapter 9).

19 Steering geometry - checking and adjustment

1   Unless the front axle and suspension has been damaged, the castor

Fig. 11.22. Steering column lock showing shear head bolts (arrowed)

Fig. 11.21. The steering column lock used on later models
The pushbutton is on the underside of the canopy

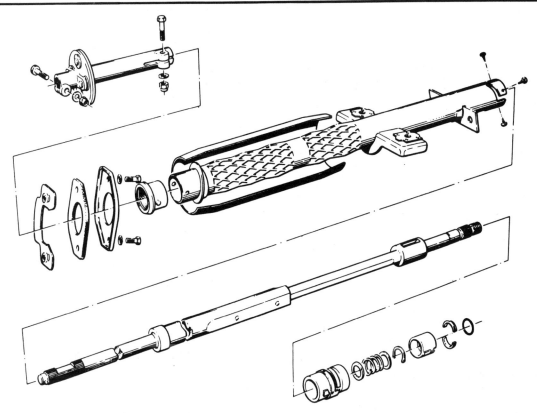

Fig. 11.23. Steering column and shaft - detailed illustration

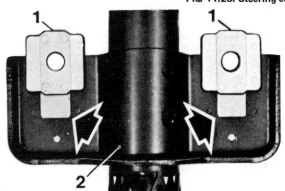

Fig. 11.24. Steering column upper mounting bracket (early type - also see Fig. 11.31)

1 Shear type mountings
2 Column

Arrows point to gaps indicating collapse of column

Fig. 11.25. Steering column and shaft. Withdrawing the shaft and bearing together from the column

angle, camber angle and steering pivot angles will not alter, provided, of course, that the suspension balljoints and wishbone fulcrum pin bushes are not worn in any way.

2   The toe-in of the front wheels is a measurement which may vary more frequently and could pass unnoticed if, for example, a steering tie rod was bent. When fitting new tie rod balljoints, for example, it will always be necessary to reset the toe-in. Similarly, the control rods running back from the lower suspension arm, if bent, would affect the castor angle.

3   Indications of incorrect wheel alignment (toe-in) are uneven tyre wear on the front tyres and erratic steering particularly when turning. To check toe-in accurately needs optical aligning equipment, so get a garage to do it. Ensure that they examine the tie rods for straightness and all balljoints and wheel bearings at the same time, if you have not done so yourself.

20 Steering wheel - removal and replacement

1   The steering wheel is located on splines to the column shaft, seats on tapered split collars and is secured by a nut.

2   First remove the centre medallion by undoing the two screws on the underside of the spoke.

3   Undo the nut with a tubular spanner and then mark the relative position of the wheel to the shaft by making two marks with a centre punch. Then pull the wheel off.

4   Replacement is a reversal of the removal procedure noting the following points: Check that the roadwheels point straight-ahead and the wheel spoke is in the 'twenty past eight' position, if you have not made a mark. The split collars should be held in position on the column with a rubber band to aid assembly. The direction indicator cancelling sleeve should be positioned so that it lines up with the lugs on the wheel hub boss.

21 Steering shaft coupling - removal and replacement

1   The coupling is supplied complete and a new one should be fitted if any signs of wear are apparent.

2   To remove the coupling, the steering gear mounting bolts should be slackened to allow it to drop down sufficiently for the coupling to be drawn off. Once the pinch bolts are slackened on the upper and lower halves it can be drawn off. Any tendency to stick must be overcome by rocking from side to side. Impacts from hitting it with a hammer could render useless the shock absorbing material of the steering column.

3   When replacing the coupling, follow the procedure described in paragraph 12, of Section 15.

22 Steering colum lock

1   The ignition and starter switch key also operates a lock on to the

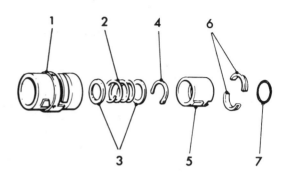

Fig. 11.26. Steering shaft bearing details

1   Bearing assembly   5   Indicator cancelling sleeve
2   Spring   6   Split collars
3   Retainer washers   7   Collar retaining band
4   Circlip

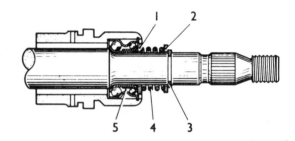

Fig. 11.27. Steering column and shaft upper bearing assembly - cross
                                section

1   Thick washer   4   Spring
2   Thin washer   5   Bearing
3   Circlip

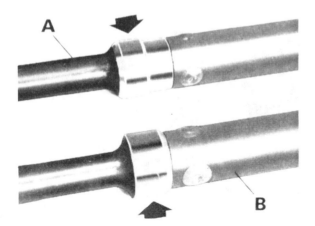

Fig. 11.28. The steering shaft and bearing

A   Later shaft   C   Later type bearing
B   Earlier shaft   D   Earlier type bearing

steering column. Great care must be taken to ensure that if the car is moved or towed without the engine running that the key is not in the lock position. Otherwise the steering will be inoperative. Later models have a push button on the underside of the column which makes operation of the lock a two-handed process to prevent inadvertent switching to the lock position whilst the car is in motion.

2   In order to remove the lock for any reason, the steering column assembly must be removed first. The lock is clamped to the column and two shear head bolts are used which must be drilled out with a 1/8 inch (No 31) drill and removed with a screw extractor (Fig. 11.22).

3   When fitting the lock use only shear head bolts. Tighten them sufficiently to hold the lock in position for testing and finally tighten until the heads shear off.

23 Steering column, steering shaft and bearings - removal, inspection and replacement

1   The steering column assembly is designed to collapse under impact to lessen the risk of injury to the driver. The column has a central section of expanded metal and the steering shaft is telescopic. The telescopic halves are maintained in their normal operating position by a plastic substance injected between them which shears on impact.

It is most important that the assembly and its components are handled with care. Any damage causing them to bend or lose their correct dimensions means that they will have to be renewed.

2   The steering column and mounting bracket may be inspected in-situ. The upper mounting bracket (do not confuse it with the upper column brace bracket) under the dash panel is mounted on shear type pads which will also break if an excessive load is imparted on the steering wheel.

Examine the bracket to see whether there is any gap between the pads and the metal part of the bracket. If there is, it means that the bracket must have moved forward - indicating that the column has collapsed to a certain extent. The column must, therefore be renewed (Fig. 11.24).

3   To remove the column assembly, remove the steering wheel (Section 20) and slacken the pinch bolt securing the upper half of the coupling flange assembly (Section 21).

Remove the shroud surrounding the upper part of the column by taking out the screws (Fig. 11.25). Where a two-handed steering column lock is fitted, the pushbutton and key must be removed first.

Disconnect the leads from the combined horn/dipper/flasher switch and from the ignition switch.

4   Undo the bolts securing the upper support brace and the upper mounting bracket.

5   Slacken the bolts holding the plate at the bottom of the column and lift the whole assembly out.

6   The upper bearing and shaft are removed from the column together after the two screws securing the bearing to the column have been taken

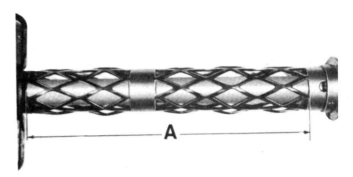

Fig. 11.29. Steering column collapsible section. Dimension 'A' is 10.37 inches minimum

Fig. 11.30. Steering column lower shaft bearing. Prising out bush from column

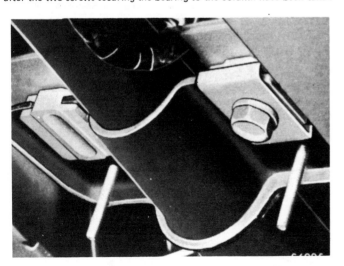

Fig. 11.31. The later type mounting bracket pads and U-shaped location plates

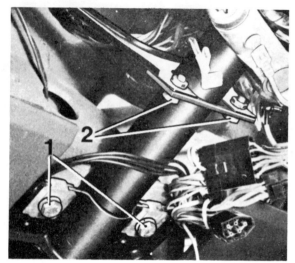

Fig. 11.32. Steering column. Upper attaching bolts at: 1 mounting bracket and 2 upper brace

out. The bearing is a bayonet fit and after turning it anticlockwise it can be drawn out (Figs. 11.25 and 11.26).

7   If the bearing is worn out it is best to replace the complete unit. Remove the retaining circlip, split collars and indicator cancelling sleeve to take it off the shaft (Fig. 11.27).

8   The shaft is checked by measuring its length which should be within 35.96/35.88 inch (91.34/91.14 cm). If outside these dimensions it should be renewed. A modified shaft is used on later cars to overcome the problem of steering column creak (Fig. 11.28). Whether the later type of shaft is used or the earlier type, the correct bearing must be used; the bearing for the later shaft is coloured black whereas the earlier bearing is light in colour (see paragraph 10).

9   The lattice work Section of the column should not be less than 10.37 inch (26.34 cm) in length. The lattice work is covered by a plastic shroud which can be prised off in two halves. The two halves can be refitted by tacking them with a hot iron in five or six spots along the seam.

10   The bearing at the bottom of the column is a nylon bush. Two small lugs on it engage in a snap fit into two holes in the column. To renew it prise it out and push in another (Fig. 11.30).

11   When fitting a new upper bearing to the shaft it will be necessary to drill two holes in the outer sleeve with a No 31 drill to accept the retaining screws. Do this when the bearing has been fitted into the column.

12   If the lower support bracket has inadvertently come apart due to undoing the screws too much, note that the nut plate (on the front side of the panel) should be replaced with the flat side against the panel and the open 'U' facing the centre line of the car. The insulation pad should be in good condition and, to assist pushing the column back into it, smear the inner edges with soap.

13   Reassembly and replacement of the column and shaft is a straight-forward reversal of the removal procedure. If the lower support bracket bolts were not slackened when the column was lifted out slacken them now and first introduce the bottom end of the column through it. Make sure that the peg on the end of the shaft engages the slot in the coupling. If the shear-type pads on the column mounting have slotted holes instead of the earlier round holes, ensure that U-shaped location plates are fitted (Fig. 11.31). Reassemble all the bracket bolts and tighten them in the following order: 1 Upper support bracket; 2 Lower bracket to dash panel; 3 Upper column brace bracket; 4 Coupling flange pinch bolt. Finally tighten the upper support bracket bolts to the specified torque.

14   Replace the steering wheel and column shroud. Where applicable, replace the steering lock pushbutton.

24 Wheels and tyres

1   To provide equal, and minimum wear from all the tyres, they should be rotated on the car at intervals of 6000 miles to the following pattern (this is only recommended for crossply and steel braced radial tyres):

Spare to offside rear
Offside rear to nearside front
Nearside front to nearside rear
Nearside rear to offside front
Offside front to spare

Wheels should be re-balanced when this is done. However, some owners baulk at the prospect of having to buy five new tyres all at once and tend to let two run on and replace a pair only. In this case the new pair should always be fitted to the front wheels, as these are the most important from the safety aspect of steering and braking.

2   Never mix tyres of a radial and crossply construction on the same car, as the basic design differences can cause unusual and, in certain conditions, very dangerous handling and braking characteristics. If an emergency should force the use of two different types, make sure the radials are on the rear wheels and drive particularly carefully. If three of the five wheels are fitted with radial tyres then make sure that no more than two radials are in use on the car (and those at the rear). At the earliest opportunity, revert to the radial ply tyres which were originally fitted as standard equipment. These have new roadholding characteristics which are far superior to crossply tyres.

3   Wheels are normally not subject to servicing problems but when tyres are renewed or changed the wheels should be balanced to reduce vibration and wear. If a wheel is suspected of damaged - caused by hitting a kerb or pot hole which could distort it out of true, change it and have it checked for balance and true running at the earliest opportunity.

4   When refitting wheels, ensure that the screw threads are clean, then apply a little general purpose grease. Do not overtighten the nuts. The maximum possible manual torque applied by the manufacturer's wheel brace is adequate. It also prevents excessive struggle when the same wheel brace has to be used in an emergency to remove the wheels. Overtightening may also distort the stud holes in the wheel causing it to run off centre and off balance.

25 Fault diagnosis - suspension and steering

Before diagnosing faults from the following chart, check that any irregularities are not caused by:

    1   Binding brakes.
    2   Incorrect 'mix' of radial and crossply tyres.
    3   Incorrect tyre pressures.
    4   Misalignment of the body frame or rear axle.

Symptom	Reason/s	Remedy
Steering wheel can be moved considerably before any sign of movement of the wheels is apparent	Wear in the steering linkage, gear and column coupling	Check movement in all joints and steering gear and overhaul and renew as required.
Vehicle difficult to steer in a consistent straight line - wandering	As above Wheel alignment incorrect (indicated by excessive or uneven tyre wear) Front wheel hub bearings loose or worn Worn balljoints, trackrods or suspension arms	As above. Check wheel alignment. Adjust or renew as necessary. Renew as necessary.
Steering stiff and heavy	Incorrect wheel alignment (indicated by excessive or uneven tyre wear) Excessive wear or seizure in one or more of the joints in the steering linkage or suspension arm balljoints Excessive wear in the steering gear unit	Check wheel alignment. Renew as necessary or grease the suspension unit balljoints. Adjust if possible or renew.
Wheel wobble and vibration	Roadwheels out of balance Roadwheels buckled Wheel alignment incorrect Wear in the steering linkage, suspension arm balljoints or suspension arm pivot bushes Broken front spring	Balance wheels. Check for damage. Check wheel alignment. Check and renew as necessary. Check and renew as necessary.
Excessive pitching and rolling on corners and during braking	Defective dampers and/or broken spring	Check and renew as necessary.

Chapter 12 Bodywork and fittings

Contents

Bonnet and boot lid and locks - elimination of rattles, removal and replacement 15	
Door catches - removal and replacement 12	
Door glasses - removal and replacement 10	
Doors - tracing of rattles and setting of latch striker pin 8	
Door trim panel and winder handles - removal and replacement ... 9	
Estate car - rear door hinges and lock 16	
Exterior door handles and latch buttons - removal and replacement 13	
Fan and ventilation/heater unit - removal and replacement ... 21	
Front and rear bumpers - removal and replacement 6	
General description 1	
Glovebox lid catch - removal, dismantling and replacement ... 23	

Grilles and exterior trim 18
Heater controls - adjustment and cable renewal 20
Heater/demister and ventilating system - general description ... 19
Interior latch handles - removal and replacement 14
Maintenance - bodywork and underframe 2
Maintenance - interior 3
Major bodywork damage - repair 5
Minor bodywork damage - repair 4
Seats 22
Weatherstrips 17
Window winder mechanism - removal and replacement 11
Windscreen, rear window and rear quarter fixed glass - removal and replacement 7

1 General description

The combined bodyshell and underframe is an all welded unitary structure of sheet steel. Openings in it provide for the engine compartment, luggage compartment, doors and front and rear windows. The rear axle is attached to the body by arms bolted directly to it on rubber bushes, and a detachable crossmember across the bottom of the engine compartment provides support for the engine and front suspension. A second detachable item is a central crossmember bridging the transmission tunnel which is the rear support of the engine/gearbox unit.

The body styles of the Magnum models have all appeared on other cars in the Vauxhall range. The 2-door and 4-door Saloons have the same basic bodyshell as the Viva HC models, and the Estate version is basically the Viva HC estate car. The Coupe version has the earlier Firenza bodyshell which was modified from the original Viva HC shape at the rear to give a fastback style.

2 Maintenance - bodywork and underframe

1 The general condition of a car's bodywork is the one thing that significantly affects its value. Maintenance is easy but needs to be regular and particular. Neglect, particularly after minor damage, can lead quickly to a further deterioration and costly repair bills. It is important also to keep watch on those parts of the car not immediately visible, for instance the underside, inside all the wheel arches and the lower part of the engine compartment. If your car is not fitted with mud flaps at the front, it is strongly recommended that they are installed. Vauxhall agents will supply them made to measure for the car at a very fair price. These protect the door undersills which are otherwise soon stripped to the bare metal by the water/grit slurry thrown up by the front wheels in wet weather.
2 The basic maintenance routine for the bodywork is washing - preferably with a lot of water, from a hose. This will remove all the loose solids whicy may have stuck to the car. It is important to flush these off in such a way as to prevent grit from scratching the finish. The wheel arches and underbody need washing in the same way to remove any accumulated mud which will retain moisture and tend to encourage rust. Paradoxically enough, the best time to clean the

underbody and wheel arches is in wet weather when the mud is thoroughly wet and soft. In very wet weather the underbody is usually cleaned of large accumulations automatically and this is a good time for inspection.
3 Periodically, it is a good idea to have the whole of the underside of the car steam cleaned, engine compartment included, so that a thorough inspection can be carried out to see what minor repairs and renovations are necessary. Steam cleaning is available at many garages and is necessary for removal of accumulations of oily grime which sometimes cakes thick in certain areas near the engine, gearbox and back axle. If steam facilities are not available, there are one or two excellent grease solvents available which can be brush applied. The dirt can then be simply hosed off.
4 After washing paintwork, wipe it off with a chamois leather to give an unspotted clear finish. A coat of clear protective wax polish will give added protection against chemical pollutants in the air. If the paintwork sheen has dulled or oxidised, use a cleaner/polisher combination to restore the brilliance of the shine. This requires a little more effort, but the condition is usually caused because regular washing has been neglected. Always check that door and ventilator opening drain holes and pipes are completely clear so that the water can drain out. Bright work should be treated the same way as paintwork. Windscreens and windows can be kept clear of the smeary film which often appears if a little ammonia is added to the water. If they are scratched, a good rub with a proprietary metal polish will often clear them. Never use any form of wax or chromium polish on glass. Plastic roof covering material should be cleaned with lukewarm water and a little neutral soap applied with a soft bristle nailbrush. It must be thoroughly rinsed afterwards and finished off using a chamois leather.

3 Maintenance - interior

1 Mats and carpets should be brushed or vacuum cleaned regularly to keep them free of grit. If they are badly stained remove them from the car for scrubbing or sponging and make quite sure they are dry before replacement. Seats and interior trim panels can be kept clean by a wipe over with a damp cloth. If they do become stained (which can be more apparent on light coloured upholstery) use a little liquid detergent and a soft nail brush to scour the grime out of the grain of the material. Do not forget to keep the headlining clean in the same

way as the upholstery. When using liquid cleaners inside the car do not over-wet the surfaces being cleaned. Excessive damp could get into the seams and padded interior causing stains, offensive odours or even rot. If the inside of the car gets wet accidentally it is worthwhile taking some trouble to dry it out properly, particularly where carpets are involved. **Do not** leave oil or electric heaters inside the car for this purpose.

4 Minor body damage - repair

The photo sequence on pages 164, 165 and 166 illustrate the operations detailed in the following sub-Sections.

Repair of minor scratches in the car's bodywork

If the scratch is very superficial, and does not pepetrate to the metal of the bodywork, repair is very simple. Lightly rub the area of the scratch with a paintwork renovator (eg; T-Cut), or a very fine cutting paste, to remove loose paint from the scratch and to clear the surrounding bodywork of wax polish. Rinse the area with clean water.

Apply touch-up paint to the scratch using a thin paintbrush, continue to apply thin layers of paint until the surface of the paint in the scratch is level with the surrounding paintwork. Allow the new paint at least two weeks to harden; then blend it into the surrounding paintwork by rubbing the paintwork, in the scratch area with a paint-work renovator (eg; T-Cut) or a very fine cutting paste. Finally apply wax polish.

An alternative to painting over the scratch is to use Holts "Scratch-Patch". Use the same preparation for the affected area; then simply pick a patch of a suitable size to cover the scratch completely. Hold the patch against the scratch and burnish its backing plate; the patch will adhere to the paintwork, freeing itself from the backing paper at the same time. Polish the affected area to blend the patch into the surrounding paintwork. Where the scratch has penetrated right through to the metal of the bodywork, causing the metal to rust, a different repair technique is required. Remove any loose rust from the bottom of the scratch with a penknife, then apply rust inhibiting paint (eg; Kurust) to prevent the formation of rust in the future. Using a rubber nylon applicator, fill the scratch with bodystopper paste. If required, this paste can be mixed with cellulose thinners to provide a very thin paste which is ideal for filling narrow scratches. Before the stopper-paste in the scratch hardens, wrap a piece of smooth cotton rag around the top of a finger. Dip the finger in cellulose thinners and then quickly sweep it across the surface of the stopper-paste in the scratch; this will ensure that the surface of the stopper-paste is slightly hollowed. The scratch can now be painted over as described earlier in this Section.

Repair of dents in the car's bodywork

When deep denting of the car's bodywork has taken place, the first task is to pull the dent out, until the affected bodywork almost attains its original shape. There is little point in trying to restore the original shape completely, as the metal in the damaged area will have stretched on impact and cannot be reshaped fully to its original contour. It is better to bring the level of the dent up to a point which is about 1/8 inch (3 mm) below the level of the surrounding bodywork. In cases where the dent is very shallow anyway, it is not worth trying to pull it out at all.

If the underside of the dent is accessible, it can be hammered out gently from behind, using a mallet with a wooden or plastic head. Whilst doing this, hold a suitable block of wood firmly against the impact from the hammer blows and thus prevent a large area of bodywork from being 'belled-out'.

Should the dent be in a section of the bodywork which has a double skin or some other factor making it inaccessible from behind, a different technique is called for. Drill several small holes through the metal inside the dent area - particularly in the deeper sections, then screw long self-tapping screws into the holes just sufficiently for them to gain a good purchase in the metal. Now the dent can be pulled out by pulling on the protruding heads of the screws with a pair of pliers.

The next stage of the repair is the removal of the paint from the damaged area, and from an inch or so of the surrounding 'sound' bodywork. This is accomplished most easily by using a wire brush or abrasive pad on a power drill, although it can be done just as effectively by hand using sheets of abrasive paper. To complete the preparations for filling, score the surface of the bare metal with a screwdriver or the tang of a file, alternatively, drill small holes in the effected area. This will provide a really good 'key' for filler paste.

To complete the repair see the sub-Section on filling and respraying.

Repair of rust holes or gashes in the car's bodywork

Remove all paint from the affected area and from an inch or so of the surrounding 'sound' bodywork, using an abrasive pad or a wire brush on a power drill. If these are not available a few sheets of abrasive paper will do the job just as effectively. With the paint removed you will be able to gauge the severity of the corrosion and therefore decide whether to replace the whole panel (if this is possible) or to repair the affected area. Replacement body panels are not as expensive as most people think and it is often quicker and more satisfactory to fit a new panel than to attempt to repair large areas of corrosion.

Remove all fittings from the affected area except those which will act as a guide to the original shape of the damaged bodywork (eg; headlamp shells etc.). Then, using tin snips or a hacksaw blade, remove all loose metal and any other metal badly affected by corrosion. Hammer the edges of the hole inwards in order to create a slight depression for the filler paste.

Wire brush the affected area to remove the powdery rust from the surface of the remaining metal. Paint the affected area with rust inhibiting paint (eg; Kurust), if the back of the rusted area is accessible treat this also.

Before filling can take place it will be necessary to block the hole in some way. This can be achieved by the use of one of the following materials: Zinc gauze, Aluminium tape or Polyurethane foam.

Zinc gauze is probably the best material to use for a large hole. Cut a piece to the appropriate size and shape of the hole to be filled, then position it in the hole so that its edges are below the level of the surrounding bodywork. It can be retained in position by several blobs of filler paste around its periphery.

Aluminium tape should be used for small or very narrow holes. Pull a piece off the roll and trim it to the approximate size and shape required, then pull off the backing paper (if used) and stick the tape over the hole; it can be overlapped if the thickness of one piece is insufficient. Burnish down the edges of the tape with the handle of a screwdriver or similar, to ensure that the tape is securely attached to the metal underneath.

Polyurethane foam is best used and where the hole is situated in a section of bodywork of complex shape, backed by a small box section (eg; where the sill panel meets the rear wheel arch - most cars). The unusual mixing procedure for this foam is as follows: Put equal amounts of fluid from each of the two cans provided in the kit, into one container. Stir until the mixture begins to thicken, then quickly pour this mixture into the hole, and hold a piece of cardboard over the larger apertures. Almost immediately the polyurethane will begin to expand, gushing frantically out of any small holes left unblocked. When the foam hardens it can be cut back to just below the level of the surrounding bodywork with a hacksaw blade.

Bodywork repairs - filling and re-spraying

Before using this sub-Section, see the sub-Section on dent, deep scratch, rust hole, and gash repairs.

Many types of bodyfiller are available, but generally speaking those proprietary kits which contain a tin of filler paste and a tube of resin hardener (eg; Holts Cataloy) are best for this type of repair. A wide, flexible plastic or nylon applicator will be found invaluable for imparting a smooth and well contoured finish to the surface of the filler.

Mix up a little filler on a clean piece of card or board - use the hardener sparingly (follow the maker's instructions on the packet) otherwise the filler will set very rapidly.

Using the applicator, apply the filler paste to the prepared area; draw the applicator across the surface of the filler to achieve the correct contour and to level the filler surface. As soon as a contour that approximates to the correct one is achieved, stop working the paste - if you carry on too long the paste will become sticky and begin to 'pick-up' on the applicator. Continue to add thin layers of filler paste at twenty-minute intervals until the level of the filler is just 'proud' of the surrounding bodywork.

Once the filler has hardened, excess can be removed using a Surform plane or Dreadnought file. From then on, progressively finer grades of abrasive paper should be used, starting with a 40 grade production paper and finishing with 400 grade 'wet-and-dry' paper. Always wrap the abrasive paper around a flat rubber, cork, or wooden block - otherwise the surfaces of the filler will not be completely flat. During the smoothing of the filler surface the 'wet-and-dry' paper should be

Typical example of rust damage to a body panel. Before starting ensure that you have all of the materials required to hand. The first task is to ...

... remove body fittings from effected area, except those which can act as a guide to the original shape of the damaged bodywork - the headlamp shell in this case.

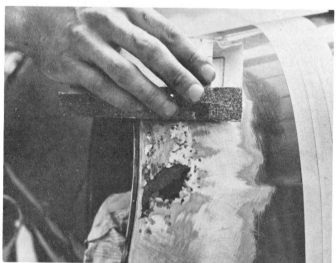

Remove all paint from the rusted area and from an inch or so of the adjoining 'sound' bodywork - use coarse abrasive paper or a power drill fitted with a wire brush or abrasive pad. Tap in the edges of the hole to provide a hollow for the filler.

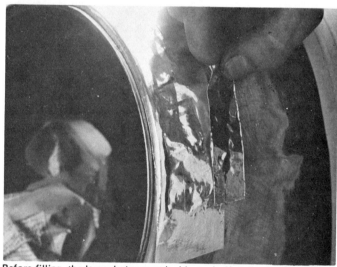

Before filling, the larger holes must be blocked off. Adhesive aluminium tape is one method; cut the tape to the required shape and size, peel off the backing strip (where used), position the tape over the hole and burnish to ensure adhesion.

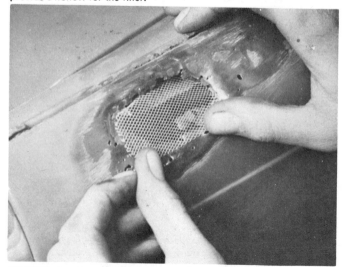

Alternatively, zinc gauze can be used. Cut a piece of the gauze to the required shape and size; position it in the hole below the level of the surrounding bodywork; then ...

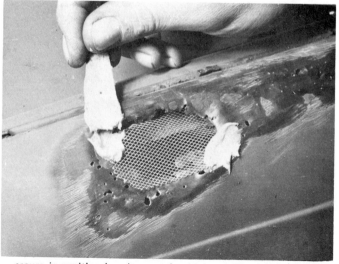

... secure in position by placing a few blobs of filler paste around its periphery. Alternatively, pop rivets or self-tapping screws can be used. Preparation for filling is now complete.

Mix filler and hardener according to manufacturer's instructions - avoid using too much hardener otherwise the filler will harden before you have a chance to work it.

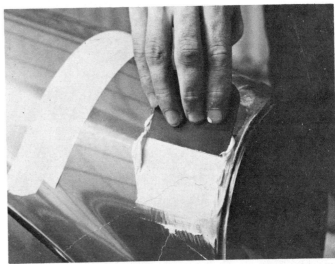

Apply the filler to the affected area with a flexible applicator - this will ensure a smooth finish. Apply thin layers of filler at 20 minute intervals, until the surface of the filler is just 'proud' of the surrounding bodywork. Then ...

... remove excess filler and start shaping with a Surform plane or a dreadnought file. Once an approximate contour has been obtained and the surface is relatively smooth, start using ...

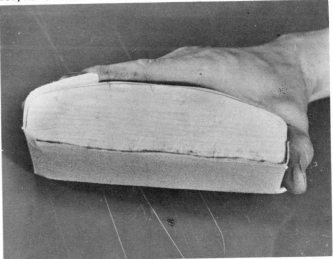

... abrasive paper. The paper should be wrapped around a flat wood, cork or rubber block - this will ensure that it imparts a smooth surface to the filler.

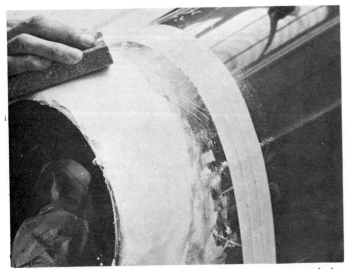

40 grit production paper is best to start with, then use progressively finer abrasive paper, finishing with 400 grade 'wet-and-dry'. When using 'wet-and-dry' paper, periodically rinse it in water ensuring also, that the work area is kept wet continuously.

Rubbing-down is complete when the surface of the filler is really smooth and flat, and the edges of the surrounding paintwork are finely 'feathered'. Wash the area thoroughly with clean water and allow to dry before commencing re-spray.

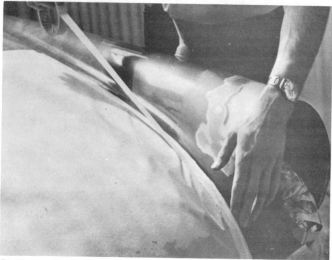

Firstly, mask off all adjoining panels and the fittings in the spray area. Ensure that the area to be sprayed is completely free of dust. Practice using an aerosol on a piece of waste metal sheet until the technique is mastered.

Spray the affected area with primer - apply several thin coats rather than one thick one. Start spraying in the centre of the repair area and then work outwards using a circular motion - in this way the paint will be evenly distributed.

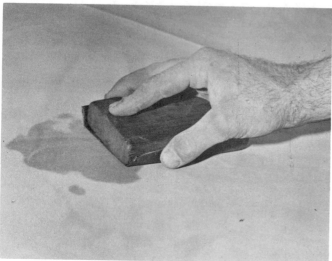

When the primer has dried inspect its surface for imperfections. Holes can be filled with filler paste or body-stopper, and lumps can be sanded smooth. Apply a further coat of primer, then 'flat' its surface with 400 grade 'wet-and-dry' paper.

Spray on the top coat, again building up the thickness with several thin coats of paint. Overspray onto the surrounding original paintwork to a depth of about five inches, applying a very thin coat at the outer edges.

Allow the new paint two weeks, at least, to harden fully, then blend it into the surrounding original paintwork with a paint restorative compound or very fine cutting paste. Use wax polish to finish off.

The finished job should look like this Remember, the quality of the completed work is directly proportional to the amount of time and effort expended at each stage of the preparation.

periodically rinsed in water. This will ensure that a very smooth finish is imparted to the filler at the final stage.

At this stage the 'dent' should be surrounded by a ring of bare metal which in turn should be encircled by the finely 'feathered' edge of the good paintwork. Rinse the repair area with clean water, until all the dust produced by the rubbing-down operation is gone.

Spray the whole repair area with a light coat of grey primer - this will show up any imperfections in the surface of the filler. Repair these imperfections with fresh filler paste or bodystopper and once more smooth the surface with abrasive paper. If bodystopper is used, it can be mixed with cellulose thinner to form a really thin paste which is ideal for filling small holes. Repeat this spray and repair procedure until you are satisfied that the surface of the filler, and the feathered edge of the paintwork are perfect. Clean the repair area with clean water and allow to dry fully.

The repair area is now ready for spraying. Paint spraying must be carried out in a warm, dry, windless and dust free atmosphere. This condition can be created artificially if you have access to a large indoor working area, but if you are forced to work in the open, you will have to pick your day very carefully. If you are working indoors, dousing the floor in the work area with water will 'lay' the dust which would otherwise be in the atmosphere. If the repair area is confined to one body panel, mask off the surrounding panels; this will help to minimise the effects of a slight mis-match in paint colours. Bodywork fittings (eg; chrome strips, door handles etc.), will also need to be masked off. Use genuine masking tape and several thicknesses of newspaper for the masking operation.

Before commencing to spray, agitate the aerosol can, thoroughly, then spray a test area (an old tin, or similar) until the technique is mastered. Cover the repair area with a thick coat of primer; the thickness should be built up using several thin layers of paint rather than one thick one. Using 400 grade 'wet-and-dry' paper, rub down the surface of the primer until it is really smooth. While doing this, the work area should be thoroughly doused with water, and the 'wet-and-dry' paper periodically rinsed in water. Allow to dry before spraying on more paint.

Spray on the top coat, again building up the thickness by using several thin layers of paint. Start spraying in the centre of the repair area and then, using a circular motion, work outwards until the whole repair area and about 2 inches of the surrounding original paintwork is covered. Remove all masking material 10 to 15 minutes after spraying on the final coat of paint.

Allow the new paint at least 2 weeks to harden fully; then, using a paintwork renovator (eg; T-Cut) or a very fine cutting paste, blend the edges of the new paint into the existing paintwork. Finally, apply wax polish.

5 Major bodywork damage - repair

Where serious damage has occurred or large areas need renewal due to neglect, it means certainly that completely new sections or panels will need welding in and this is best left to professionals. If the damage is due to impact it will also be necessary to completely check the alignment of the bodyshell structure. Due to the principle of construction, the strength and shape of the whole can be affected by damage to a part. In such instances the services of a Vauxhall agent with specialist checking jigs are essential. If a body is left mis-aligned, it is first of all dangerous as the car will not handle properly - and secondly, uneven stresses will be imposed on the steering, engine and transmission, causing abnormal wear or complete failure. Tyre wear will also be excessive.

6 Front and rear bumpers - removal and replacement

1   The front and rear bumpers are mounted similarly - that is on brackets which in turn are bolted to the longitudinal side rails at the front and to the end panel at the back. The ends of the bumper are attached to the body panels also. When removing bumpers, remove the bolts securing the brackets to the car so that the whole lot can be lifted off together.

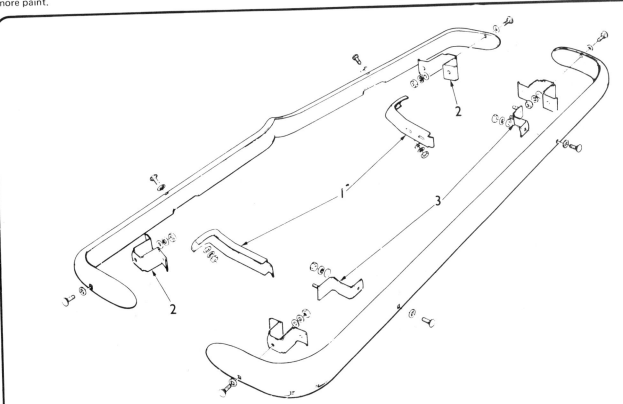

Fig. 12.1. Front and rear bumpers and brackets - details

1   *Front bumper mounting brackets*   2   *Front bumper end brackets*   3   *Rear bumper brackets*

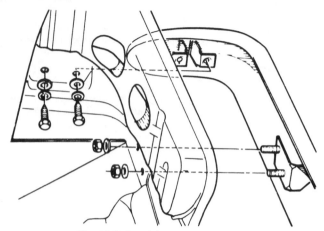

Fig. 12.2. Rear bumper end fixings

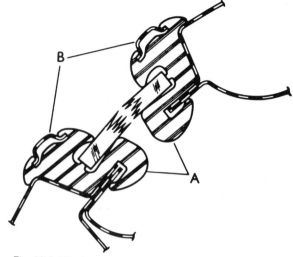

Fig. 12.3. Windscreen glazing strip - cross section

A Glazing channel   B Moulding insert

Fig. 12.4. Heated rear window - printed circuit terminations
arrowed

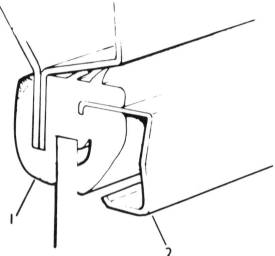

Fig. 12.5. Rear fixed quarter light glass

1 Glazing strip   2 Moulding

Fig. 12.6. Rear fixed quarter light glass
Pop rivets (arrowed) securing moulding to body panel

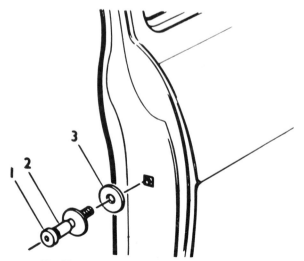

Fig. 12.7. Door latch striker pin fixing

1 Striker   3 Packing washer
2 Silencing bush

2 On estate cars the cargo floor must be lifted up to get at the bolts.
3 When replacing the rear bumper, the bolt holes must have sealing putty applied before the nuts and bolts are tightened. Otherwise water can get into the boot.

7 Windscreen, rear window and rear quarter fixed glass - removal and replacement

1 Unless the glass has been broken it is assumed that it is being removed because the sealing strip is leaking. If you are buying a secondhand screen from a breaker's yard, ask them to remove it for you before paying for it, but if the screen is already removed check the edges very carefully for signs of chipping. The screen should be smoothly ground all round the edge and any chip is a potential starter for a future crack.
2 Check whether the screen is made of toughened or laminated glass.
3 Remove the windscreen wiper arms by slackening the wedge screw, tapping it to loosen the wedge and lifting the wiper off. Disconnect the battery and remove the interior mirror.
4 Toughened glass screens can be removed by bumping the glass from inside with the flat of the hand. Wear stout gloves as a precaution. If moderate bumping fails, use foot pressure with pads under the feet to distribute pressure.
5 With laminated glass remove the glazing channel insert strip, where fitted, and cut away the lip of the glazing channel on the outside of the glass. Apply firm steady pressure from inside. Do not bump the glass or it may crack.
6 If a broken screen is being removed, cover up the scuttle ventilation grille to prevent pieces falling into the heater or ventilator.
7 To replace the glass, first clean all old sealing compound off the frame and sealing strip if the sealing strip can be re-used. If the screen is being replaced because of vehicle damage, make sure the frame is not distorted in any way. This can be checked by carefully holding the new screen in position to see that its contour and shape is reasonably well matched. Take care not to chip the glass edges.
8 Fit the glazing channel to the screen with the securing lip towards the inner (concave) side. Fig. 12.3 gives a cross-section showing chrome inserts which may be fitted.
9 Fit a piece of thin, strong cord into the inner groove so that a loop is left in the top centre and the ends come out at the bottom centre. Make sure that the cord crosses over in the channel at the loop and ends (otherwise the centre pieces of the glazing channel cannot be pulled over the flange with the cord). Identify each end and the halves of the loop so that the running direction of each piece of cord is known.
10 Using a suitable container fitted with a fine nozzle, apply sealer (Bostik No. 6) to the bottom of the corner of the body frame flange and also around the front edge of the glass between the glass and the glazing strip.
11 Place the screen in position, pressing lightly from the outside, and pull the strings from the bottom edge so that the glazing channel comes over the edge of the bottom flange up to within six inches of each

bottom corner. Make sure the glass is kept central and repeat the procedure along the top edge followed last of all by the sides. Check that the screen is properly seated both inside and out, and clear away surplus sealing compound.
12 The rear window removal and replacement procedure is similar to that for the windscreen. A similar type of insert may be fitted, but it is assembled in 4 pieces with an escutcheon at each corner. It is recommended that a soap and water solution is used when installing the escutcheons to prevent damage to the channel lips.
13 Where a heated rear window is installed, ensure that the wires are disconnected from the terminals and take great care that the printed circuit on the inner surface is not scratched or abraded. Minor repairs to the printed circuit can be repaired using a high conductivity paint.
14 The rear quarter fixed windows may be removed in the same manner as the windscreen, but first of all the 2 or 3 pop rivets must be drilled out of the forward edge of the reveal mounding (Figs. 12.5 and 12.6).

8 Doors - tracing of rattles and setting of latch striker pin

1 Check first that the door is not loose at the hinges and that the latch is holding it firmly in position. Check also that the door lines up with the aperture in the body.
2 If the hinges are loose, or the door is out of alignment, the hinge securing bolts should be tightened up first. If necessary, new hinge pins should be fitted. If the door is still out of alignment then the problem is more serious and the hinges may need renewal. As they are welded to the door this needs specialist attention.
3 If the latch is holding the door correctly it should be possible to press the door inwards fractionally against the rubber weatherstrip. If not, adjust the striker pin which is screwed into a plate behind the door pillar either inwards or outwards as required. Use an Allen key to undo the striker sufficiently to move it as needed. If the striker should need moving forward or backwards (relative to the front and rear of the car) packing washers can be fitted as necessary so that the lock fork engages over the pin where the rubber silencing bush is fitted (Fig. 12.7).

9 Door trim panel and interior handles - removal and replacement

1 Remove the window regulator (winder) handle by first prising out the trim cover and undoing the screw. Do not lose the wearing washer fitted behind (Fig. 12.8).
2 Remove the arm rest by undoing the 2 mounting screws and pushing downwards to release the lug at the extended end. Remove the escutcheon round the latch handle; it is a press fit and will lever off.
3 Unscrew the inside lock button.
4 Slide a thin stiff blade (such as a putty knife) behind the edge of the trim, run it round next to each fixing clip in turn and prise the clip out of the hole in the door. Do not prise anywhere except next to a clip, or the clip will probably tear out of the trim panel.

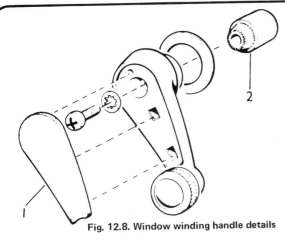

Fig. 12.8. Window winding handle details

1 *Spring fit insert*
2 *Extension piece*

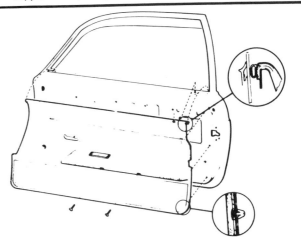

Fig. 12.9. Door trim pad - shown (inset) fixing over window sill and clip fixing

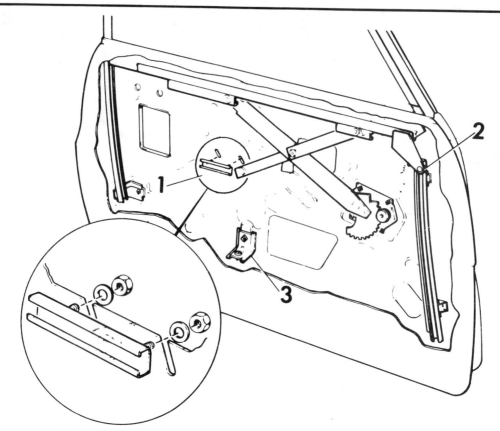

Fig. 12.10. Window winding mechanism - front doors inset - detail of horizontal channel

1   Support channel   2   Fixed roller in guide channel   3   Stop buffer bracket

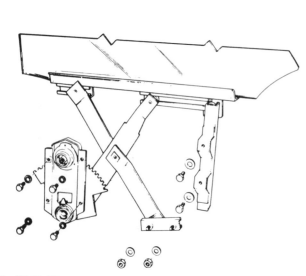

Fig. 12.11. The lower balance arm support channel used on 4 door models

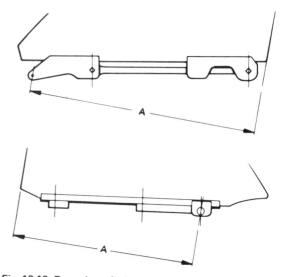

Fig. 12.12. Door glass - fitting position in support channel

Top	2 door models A = 37.80 inches
Centre	4 door models - front door A = 26.80 inches
Bottom	4 door models - rear doors A = 23.20 inches

Fig. 12.13. Window winding mechanism - rear doors of 4 door saloon

5   On estate car rear doors the pad is held by clips which are prised off in the same manner.

6   The remote control latch handle is fixed to the door and the trim pad can be taken off over it.

7   Under the trim pad there is a polythene sheet stuck to the lower half of the door panel as a water deflector (to keep water that gets inside the door from soaking the trim pad before it runs out of the bottom of the door). This should be securely fixed - particularly along the bottom edge.

8   Replacement is a straightforward reversal of the removal procedure.

10 Door glasses - removal and replacement

1   Remove the trim pad as described in the previous Section and the sealing strips along the door aperture.

2   Referring to Fig. 12.10, if the horizontal support is removed from the door panel the regulator arms can then be disengaged from the roller runs in the glass support channel. If the support channel fixed roller at the forward end is then disengaged from the vertical channel, the glass can be tipped and drawn out from the top of the door. On four door cars the front window horizontal guide channel is bolted to the window support channel. Note that these have a cranked lower balance arm support channel, the longer section of which (A) faces towards the front of the car (Fig. 12.11).

3   On replacement it is possible to adjust the vertical channels to keep the glass in position against the weatherstrip on the outer door window sill. Access to the adjusting bolts from the top ends of both channels is through holes in the front and rear edges of the doors. The holes are covered by press in plugs.

4   If new glass is being fitted into the channels make sure that they are positioned according to the dimensions given in Fig. 12.12.

5   Rear door glasses on four door cars are removed according to the same principles.

6   When the lower horizontal support channel is replaced it should be adjusted in its slots so that the top edge of the glass is parallel with the door frame.

11 Window winder mechanism - removal and replacement

If the window mechanism operating arms are disengaged from their channels as described in the previous Section, the securing screws can be removed and the regulator mechanism taken out through the door panel aperture.

12 Door catches - removal and replacement

1   Remove the interior trim panel and close the window of the door in question.

2   Remove the glass run channel securing screws.

3   On the front doors of 2-door models, remove the exterior door handle (Section 13).

4   Remove the lock securing screws and the lock can then be detached from the control rods and taken out (Fig. 12.14, 12.16 and 12.17). Note that the release rod is connected in the upper hole of the lock mechanism on 2-door models and an anti-rattle spring is fitted.

5   On replacement, smear the lock mechanism and rod ends with a general purpose high melting point grease.

13 Exterior door handles and latch buttons - removal and replacement

1   All door handles are secured by nuts on studs in the handle which are accessible from inside the door once the trim pad has been removed (Fig. 12.15).

2   Once the handle has been removed the push button and spring can be released by removing the three screws securing the cover plate.

3   The lock barrel may be removed from the push button by pressing down the spring loaded plunger in the end of the lock barrel and removing the extension. The barrel will then come out and another may be fitted.

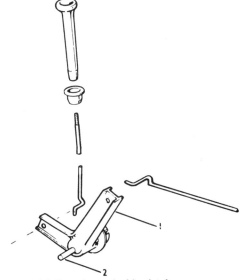

Fig. 12.14. Rear doors - locking latch

1   Bell crank   2   Pivot pin

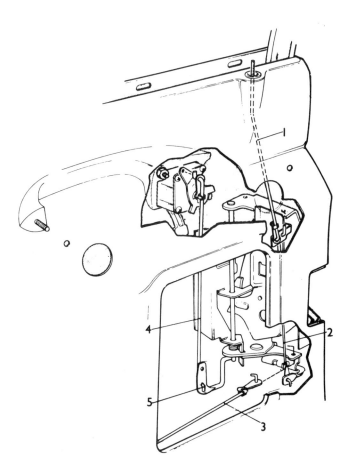

Fig. 12.15. Front door lock and catch mechanism detail - 4 door models

1   Internal lock button link rod
2   Internal lock button link rod
3   Door latch interior release handle rod
4   Door latch exterior release rod
5   Rod link - no anti-rattle clip fitted

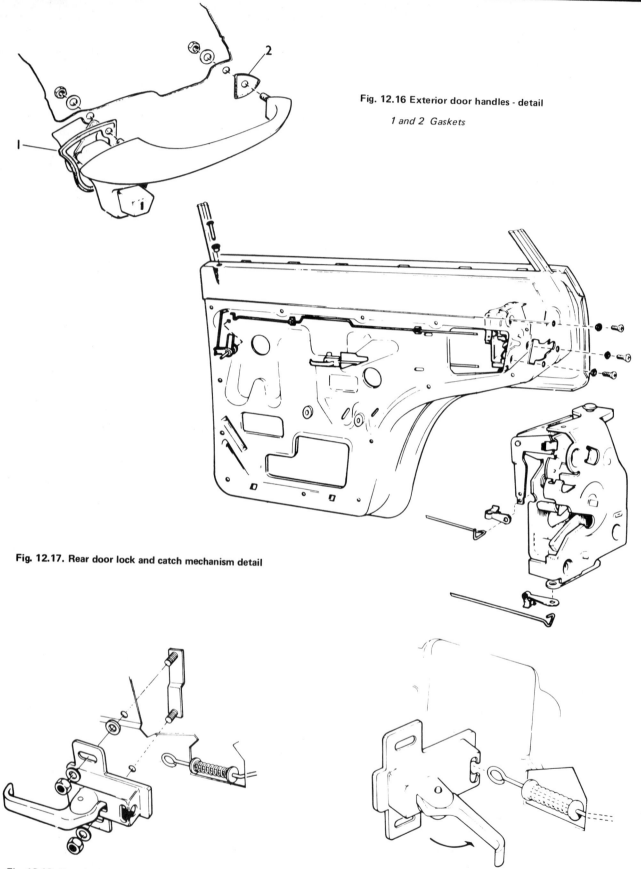

Fig. 12.16 Exterior door handles - detail

1 and 2 Gaskets

Fig. 12.17. Rear door lock and catch mechanism detail

Fig. 12.18. Door locks - interior release handle details
Move in direction of arrow to detach from rod

Fig. 12.19. Door locks - interior release handle details
Move in direction of arrow to detach from rod

14 Interior latch handles - removal and replacement

With the door trim pad removed, the latch assembly can be undone by removing the two securing nuts. If it is then turned at right angles horizontally it can be unhooked from the connecting rod (Fig. 12.18 and 12.19).

15 Bonnet and boot lids and locks - elimination of rattles, removal and replacement

1   Rattles traced to the bonnet are usually due to maladjustment or wear of the catch.
2   Both front and rear ends of the bonnet are adjustable for height. Before altering the front on the catch ensure that the rear is flush with the bodywork and centrally positioned. Adjustment can be made on the hinge bracket mountings which are slotted.
3   If extreme pressure is required to close the bonnet so that the catch grips, or if the catch engages and the front of the bonnet can still be pressed down a noticeable amount, then the dovetail bolt which engages in the catch needs adjustment. If the locknut is slackened, the bolt may be screwed in or out as necessary (Fig. 12.20).
4   If the latch mechanism is faulty it can be removed. First mark the position to assist line-up when another is fitted, remove the radiator grille left-hand insert and undo the three nuts holding the latch mechanism to the support rail (Fig. 12.21).
5   On models fitted with a cable operated release mechanism, release the cable outer retaining clip and the end of the cable can then be detached from the release lever.
   If the cable should break it will be necessary to detach the release lever mechanism from the side of the scuttle by undoing the two self-tapping screws and drilling out the pop rivet. The inner end of the cable may then be unhooked (Fig. 12.22 and 12.23).
6   Removal and replacement of the bonnet is quite straightforward. Make sure that there is another person available to support it. Mark the position of the upper hinge brackets on the bonnet and then remove the two bolts at each side when it may be lifted off.
7   The boot lid is hinged with integral torsion bars which hold it open. The torsion bar hooks into one of three slots to give the most suitable tension. The latch engages a striker loop which is clamped to the rear panel and may be raised or lowered so that the lid may be closed with the correct amount of firm hand pressure.
8   When removing the boot lid, mark the hinges and note any packing wedges that may have been installed between hinge and lid to maintain the correct height in relation to the surrounding bodywork. If the hinges are being removed from the bodywork it will be necessary to remove the rear seat, squab and parcel shelf first in order to get at the upper mounting bolt.
9   To remove the lock assembly requires a spring retainer plate to be moved sideways. This retainer plate is accessible through an aperture on the inside of the lid.
10 The lock may be dismantled after the lock support and nut are removed and the striking lever taken off. Next, release the spring and remove the extension from the body. The lock barrel may be removed from the body after inserting the key. Before reassembling, lubricate the barrel wards with a dry lubricant such as WD-40, Loclube or dry graphite (pencil 'lead').
11 When reassembling, ensure that the spring lugs on the extension and body are diametrically opposed. Assemble the lock lever so that its position relative to the extension lug is as shown in Fig. 12.25.
12 The latch mechanism can be taken out after removal of the turn button assembly, by undoing the mounting screws through the same aperture.

16 Estate car - rear door hinges and lock

1   The rear door lock is similar to the saloon and coupe boot locks, except that a turn button is also incorporated. The turn button lever is connected to the latch by a link rod.
2   The door catch can be removed after removal of the trim pad, then pushing the retainer plate towards the turn button and releasing the turn button from the connecting rod.
3   When installing, lubricate the door catch and rod ends with a high melting point general purpose grease and engage the end of the rod in the catch release plate hole furthest from the turn button.

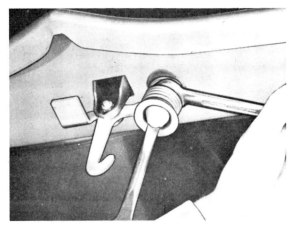

Fig. 12.20. Bonnet catch dovetail bolt - adjustment

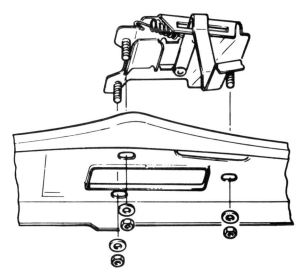

Fig. 12.21. Bonnet release catch - detail of fixing

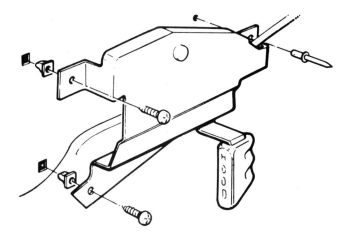

Fig. 12.22. Bonnet release cable lever - detail of fixing

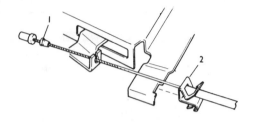

Fig. 12.23. Bonnet latch cable release detail

1   *Lever retaining sleeve*   2   *Cable outer clip*

Fig. 12.24. Boot lid lock assembly - detail

1   *Lock barrel*   4   *Extension*
2   *Body*   5   *Lock lever*
3   *Spring*   6   *Nut*

Fig. 12.25. The correct position of the boot lock extension lug (arrowed)

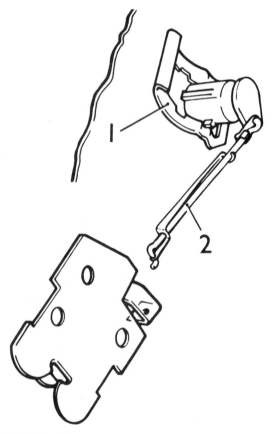

Fig. 12.26. Rear door - estate car, turn button and latch arrangement

1   *Turn button retaining plate*   2   *Link rod*

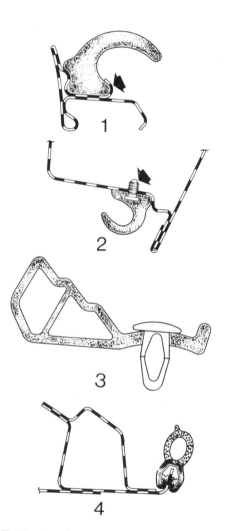

Fig. 12.27. Weatherstrips - cross sections

1   *Door upper part - retained in channel (arrowed)*
2   *Door lower section - held by push fit fasteners (arrowed)*
3   *Bonnet landing weatherstrip held by push fit fastener*
4   *Boot aperture and estate car rear door strip*

4   Access to the rear door hinges is possible after removing the cover assembly. This can be lowered, complete with lamp unit, after the nine attaching screws have been removed. Detach the wires from the lamp, and the cover can be taken out.

5   The rear door hinges also incorporate torque rods to keep the door in the raised position when opened. Mark the hinges on the door panel before removing the door from the hinges. If the hinges are to be removed, take the door off first.

17 Weatherstrips

1   The doors, bonnet and boot are all fitted with rubber weatherstrips to keep water out (and in the case of the bonnet to prevent engine fumes from entering the ventilation air inlet). Damaged weatherstrips should be renewed without delay as deterioration of the bodywork interior will otherwise result.

2   The bonnet landing strip is fixed to the upper edge of the ventilation cover panel by press in studs. When fitting a new strip, the raised section must face the front of the car.

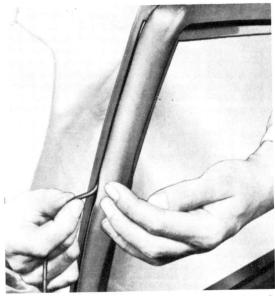

Fig. 12.28. Inserting a rubber fillet strip into the weatherstrip

Fig. 12.29. The fillet strip dimension for front doors

A = 16 in. (41 cm)

Fig. 12.30. The fillet strip installation dimensions for rear doors

A = 0.50 in. (12.7 mm)   C = 14 in. (35.6 cm)
B = 1.0 in. (2.54 cm)

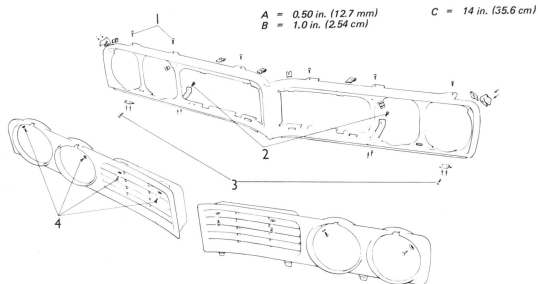

Fig. 12.31. The radiator grille and inserts

1   Top fixing screws (6)   3   Headlamp mounting panel
2   Screws in engine compartment   screws (2)
    (2)   4   Insert screws and washers (4)

3   The boot aperture weatherstrip is simply pressed over the flange,
although it can help to use an adhesive to hold it in position. It is
important to see that the ends of the strip are butted neatly together
and sealed with adhesive. If the smooth outer skin of the strip is
broken, the whole article will absorb water and encourage rust.

4   Door weatherstrips are held to the frame at the top in a channel. The
lower edge is secured by press-in plastic fasteners. On the estate car the
rear door strip is similar to that used on a saloon car boot; ensure that
the lip faces towards the body aperture.

5   Selective use of a rubber filler strip is made on some cars to prevent
damage and distortion to weatherstrips. This can be renewed (or fitted),
if found necessary where not previously used), by inserting at the rear
edge of the door (Fig. 12.28). On rear doors it is also necessary to drill
a 7/32 in. (5.56 mm) in the door panel where shown in Fig. 12.30 and
to insert a special fastener.

18 Grilles and exterior trim

1   The radiator grille frame is secured to the front end panel by 6
screws along the top, 2 screws accessible from the engine compartment
and 2 further screws on the headlamp mounting panel. The inserts are
secured to the grille frame by 4 screws and washers at the top and by
3 tongues at the bottom.

2   Door sill mouldings, if fitted, are attached by 7 pop rivets which
must be drilled out to remove them.

3   The body side and rear end mouldings incorporate an integral
plastic strip and are retained by plastic fasteners and clips. A sealing
washer is placed between the clip and the panel on the rear quarter side
panel and back door panel.

4   To gain access to the moulding clip attaching nuts, the trim pads
and rear lamps must first be removed, and the water deflectors released
from the front and rear door inner panels. A thin knife blade can be
used to spring the mouldings from the fasteners.

5   The moulding fastener has a central pin which expands the fastener
behind the panel when installed. This fastener can be released from the
panel by punching through the pin.

6   Door aperture tread plates are held by studs engaging in keyhole
slots and a single plastic push-fit stud at the rear end. To remove the
tread plate pull out the stud, slide the plate forward and lift it off
(Fig. 12.34).

7   Fixed window reveal mouldings are retained by the glazing strip
and, to remove them, the window assembly must be taken out (refer
to Section 7).

19 Heater/demister and ventilating system - general description

Ventilation of all models is provided by a pair of intakes in front
of the windscreen which duct air to face level outlets at each end of
the instrument panel. Air is exhausted from the car through slots under
the rear screen or above the rear door on estate cars.

In addition there is a ventilation assembly centrally mounted in the
scuttle which incorporates a booster fan and heater battery where
specified. The controls for this are independent of the air inlets at the
ends of the instrument panel.

The ventilator assembly is a moulding with a series of ducts in it
and two flaps.

Each flap is controlled by one of the two levers. The left-hand lever
controls the outflow of air to either the car or the screen, and the
right-hand lever controls the inflow of air past the heater, fully,
partially or not at all. On early models, there is no hot water control
valve, and to prevent warm air from entering the car when the heat
control is in the cold (upward) position, the air control lever should be
placed fully downwards.

Where fitted, the hot water control valve is attached to the forward
side of the ventilator shroud panel by 2 screws; the valve is cable
operated. The valve is connected by hoses to an adaptor in the intake
manifold and the heater radiator inlet pipe.

The heater control escutcheon will vary in style according to
whether or not a hot water control valve is used.

20 Heater controls - adjustment and cable renewal

1   The controls are mounted in the centre of the instrument panel.

Fig. 12.32. Sill mouldings - inset, cross section

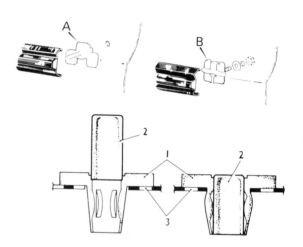

Fig. 12.33. Side and rear end moulding retainers

A Moulding fastener   B Moulding clip
1 Moulding fastener   3 Body panel
2 Central pin

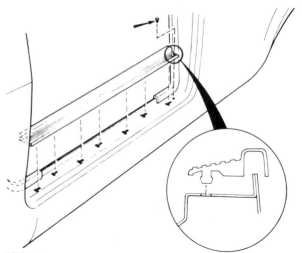

Fig. 12.34. Door aperture tread plate with (inset) cross sectional view

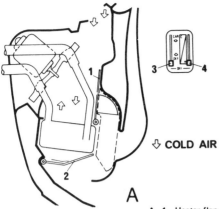

⇩ COLD AIR

A

A 1 Heater flap open
  2 Outlet to car flap closed
  3 Outlet to car flap control lever (off)
  4 Heater flap control lever (hot and off position)

Fig. 12.36. Heater control escutcheon - removal of lever knobs and escutcheon retaining screw

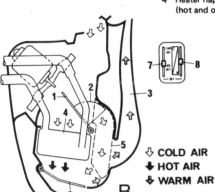

⇩ COLD AIR
⬇ HOT AIR
⇩ WARM AIR

B

B 1 Heater flap ½ open
  2 Deflectors on upper flap
  3 De-mist duct
  4 Heater radiator
  5 Bypass chute
  6 Lower flap
  7 Lower flap control at screen defrost position
  8 Heater flap control at mixing position

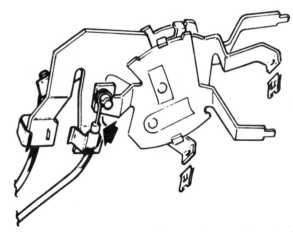

Fig. 12.37. Heater control levers. Note maximum cable protrusion of 1/8 inch (arrowed)

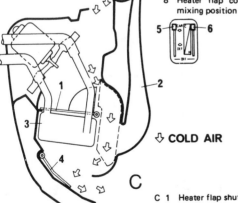

⇩ COLD AIR

C

C 1 Heater flap shut
  2 De-mist duct
  3 Heater radiator
  4 Lower flap
  5 Lower flap control at car in hot position
  6 Heater flap control at cold

Fig. 12.35. Ventilator unit - cross section of typical settings
(Early type control shown)

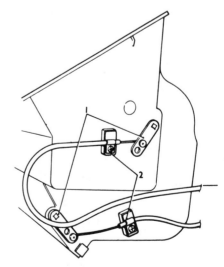

Fig. 12.38. Ventilator flap control cable fixings
(Heater without hot water control valve)

1 Flap spindles   2 Cable outer clips

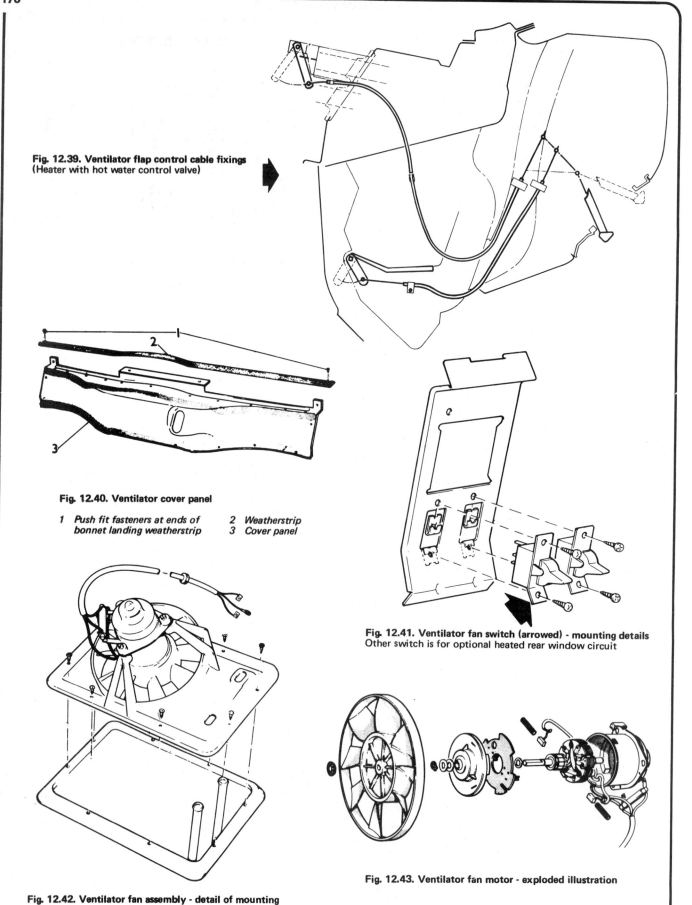

Fig. 12.39. Ventilator flap control cable fixings
(Heater with hot water control valve)

Fig. 12.40. Ventilator cover panel

1 *Push fit fasteners at ends of*   2 *Weatherstrip*
  bonnet landing weatherstrip   3 *Cover panel*

Fig. 12.41. Ventilator fan switch (arrowed) - mounting details
Other switch is for optional heated rear window circuit

Fig. 12.43. Ventilator fan motor - exploded illustration

Fig. 12.42. Ventilator fan assembly - detail of mounting

Pull off the control lever knobs, remove the screw at the bottom of the escutcheon and lift out the escutcheon.

Remove the filler panel next to the steering column and then undo the two screws holding the lever assembly to the instrument panel. The control can be withdrawn from below (Fig. 12.36).

2 Cables should be clipped to the control so that no more than 1/8 inch protrudes above the clip. Otherwise the movement of the lever will be restricted (Fig. 12.37).

3 Adjustment of the cables is at the ventilation end. Both cable clips should be slackened and, with both control levers in the 'off' (down) position the upper flap should be fully forward (anticlockwise) and the lower flap fully back (clockwise) viewed from the flap lever side of the ventilation casing. For models with a hot water control valve, ensure that the water valve lever is in the rearwards (closed) position and the heat control lever is downwards before tightening the water valve lever clamp screw.

4 To detach the cables from the flaps, remove the clips and prise the levers off the ends of the flap spindles,

---

21 Fan and ventilator/heater unit - removal and replacement

Fan and motor - early models (fan motor without a hole in the end of the casing)

1 To remove the fan and motor it is first necessary to detach the ventilator cover panel under the bonnet. Prise out the two end fasteners holding the bonnet landing weatherstrip, remove the fourteen screws securing the panel and disconnect the heater hoses. The panel can then be lifted off (Fig. 12.40).

2 Remove the heater control escutcheon (Section 20) and disconnect the fan motor switch by removing the two screws and pulling the connections off the back (Fig. 12.41).

3 Undo the fan motor earth wire bolt which is screwed into the dashpanel behind the ashtray.

4 Remove the eight screws holding the fan motor and cover to the top of the ventilator housing and lift it out (Fig. 12.42). (On left-hand drive cars disconnect the windscreen wiper right-hand link at the motor).

5 If it is wished to renew the fan motor brushes, remove the motor from the cover, detach the fan from the spindle, remove the circlip also on the spindle and undo the three spring clips holding the motor casing to the end cover (Fig. 12.43).

6 When replacing the fan to the motor, fit the thicker sides of the blades towards the motor and the toothed retaining lockwasher with the concave side against the fan hub.

7 When refitting the fan assembly to the top of the ventilator, the screw holes and heater pipe apertures should be sealed to prevent water getting inside the car.

8 The fan wires should be correctly connected at the switch blue/black to No. 1 (top), green to No. 2 (centre) and green/yellow to No. 3 (lowest) terminals.

Fan and motor - later models (fan motor with a hole in the end of the casing)

9 To remove the fan and motor, first remove the carburettor air cleaner (refer to Chapter 3, if necessary).

10 Remove the screws which retain the ventilator shroud panel and release the push-fit rivets at each end of the bonnet landing. Without disconnecting the heater hoses, move the shroud panel as far as possible to provide maximum access to the heater motor.

11 On right-hand drive cars remove the heater control escutcheon so that the motor switch wires can be seen (Section 20).

12 Remove the filler panel adjacent to the steering column, disconnect the wires from the heater motor switch and remove the earthing bolt forward of the ashtray.

13 Using strips of adhesive tape to retain the anchor nuts in their recesses, remove the three retaining screws. Remove the motor, noting the washer fitted between the cover lug and the motor (two washers at the lower lug - see Fig. 12.44).

14 Rotate the motor anticlockwise until the resistor is over the lower lug, then tilt it upwards so that its body passes between the two upper lugs and contacts the perimeter of the fan aperture with the fan rim contacting the tip of the lower lug.

15 Rotate the motor further to permit the fan rim to pass the lower lug and the assembly to be removed.

Fig. 12.44. The installed position of the later type fan
(The arrow indicates the two washers at the lower lug)

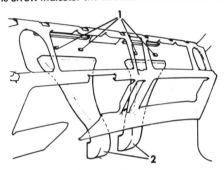

Fig. 12.45. Ventilator demist ducts

1 Outlet aperture clips
2 Lower ends - push fit into main ventilation casing

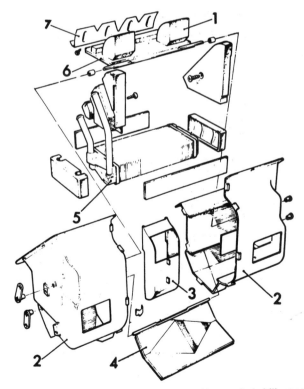

Fig. 12.46. Ventilator/heater casing assembly - exploded illustration

1 Deflectors
2 Casing halves
3 Bypass chute
4 Lower flap
5 Heater radiator
6 Upper flap
7 Graduation plate

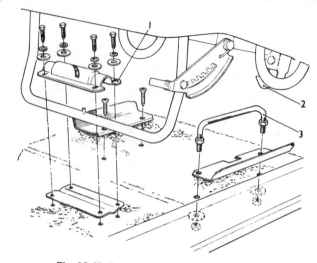

Fig. 12.47. Front seat fixing details

1 Stirrup retaining plate
2 Anti-tip safety catch (two door models)
3 Retaining loop

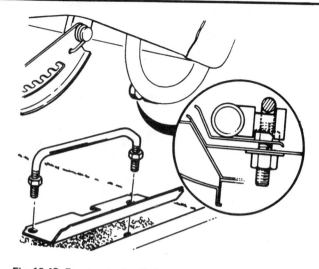

Fig. 12.48. Front seat - detail of non-tip retaining lug on four door models

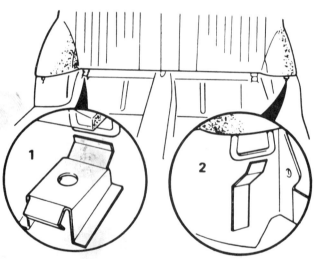

Fig. 12.49. Rear seat squab retaining loop details (inset)

1 Floor bracket (for cushion also)
2 Wheel arch clip

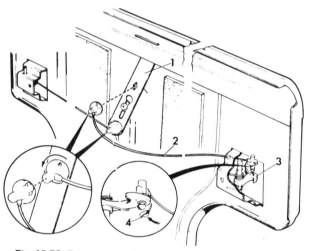

Fig. 12.50. Rear seat squab - estate car, detail of upright position retaining latches

1 Release lever
2 Cables
3 Release latches
4 Cable retaining washer

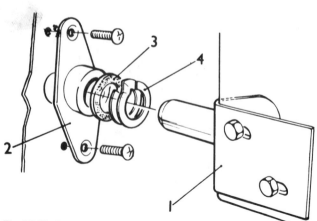

Fig. 12.51. Rear seat cushion - estate car, detail of pivot pin and bush

1 Pivot pin bracket
2 Bush
3 Friction washer
4 Anti-rattle spring

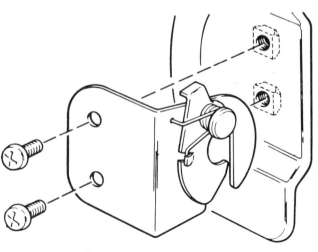

Fig. 12.52. Rear seat - estate car

Squab pivot catch

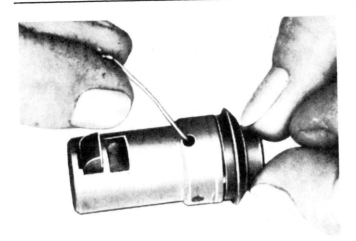

Fig. 12.53. Depressing the retaining wards to remove the glovebox lock press-button

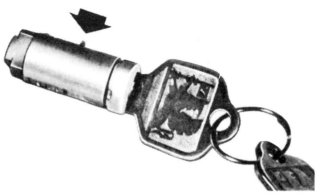

Fig. 12.54. The one ward (arrowed) which retains the lock barrel when the key is inserted

16 Refer to paragraph 5 for renewal of the fan motor brushes.
17 Replacement is the reverse of the removal procedure, but ensure that the resistor is positioned as shown in Fig. 12.44.

Ventilator and heater assembly
18 If it is wished to remove the ventilator and heater assembly, first remove the instrument panel cover and instrument assembly (see Chapter 10), glovebox and parcel shelf.
19 The demist ducts are a push-fit into the ventilator box at the bottom and are held by clips up to the outlet slots at the top. Take these off. Disconnect the control cables at the ventilator bore. Provided the fan wires are disconnected, and ventilator shrouds are already removed, the whole unit can be lifted out (Figs. 12.45 and 12.46).
20 On replacement, make sure that the demist ducts are properly secured into their clips at the outlet slots.

22 Seats

1   All Magnum models are fitted with reclining front seats. On 2-door models, the reclining mechanism is integral with the squab frame; on 4-door models it is integral with the seat frame.
2   On 2-door models, front seats tip forward and their adjustment consists of pivoting forward and backwards on the front support frame member which is hinged at the floor. A safety catch latches the rear of the seat to the floor to prevent forward tipping in emergency (Fig. 12.47).
3   On 4-door models, the front seat is the same except that the tipping safety catch is replaced by a peg which hooks under the retainer hoop. The retainer can be adjusted vertically to eliminate any rattle which might develop (Fig. 12.48).
4   The saloon rear seat cushion is held in position by two studs and nuts under the front edge of the seat. The rear of the cushion has two wire loops which hook into brackets on the floor.
5   The saloon squab can be removed only after the cushion has been taken out. It is held by two wire loops to the same brackets holding the cushion and by two smaller loops which hook over malleable clips

on the wheel arches. These clips are simply bent to release the loops (Fig. 12.49).
6   The estate car rear seats fold to form a load carrying area. The cushion hinges forward into a vertical position and the squab folds flat forward to provide a platform (Fig. 12.50).
    The cushion pivots on a pin at each side fixed to a bracket and this engages in a bush in the body side panel. In order to remove the cushion the pivot pin brackets must be unbolted from the seat (Fig. 12.51). The squab pivots on pins fixed to the side panels. Two hooks with spring catches fixed to the sides of the squab engage the pins. This is a quick release method as the spring catches can release the squab from the pivot pins so that it may be lifted out completely (Fig. 12.52).
    In addition there are two latches fitted to keep the squab upright. Should it be necessary to renew a latch release cable, remove the securing washer from the latch end and turn the cable through 90° at the release lever end to disengage it from the lever.

23 Glovebox lid catch - removal, dismantling and replacement

Early models - with escutcheon
1   Remove the press-button or lock barrel by depressing the retaining wards with a thin stiff wire while pulling the assembly outwards (Fig. 12.53).
2   The escutcheon can now be unscrewed if necessary. A suitably sized bolt head in the hexagonal recess will enable this to be done.
3   The press button is retained by two wards which must be depressed in turn while pulling the button outwards. Access is through the upper hole in the catch body.
4   To remove the lock barrel, insert the key then depress the single protruding ward through the upper hole if the barrel is locked or through the right-hand hole if unlocked. If the key is not available, each of the five wards must be depressed in turn whilst pulling the lock barrel outwards (Fig. 12.54).
5   Replacement is a straightforward reversal of the removal procedure.

Later models - with turnbutton
6   The turnbutton catch can be removed by unscrewing the flanged threaded ring. When installing, ensure that the rubber buffers are undamaged; adjust the striker in or out so that the lid closes after applying firm hand pressure.

Metric conversion tables

Inches	Decimals	Millimetres
1/64	0.015625	0.3969
1/32	0.03125	0.7937
3/64	0.046875	1.1906
1/16	0.0625	1.5875
5/64	0.078125	1.9844
3/32	0.09375	2.3812
7/64	0.109375	2.7781
1/8	0.125	3.1750
9/64	0.140625	3.5719
5/32	0.15625	3.9687
11/64	0.171875	4.3656
3/16	0.1875	4.7625
13/64	0.203125	5.1594
7/32	0.21875	5.5562
15/64	0.234375	5.9531
1/4	0.25	6.3500
17/64	0.265625	6.7469
9/32	0.28125	7.1437
19/64	0.296875	7.5406
5/16	0.3125	7.9375
21/64	0.328125	8.3344
11/32	0.34375	8.7312
23/64	0.359375	9.1281
3/8	0.375	9.5250
25/64	0.390625	9.9219
13/32	0.40625	10.3187
27/64	0.421875	10.7156
7/16	0.4375	11.1125
29/64	0.453125	11.5094
15/32	0.46875	11.9062
31/64	0.484375	12.3031
1/2	0.5	12.7000
33/64	0.515625	13.0969
17/32	0.53125	13.4937
35/64	0.546875	13.8906
9/16	0.5625	14.2875
37/64	0.578125	14.6844
19/32	0.59375	15.0812
39/64	0.609375	15.4781
5/8	0.625	15.8750
41/64	0.640625	16.2719
21/32	0.65625	16.6687
43/64	0.671875	17.0656
11/16	0.6875	17.4625
45/64	0.703125	17.8594
23/32	0.71875	18.2562
47/64	0.734375	18.6531
3/4	0.75	19.0500
49/64	0.765625	19.4469
25/32	0.78125	19.8437
51/64	0.796875	20.2406
13/16	0.8125	20.6375
53/64	0.828125	21.0344
27/32	0.84375	21.4312
55/64	0.859375	21.8281
7/8	0.875	22.2250
57/64	0.890625	22.6219
29/32	0.90625	23.0187
59/64	0.921875	23.4156
15/16	0.9375	23.8125
61/64	0.953125	24.2094
31/32	0.96875	24.6062
63/64	0.984375	25.0031

Millimetres to Inches		Inches to Millimetres	
mm	Inches	Inches	mm
0.01	0.00039	0.001	0.0254
0.02	0.00079	0.002	0.0508
0.03	0.00118	0.003	0.0762
0.04	0.00157	0.004	0.1016
0.05	0.00197	0.005	0.1270
0.06	0.00236	0.006	0.1524
0.07	0.00276	0.007	0.1778
0.08	0.00315	0.008	0.2032
0.09	0.00354	0.009	0.2286
0.1	0.00394	0.01	0.254
0.2	0.00787	0.02	0.508
0.3	0.01181	0.03	0.762
0.4	0.01575	0.04	1.016
0.5	0.01969	0.05	1.270
0.6	0.02362	0.06	1.524
0.7	0.02756	0.07	1.778
0.8	0.03150	0.08	2.032
0.9	0.03543	0.09	2.286
1	0.03947	0.1	2.54
2	0.07874	0.2	5.08
3	0.11811	0.3	7.62
4	0.15748	0.4	10.16
5	0.19685	0.5	12.70
6	0.23622	0.6	15.24
7	0.27559	0.7	17.78
8	0.31496	0.8	20.32
9	0.35433	0.9	22.86
10	0.39370	1	25.4
11	0.43307	2	50.8
12	0.47244	3	76.2
13	0.51181	4	101.6
14	0.55118	5	127.0
15	0.59055	6	152.4
16	0.62992	7	177.8
17	0.66929	8	203.2
18	0.70866	9	228.6
19	0.74803	10	254.0
20	0.78740	11	279.4
21	0.82677	12	304.8
22	0.86614	13	330.2
23	0.90551	14	355.6
24	0.94488	15	381.0
25	0.98425	16	406.4
26	1.02362	17	431.8
27	1.06299	18	457.2
28	1.10236	19	482.6
29	1.14173	20	508.0
30	1.18110	21	533.4
31	1.22047	22	558.8
32	1.25984	23	584.2
33	1.29921	24	609.6
34	1.33858	25	635.0
35	1.37795	26	660.4
36	1.41732	27	685.8
37	1.4567	28	711.2
38	1.4961	29	736.6
39	1.5354	30	762.0
40	1.5748	31	787.4
41	1.6142	32	812.8
42	1.6535	33	838.2
43	1.6929	34	863.6
44	1.7323	35	889.0
45	1.7717	36	914.4

1   Imperial gallon = 8 Imp pints = 1.16 US gallons = 277.42 cu in = 4.5459 litres

1   US gallon = 4 US quarts = 0.862 Imp gallon = 231 cu in = 3.785 litres

1   Litre = 0.2199 Imp gallon = 0.2642 US gallon = 61.0253 cu in = 1000 cc

Miles to Kilometres		Kilometres to Miles	
1	1.61	1	0.62
2	3.22	2	1.24
3	4.83	3	1.86
4	6.44	4	2.49
5	8.05	5	3.11
6	9.66	6	3.73
7	11.27	7	4.35
8	12.88	8	4.97
9	14.48	9	5.59
10	16.09	10	6.21
20	32.19	20	12.43
30	48.28	30	18.64
40	64.37	40	24.85
50	80.47	50	31.07
60	96.56	60	37.28
70	112.65	70	43.50
80	128.75	80	49.71
90	144.84	90	55.92
100	160.93	100	62.14

lb f ft to Kg f m		Kg f m to lb f ft		lb f/in^2: Kg f/cm^2		Kg f/cm^2: lb f/in^2	
1	0.138	1	7.233	1	0.07	1	14.22
2	0.276	2	14.466	2	0.14	2	28.50
3	0.414	3	21.699	3	0.21	3	42.67
4	0.553	4	28.932	4	0.28	4	56.89
5	0.691	5	36.165	5	0.35	5	71.12
6	0.829	6	43.398	6	0.42	6	85.34
7	0.967	7	50.631	7	0.49	7	99.56
8	1.106	8	57.864	8	0.56	8	113.79
9	1.244	9	65.097	9	0.63	9	128.00
10	1.382	10	72.330	10	0.70	10	142.23
20	2.765	20	144.660	20	1.41	20	284.47
30	4.147	30	216.990	30	2.11	30	426.70

Index

A

Accelerator cable and pedal - 63
Air filter - 48
Alternators - 117, 121
Antifreeze - 45
Automatic transmission
    adjustment and attention - 95
    description - 93
    fluid level - 95
    removal and replacement - 95
    specifications - 80
Auxiliary shaft:
    drivebelt - 18
    pulley - 21
    removal and inspection - 24
    replacement - 35

B

Battery - 116, 117
Bellhousing and cover plate - 18
Big-end bearings:
    examination and renovation - 26
    removal - 24
Bodywork and fittings:
    exterior trim - 171, 176
    general description - 162
    grilles - 176
    maintenance - 162
    major body damage - 167
    minor body damage - 163
    rear quarter fixed glass - 169
    rear window - 169
    seats - 181
    weatherstrips - 175
    window winder mechanism - 171
Bonnet - 173
Boot lid - 173
Braking system:
    bleeding hydraulic system - 104
    brake pedal - 77
    disc brakes - caliper - 109
    disc brake pads - 107
    disc run-out check - 109
    drum brakes - hydraulic wheel cylinders - 108
    drum brake shoes - 104
    fault diagnosis - 114
    general description - 103
    handbrake - 107
    hydraulic pipes - 107
    master cylinder - 109
    specifications - 103
    vacuum servo unit - 111
Bumpers - 167

C

Camshaft:
    drivebelt - 18

    housing assembly - 35
    pulley - 21
    removal and inspection - 21
    replacement - 33
Carburettors - 63
    stromberg 175CD-2SE - 55, 59
    stromberg 175CD-2SET - 60
    zenith 36IVE - 51, 53, 55
Clutch:
    actuating lever and thrust release bearing - 77
    adjustment - 74
    assembly - removal and inspection - 77
    assembly - replacement - 77
    pedal - 4
    fault diagnosis - 78
    description - 74
    shaft - 77
    bearing - 77
    specifications - 74

    crankshaft - 31
    removal - 24
    replacement - 27
Contact breaker points:
    adjustment - 66
    removal and replacement - 67
Cooling system:
    antifreeze - 45
    draining - 41
    fault diagnosis - 46
    filling - 42
    flushing - 42
    general description - 40
    specifications - 40
Crankshaft:
    removal and inspection - 26
    replacement - 29
    seals - 29
Crankshaft pulley:
    removal and replacement - 21
Cylinder bores:
    examination and renovation - 24
Cylinder head - 29, 31
    removal, inspection and renovation - 22
    replacement - 33

D

Dampers:
    front - 146
    rear - 150
Distributor:
    dismantling and reassembly - 68
    removal and replacement - 68
    rotor - 66
Doors - 169
Drivebelt - 18, 37

E

Electrical system:
    battery - 116, 117
    flasher bulbs - 127
    flasher circuit - 124
    fusible links, fuses and thermal circuit breaker - 124
    general description - 116
    heater control - 134
    instrument panel - 133
    instrument voltage stabilizer unit - 124, 133
    rear lights - 127
    reverse lamp and starter inhibitor switch - 135
    sidelamps - 127
    specifications - 115
    steering column stalk - 134
    stop lamp switch - 135
    wiring - general - 124
    wiring diagrams - 136 - 143
Engine:
    ancillaries - removal - 18
    dismantling - general - 16
    exhaust manifold - 22
    fault diagnosis - 39
    final reassembly of major overhaul - 38
    general description - 23
    inlet manifold - 22
    major operations - engine in chassis - 14
    major operations - engine removed - 14
    mountings - removal and replacement - 18
    reassembly - general - 26
    removal - 14
    replacement - 38
    specifications - 11
Exhaust manifold - 22, 63
Exhaust system - 63

F

Fan belt - 45
    removal, inspection and renovation - 18
    replacement - 31
Fuel gauge - sender unit - 63
Fuel pump - 51
Fuel system and carburation:
    fault diagnosis -
    general description - 48
    specifications - 47
Fuel tank - 61

G

Gearbox (manual):
    dismantling - 82
    extension housing oil seal - 93
    fault diagnosis - 93
    gearchange mechanism - 93
    general description - 80
    inspection - 85
    reassembly - 88
    removal - 80
    replacement - 91
    specifications - 79

H

Halfshafts:
    bearings and oil seals - 102
    removal and replacement - 102
Handbrake - 107
Headlamps - 126
Heater - 176, 179
Horns - 126

I

Ignition system:
    fault diagnosis - 72, 73
    general description - 66
    specifications - 65
    timing - 71

Inlet manifold - 22, 63

L

Lubricants:
    recommended - 6

M

Main bearings:
    inspection and renewal - 26
Metric conversion tables - 182

O

Oil filter and adaptor - 18
Oil pump:
    removal and inspection - 22
    replacement - 35
Oil suction pipe and strainer - 24

P

Pistons and rings:
    inspection and renovation - 24
    removal - 24
    replacement - 27
Propeller shaft:
    general description - 97
    removal, inspection and replacement - 97
    specifications - 97
    universal joints - 99

R

Radiator - 42
Rear axle:
    general description - 100
    halfshafts - 102
    pinion, crownwheel and differential - 102
    pinion oil seal - 102
    removal and replacement - 100
    specifications - 100
Routine maintenance - 4
Rear window - 169

S

Spark plugs - 71
Springs:
    front - 146
    rear - 150
Starter motors - 121, 123
Steering:
    arm - 156
    column - 159
    column, lock - 158
    fault diagnosis - 160
    gear - 155
    general description - 145
    geometry - 156
    inspection - 155
    knuckle - 156
    shaft and bearings - 159
    shaft coupling - 158
    specifications - 144
    trackrod outer balljoints - 156
    wheel - 158
Suspension:
    arm balljoints - front - 146
    arms - front - 146
    arms - rear - 150
    control rods - front - 148
    dampers - 146, 150
    fault diagnosis - 160
    front crossmember - 149
    front springs - 146
    front wheel hub bearings - 155
    general description - 145
    rear springs - 150
    specifications - 144
    springs and dampers - inspection - 145

stabilizer bars - 152
Sump:
    removal - 24
    replacement - 31

T

Tappets:
    removal and inspection - 21
    replacement - 33
Thermostat - 42
Tyre pressures - 145
Tyres - 160

U

Universal joints - 99

V

Valves:

clearances - 37
reassembly - 33
removal, inspection and renovation - 22
Valve timing - 37
Viscous coupling fan - 45

W

Water pump - 42
Water temperature gauge - 45
Wheels - 160
Windscreen - 169
Windscreen washers - 127
Windscreen wiper motor - 127
Windscreen wipers - fault diagnosis - 127
Wiring diagrams - 136 - 143